Praise fo

"Maxwell's lived experience is
courage is unequaled. Reading
edly agree that the people and causes for which he writes have no better
advocate, nor will they likely have one again like him in our lifetimes. Bill
Maxwell is a Florida—and national—treasure, and we are all fortunate to
have shared this precious state with him for so many years."
—GREG ASBED, co-founder, Coalition of Immokalee Workers

"This is one of the most impactful books I've ever read. Not only has Bill
Maxwell led an extraordinary life, but he also writes vividly of his boyhood
as a migrant farmworker and later a civil rights activist in the Deep South,
marching on occasion with Martin Luther King Jr. It really is accountability
journalism at its best. Maxwell writes boldly and with ruthless honesty and
empathy about persistent racial inequities, environmental degradation, and
much else. Maxwell takes elected officials to task—and also the readers responsible for putting them in office."
—AMY GREEN, author of *Moving Water: The Everglades and Big Sugar*

"I thoroughly enjoyed reading *Maximum Vantage*. Maxwell's advice on how
others may or should think about these issues is thoughtful and personal to
him. I felt better informed after reading his stories."
—BETTYE A. GRABLE, Florida A&M University School of Journalism
and Graphic Communication

"A must-read that will touch your heart and inspire a more thoughtful approach to very challenging societal issues. Maxwell's words remind me personally, in most vivid terms, of the importance of being human, giving back
to your community, and never settling for less than the truth."
—LINDA FRIAR, deputy chief of public affairs, Bureau of Reclamation

"Maxwell's social and cultural commentaries provide prescient wisdom and
insight into many controversial issues within Florida and our nation as a
whole that flow from his own unique and varied life experiences. The collection highlights the essence of one of Florida's greatest writers and thinkers
whose perspectives are exceedingly relevant to the issues our society and
state continue to grapple with today."
—PATRICK FERGUSON, organizing representative for the Sierra Club,
Florida Chapter

Maximum Vantage

UNIVERSITY PRESS OF FLORIDA

Florida A&M University, Tallahassee
Florida Atlantic University, Boca Raton
Florida Gulf Coast University, Ft. Myers
Florida International University, Miami
Florida State University, Tallahassee
New College of Florida, Sarasota
University of Central Florida, Orlando
University of Florida, Gainesville
University of North Florida, Jacksonville
University of South Florida, Tampa
University of West Florida, Pensacola

MAXIMUM VANTAGE

New Selected Columns

BILL MAXWELL

Foreword by Tim Nickens

University Press of Florida

Gainesville · Tallahassee · Tampa · Boca Raton

Pensacola · Orlando · Miami · Jacksonville · Ft. Myers · Sarasota

Note to the Reader: The content of this book will necessarily engage with racism and includes graphic or intense acts of violence and racist language and terminology.

Publication of this work made possible by a Sustaining the Humanities through the American Rescue Plan grant from the National Endowment for the Humanities.

27 26 25 24 23 22   6 5 4 3 2 1

Library of Congress Control Number: 2022943140
ISBN 978-0-8130-6882-4

The University Press of Florida is the scholarly publishing agency for the State University System of Florida, comprising Florida A&M University, Florida Atlantic University, Florida Gulf Coast University, Florida International University, Florida State University, New College of Florida, University of Central Florida, University of Florida, University of North Florida, University of South Florida, and University of West Florida.

University Press of Florida
2046 NE Waldo Road
Suite 2100
Gainesville, FL 32609
http://upress.ufl.edu

Contents

Foreword

Bill Maxwell is a Florida treasure.

Over three decades, Maxwell's provocative, straightforward columns graced the opinion pages of the *St. Petersburg Times* and then the *Tampa Bay Times* when the state's largest newspaper changed its name in 2012. During that period, Maxwell provided a unique voice in Florida journalism—a Black opinion columnist with remarkable life experiences who spoke truth to power and to other Black Floridians. That often didn't win him many friends in either group, but his unvarnished honesty and keen observations always enriched the public discourse and often stimulated vigorous debate from the halls of the state Capitol in Tallahassee to the impoverished neighborhoods just south of St. Petersburg's vibrant downtown.

Phil Gailey, my predecessor as editor of editorials at the *Times*, made Maxwell his first hire for the editorial board and often called that decision one of his proudest accomplishments. Gailey read Maxwell's columns in the *Gainesville Sun*, hired him in 1994, and gave him wide latitude to write a Sunday column about whatever he pleased. By then Maxwell was nearly fifty years old, and he already had lived a full life that would inform his opinions and quickly affirm his credibility.

When he wrote about the plight of farmworkers in South Florida or in the fields east of Tampa, the Fort Lauderdale native could draw on his childhood memories as the son of migrant workers. When he wrote about education, he could remember lessons from his teaching jobs from Chicago to Texas to Florida. And when he wrote about race, he could recall his own experiences of being profiled in stores and steered away from houses in particular neighborhoods.

* * *

A less dedicated columnist could have survived by retelling old stories. After all, Maxwell attended segregated schools in Florida, enrolled in a historically Black college in Texas on a football scholarship, and dropped out to enlist in the Marines during the Vietnam War. He helped register Black residents to vote in Alabama when that risked death, and he marched with the Reverend Martin Luther King Jr. several times. By the time Maxwell joined the *Times* editorial board, he had traveled the country and seen the world.

But Maxwell was not a lazy journalist satisfied with reminiscing. When he pitched a column, he had read up on the subject. He had interviews scheduled, and he was as comfortable talking with politicians and professors as he was with farmworkers and students. And you didn't bother looking for him in the office. Maxwell was out in the neighborhoods. Or out in the Everglades. Or on a two-lane road in rural Florida, driving an old truck he didn't consider broken in until it had more than 150,000 miles on it. Cell phone? He might pick up. Or he might not. He preferred not to be in close range of editors if he could help it. In later years when he moved from a full-time *Times* employee to a correspondent, he would email his column to me and follow up shortly with a terse question: "Get column?"

This collection of Maxwell columns features some of his best work on race, farmworkers, education, the environment—and a few other favorites. They are as relevant today as when he wrote them because the issues and the public debates are still with us. Florida remains as consumed with accountability and standardized testing in public schools as when Maxwell challenged Governor Jeb Bush's push for testing and school letter grades more than two decades ago. Farmworkers continue to be exploited in the fields, working for too little pay and living in intolerable conditions. And efforts to preserve the Everglades and prevent the state from being paved over entirely remain halting works in progress.

Yet nothing resonates more now than Maxwell's honest columns about race and racism. These columns were published years before the recent protests following the killings of unarmed Black residents by police officers. Before the Black Lives Matter movement. Before serious public discussions about voter suppression and structural racism. But Maxwell's words are as relevant and powerful today as they were when they were written.

Today, unfiltered opinions flood our social media feeds. They are too often from unknown sources with unknown motives, filled with unverified claims and uninformed observations. Bill Maxwell's columns are his opinions alone, well researched, well reasoned, and enriched by a lifetime of experiences. He exposed readers to the stark realities they needed to know, not the gauzy fantasies they wanted to believe. They didn't always like the message, but they were always richer for having read it.

Tim Nickens

Tim Nickens spent more than 35 years as a journalist with the *Tampa Bay Times* (formerly the *St. Petersburg Times*) and the *Miami Herald*. He and his *Times* colleague Daniel Ruth won the 2013 Pulitzer Prize for editorial writing. Nickens retired from the *Times* in 2020 after twelve years as its editor of editorials.

Preface

As an African American columnist for a Pulitzer Prize-winning newspaper, I feel a special responsibility to be more than the average journalist. I see myself as a social critic seeking and expressing the truth. Therefore, I feel the need to cast light on subjects that most of society prefers to ignore.

My skin color is more than my physicality. It is my essence as a human, the sum of who I am, the Black columnist. I was Black before I became a writer. My Blackness shapes my views and influences my reactions to events and ideas and other people. For me to pretend otherwise is to be cynically dishonest.

These selections are offered in keeping with the mission of the University Press of Florida to produce works of global significance, regional importance, and lasting value. Although the columns are Florida-focused, they reflect our unavoidable encounters and engagement with issues that have lasting impact on all of us.

Acknowledgments

I am grateful to the *Tampa Bay Times* for publishing my columns for thirty years of my professional writing career. The newspaper's management gave me the freedom to express myself candidly and (mostly) in unvarnished language. In other words, they let me be the curmudgeon I am.

The *Times*, supportive of most of my many interests, allowed me to travel statewide, nationally, and internationally and write from each destination. Because I had been a college professor before coming to the *Times*, management allowed me to take leave on two occasions to teach, the first time at Angelo State University in San Angelo, Texas, and the second at Stillman College, a historically Black college in Tuscaloosa, Alabama.

The *Times* also allowed me to travel as part of the Florida Humanities Council's speakers program in which novelist Beverly Coyle and I read from our "Parallel Lives" essays that were published in the council's *Forum* magazine. The essays explore our experiences, white and Black, during the last years of the Jim Crow era in Florida. The essays were later developed into a stage play.

I have always loved the natural world, the environment. In 2013 I was selected as an Artist in Residence in Everglades (AIRIE) fellow. For more than a month I lived in the AIRIE studio apartment in Everglades National Park as a writer. AIRIE and the park let me live a dream.

Success is a collaborative effort. On my voyage to succeed, there are too many people to specifically identify for their contributions to my career over these past thirty years. So to my unidentified supporters herein, I earnestly say, THANK YOU.

Finally, special thanks to the people who directly made this book possible, my editors, proofreaders, legal advisers, and loyal friends who withstood my cantankerousness. Some call it contrariness. These special people are Michelle Gray, BJ Sheffield, Gail Halsey Collins, Pamela C. McMullen, Brian Sheffield, Tim Nickens, Alison Steele, Sian Hunter, and everyone at the University Press of Florida.

*   *   *

Editorial note: These columns were written over a twenty-year span most consistently using the newspaper Associated Press and *Tampa Bay Times* style. Some elements of style have changed during that period, and several have been updated in this publication.

Racism

Some Southerners understand collateral responsibility

JUNE 25, 2000

Southerners have a tortured relationship with their history. If they are not romanticizing it, they are denying it.

Rarely do Southerners look themselves in the eye and fess up to the racism, the violence and the rascality that shaped the region's character.

Merely romanticizing and denying history are no great matters unto themselves. But their consequences—the broad human damage they foment—continue to act as a ghostly blueprint that subtly determines and guides behavior, especially behavior between white people and black people.

Ultimately, though, romanticizing and denying the past ostensibly absolve Southerners of what I call collateral responsibility. I define it as our moral duty to correct the residual effects of the collective wrongs of earlier generations.

I have written about this subject several times during the past 10 years, and the response from whites always has been the same: anger and the argument that white people today bear no responsibility for the past.

Fortunately, not all whites believe such nonsense. An important example of someone who understands collateral responsibility is Florida Insurance Commissioner Bill Nelson. On Wednesday, Nelson, a Democrat running for the U.S. Senate, announced the settlement of a nation-wide class-action suit during a press conference in Tallahassee. Nelson indicated that tens of thousands of low-income blacks in the Sunshine State will receive cash refunds because of years of being charged more than white customers for the same burial and other low-value policies.

Some companies, by the way, charged blacks 33 percent more than whites, a practice that did not stop in Florida until several weeks ago, when Nelson issued a cease-and-desist order. The evil is that the practice was institutional nationwide. White and black agents throughout the South, who went door-to-door, were given two books, with two different sets of premiums.

Here is what James D. Crane, who went to work for Independent Life & Accident Insurance Co., in 1964, told the *Wall Street Journal* of orders from his Gadsden, Ala., district manager: "You write the white people out of this and the niggers out of this."

For their wrongs, these companies must shell out $206-million, not including other adjustments. And one of those so-called "niggers" is Bessie Jones, 71, a grandmother originally from Quincy, who has lived in Sarasota for more than 40 years. She, like many other blacks over the years, including my grandparents, tried to tell someone, anyone, that something "was funny" about their policies.

After a relative died, for example, many survivors discovered less than $100 in their accounts even though they had paid in as much $1,600 over many years. Jones did not give up. Nelson listened to her and others and initiated a probe that has resulted in a landmark decision.

Nelson and I have spoken often about this crisis, and I am convinced that his concern transcends burial insurance. He understands the need to set the past right, to commit oneself to collateral responsibility.

"The reason we're doing this is for the Bessie Joneses of the world," he said in a telephone interview. "There are millions of consumers who, like her, were taken advantage of by being charged more because of their race. It's inconceivable—and unconscionable—that this practice would continue up until the present."

Inconceivable? Unconscionable?

Not when people refuse to assume collateral responsibility.

Thankfully, Nelson is not the only Southerner who may have seen the light. Throughout the South, in fact, a handful of other public officials are trying to right some old wrongs, wrongs whose legacies perpetuate human cruelty.

Mike Moore, Mississippi's attorney general, the man who sparked the nationwide fight against the tobacco industry, decided to reopen the infamous 1964 case in which civil rights workers Michael Schwerner, Andrew Goldman and James Chaney were murdered by the Klan. I have spoken to Moore, and I am convinced that he understands the relationship of history to the present—of how we need to be honest with ourselves about the past's hold on us, the cyberspace living.

In Alabama, brave prosecutors have revisited the Sixteenth Street Baptist Church, where, in 1963 (the year I went to college), four black girls died in a bomb blast. Two former Klansmen have been indicted for these atrocities.

Down in Louisiana, the FBI recently restarted an investigation into the 1964 deaths of two black men whose bodies were found in a swamp. Then something unheard of in 1970, when the incident occurred, happened recently in Mississippi when a jury went over 30-year-old evidence and convicted three white men of killing a one-armed black sharecropper and throwing his body into a river.

Similar crusades are taking hold elsewhere in the South. These awful crimes are being given the attention they should have been given when they occurred. *The Economist* magazine aptly describes the men and women who are bringing some long-overdue justice to the South:

"Most of the momentum to reopen these cases comes from a defiant group of young lawyers and prosecutors, determined to discover the truth before time erodes the evidence or puts the suspects beyond reach. Many of this new generation grew up when the passions of the civil-rights struggle was still fresh in people's minds."

Simply stated, they, along with Commissioner Nelson, understand the concept of collateral responsibility—the moral duty to correct the residual effects of the collective wrongs of earlier generations.

A black man's plan for success

AUGUST 9, 2000

An open letter to black males and people who care about them:

Academics, journalists, public speakers and others used to label the black male in the United States an "endangered species." Because of political correctness, the term has fallen out of favor and is rarely used in any public forum.

If truth be told, too many black males nationwide still are in big trouble. And we black people are duty-bound to find ways to break this cycle of endangerment once and for all.

Yes, racism, especially the institutional kind, is a problem. It has destroyed generations of lives and continues to do terrible harm to the most vulnerable. But we no longer can let it prevent us from aggressively doing what we can on our own to save our boys, of instilling in them the traits, practices, habits, attitudes and philosophies that will enable them and their children to succeed.

Let me begin by describing the lay of the land: We, black males, are the least-desirable group in the United States. We are not wanted. White racists despise us, fear us and want us to evaporate or, at the very least, buy a one-way group ticket back to Africa. Most white liberals who want to help us also fear us, especially our boldest youngsters whose behavior mocks society's expectations of what is acceptable.

The bottom line is white liberals cannot help us. Welfare cannot. School reform cannot. Bill Clinton cannot. George W. Bush cannot. Al Gore cannot.

Only we can save ourselves by committing ourselves to reversing what Berkeley University linguistics professor John McWhorter calls "self-sabotage"—a counterproductive condition that encourages separatism, victimology and, perhaps worst of all, anti-intellectualism that views being smart as "being white."

Because we know from the get-go that society naturally rejects us, we must have the savvy to avoid everything that plays into the hands of the enemy. Why should we willfully set ourselves up for failure and contempt and societal abuse? Why do we re-enact all of the negative stereotypes?

I see such re-enactments each day: young brothers playing out the in-your-face style that turns off everyone else; getting arrested for stupid reasons; perpetually getting their mugs in newspapers and on prime-time TV; accumulating long rap sheets that destroy futures; roaming the streets all times of night; never reading a book or completing homework; dissing schoolmates who use their brains; refusing to master spoken and written English; rejecting the experience and wisdom of adults.

Why do we set ourselves up for mistreatment? Sometimes I believe that we want to be disliked. I hope that I am wrong. One thing I know for sure is that many brothers believe that they are getting back at white society with their behavior and attitude.

Simply stated, admissions officers do not give scholarships to those they perceive as dumb. Employers do not hire people they fear. Landlords do not rent to people they believe are destructive. Lenders do not lend to those they mistrust. Get the picture?

Yo, brothers, here is a secret I learned as a child: The best way to get back at white society—the ultimate revenge—is to succeed precisely where we are expected to fail, to do the unexpected.

What do I mean? To avoid miscasting someone else, let me use myself as an example. When I, a former migrant, arrived at the University of Chicago, few whites there expected me to succeed. Determined, I kept my nose in a book and surrounded myself with smart, well-traveled people. When I drank, I did so at Woodlawn Tap, where brilliant students and professors interacted, where I absorbed their intellectuality. I attended every play on campus and bought tickets to the Goodman and other theaters. I stalked the museums, the Art Institute and even acquired a lukewarm taste for chamber music and opera. I took part of my stipend to pay a doctoral student to teach me *The Chicago Manual of Style* so that I could write proper papers immediately. Using recordings, I even taught myself enough French to read *Madame Bovary* and appreciate Flaubert's *l'art pour l'art* as he had intended.

In other words, I had a personal plan—a black man's plan—for success beyond racism. A major part of my plan, as it is with most other successful blacks, is the simple matter of minimizing encounters with external, societal barriers to success. By avoiding external barriers, we enable ourselves to maximize our native talents and intelligence.

While continuing to battle racism as an external reality, we also must stop adopting self-sabotaging thought and conduct. Racism is never going away. Therefore, we must stop letting it be an excuse to fail. We must survive and thrive despite racism.

This confusion has no white equivalency

NOVEMBER 15, 2000

Several days ago, my colleague Elijah Gosier and I wrote columns about how we, along with other black men, are mistaken for each other all the time, mostly by white people. The pieces were intended to inform and entertain. Here in the *St. Petersburg Times* newsroom, we have had nothing but fun, with our white and black colleagues jokingly misidentifying not only us but other African Americans in the company as well.

Much of my correspondence from whites outside the company, however, has been either angry, defensive, ill-informed, recriminatory or zany.

With some overlap, the overwhelming majority of my letters, email and telephone calls have come in three main categories: attempts to show white equivalency, denial and defensiveness.

White equivalency is a logical fallacy. It attempts to show that for every black problem, whites have the same problem, and with the same import and ramifications.

In this case, white people are saying that like blacks, they also are victims of mistaken identity. A white television producer, for example, sent an email telling me that she is often mistaken for another white female producer. Her boss said, "Well, you're both producers and you both have brown hair." Yo! Dye your hair red. Elijah and I cannot change skin color unless, of course, we pull a Michael Jackson.

She writes also that people routinely mistake Marti Matthews of Channel 10 for Martie Tucker of Channel 28, "both blue-eyed blonds with the same name. Sometimes Sue Zelenko gets thrown into the confusion, too."

The woman's logic breaks down on several fronts and begs comment. Does she not know that mistaking one petite, blue-eyed blond TV news anchor for another is not the same as mistaking a black man for another? In the case of the blonds, we are talking about a specific group of people, a subset of the white race, who have been made to resemble one another because the news industry requires a generic look for its female talking heads. You had better look a lot like Marti Matthews or Martie Tucker or Jessica Savitch for that matter. If not, you are out the door, if you got through the door to begin with.

Mistaking one black man for another is not the same; we are not a generic subset of the group. Each individual black man is a generic entity in a generic group. In other words, "all niggers look alike," as a white man told me several years ago. Black computer techs here at the *Times* are mistaken for me. They are not columnists. Believe it or not, a 26-year-old *Times* employee on another floor (no gray beard or nappy gray coiffure) gets mistaken for me. No, he is not a columnist or writer. His mug is never in the newspaper.

Anyway, I have never heard of the police blowing away a petite, blue-eyed blond because she is mistaken for another petite, blue-eyed blond. We could, though, produce a long list of black males, from different professions, who have suffered this fate. In other words, no white equivalency exists.

Other readers deny that such mistakes occur at all. Still others become defensive to the point of hurling insults. The most interesting are whites married to blacks. Trying to show that they do not mistake one black for another, they became "deeply offended" by the columns, called me "ignorant," felt "betrayed" and miss the point of the pieces. Most whites married to blacks delude themselves into believing that they know as much about the black experience as I do. That offends me.

An excerpt from a typical letter in this category is worth quoting: "Yes, I am white. I am also a graduate of (historically black) Howard University and the wife of a black man. When you see me on the street, you assume I am as blind as the other white people you have encountered. You don't want to assume you are the same as any other black person, so how fair is it to judge what I might think about you when you don't know me?

"If I thought all black people looked alike, I would not know half of my family. I might have even spent my honeymoon with the wrong man. I might have asked the wrong girlfriend to be my maid of honor. And I might have sat in on the wrong lectures in college. I assure you that did not happen. People call me by the wrong name all the time, I'm just another physical therapist. It seems to me that it's natural to confuse people you don't know or have met only once. It just doesn't happen to black people."

Again, I do not know of a white, female physical therapist blown away by cops because she resembles another white, female physical therapist.

I will repeat one simple premise of my "invisible men" column: Far, far more whites than blacks mistake me and other black men for someone else. This phenomenon is a fact of life. It is not trivial. It has no white equivalency.

White America, denial won't erase racism

DECEMBER 6, 2000

The United States will never fix its race problems because too many white people simply do not recognize white privilege and refuse to con- fess, yes, confess, that they, individually and collectively, have a race problem to begin with.

Instead of seeing racism for the evil that it is, the perpetrators blame the victims for the nation's race problems. The bigot who supports Bob Jones University, for example, is not the problem. Instead, outspoken African Americans, such as the Rev. Jesse Jackson and NAACP leader Kweisi Mfume, are blamed and cast as rabble-rousers, instigators of the nation's race problems.

How absurd. No, how utterly stupid.

Solving race problems is made even more difficult because a handful of well-known black Republicans, such as Supreme Court Justice Clar- ence Thomas, U.S. Congressman J.C. Watts and California businessman Ward Connerly, pretend that racism no longer matters because they are successful.

Tens of thousands of other black people succeed without aping the lie that racism is a figment of the imagination of whining blacks and bleeding heart white liberals. These blacks succeed while acknowledging racism and fighting it directly. Racism is a nasty reality that continues to bar people from jobs, business, real estate, education, intimate relation- ships. And it needs to be acknowledged and discussed. Racism makes black life unnecessarily tough.

The 2000 presidential election magnified the gulf between whites and blacks. White men overwhelmingly voted for Texas Gov. George W. Bush. Black people, especially black males, voted overwhelmingly for Vice President Al Gore despite Bush's claim of "compassionate conser- vatism." The 2000 election pulled the lowest percentage of blacks to sup- port a Republican presidential candidate since Barry Goldwater's failed campaign in 1964.

Why did white men, even Vietnam vets, vote for Bush, a rich man who dodged service in Vietnam, a privileged child eminently unquali- fied for the presidency, a university legacy of weak intellect, someone who tried to hide his DUI arrest record, an executioner who courted the bigots of Bob Jones University, an empty suit who has no ethical problem with the Confederate flag topping off statehouses?

The answer: race. If truth be told, blacks and whites are from different planets and are treated as such. And the sooner we accept this truth, the sooner we can find solutions to some of the tough race-specific problems.

Black people are not inventing racial profiling. It actually exists. Have you heard of New Jersey or Volusia County, Fla.? Black people do not redline themselves. White bankers and insurers do. Black people do not invite cops to beat and shoot them. Cops commit these acts on their own. Blacks do not advise white employers to toss out their job applications. White employers make such decisions on golf courses.

Let me, as a black man, try to understand a few things: Am I to believe that our nappy hair means nothing? That our black skin is equivalent to a zit on a white kid's forehead, a simple, natural growth that salve can erase? That slavery has had no permanent impact on our families? That the legacy of Jim Crow's separate-but-equal public school system disappeared with passage of the 1964 Civil Rights Act? That school busing is a colorblind promenade in the park? That our segregated neighborhoods are a matter of chance?

Whites regularly intone that blacks should stop using the term African American and start being "just Americans." One such letter writer, an Italian, conveniently takes great pride in belonging to the local Italian-American Club.

When I pointed out this fact and that he and most other groups (Irish-Americans, Greek-Americans, Asian-Americans, Cuban-Americans, Polish-Americans, Jewish Americans, Swedish-American) always liked their hyphenated names until blacks hyphenated African and American, he hemmed and hawed in hypocritical fashion.

Indeed, when "African-American" came into vogue, other hyphenated groups suddenly wanted everyone, read that black people, to be "just Americans." The racist truth is that many whites cannot stand the co-mingling of the terms Africa and America.

Anything else but that.

Whites want to forget about race. For sure, they want blacks to forget about it. But people like Jesse Jackson will not give white people a soft landing so long as the imprint of racism marginalizes innocent people, limits careers, blocks education and otherwise destroys lives. He and others will stay in White America's face.

Experience colors our view of history

JANUARY 10, 2001

While on Christmas vacation in the frozen North, I heard Pulitzer Prize-winning historian Henry Allen discuss his recent book, *What It Felt Like Living in the American Century*, on National Public Radio's program *Talk of the Nation* with host Juan Williams and his call-in guests. The book is a treat for history buffs who color the past outside the lines.

During the program, callers—most of them older whites—fondly reminisced. A 94-year-old woman vividly described hardships amid the 1920s' exuberance and worship of progress, but she also cheered the postwar economy that improved life for many Americans. Another white woman, born several years before the Great Depression, spoke of how she went door-to-door in New Orleans guiding illiterate blacks through the legal maze of the voting process, a task made more difficult because many older folk did not know when or where they were born. She also described how many local whites threatened to lynch her if she did not cease and desist.

The most interesting moments came when callers were asked to identify their favorite period during the 20th century. Not surprisingly, these elderly callers loved the postwar 1950s. They warmly recalled President Dwight D. Eisenhower, newly developed tract communities of identical houses, families gathered around black-and-white TVs, dandies awash with Vitalis, 3-D movies, Formica counter tops, Marilyn Monroe, *American Bandstand*, drive-in eateries.

Yes, the 1950s were good for most whites. Listening, I was transported back to my own 1950s' childhood in the South and realized anew that people's views of history are shaped by their individual and group experiences.

For most blacks and other minorities, the 1950s were not Ike's paradise. For many blacks, especially the migrant farmworkers in my life, the 1950s were pure hell. This was the heyday of Jim Crow, when racial separation was the law, when each ingredient in the so-called melting pot (salad bowl) settled into its own niche. Allen writes: "Amid the Ford Country Squire station wagons and slate roofs, wealthier homeowners boast that neighborhood covenants still keep out Jews and Negroes."

While whites enjoyed the mid-century euphoria, most blacks cast their lot with the likes of Rosa Parks—who refused to give up her seat on a Montgomery, Ala., bus to a white man—and a young minister named Martin Luther King Jr., who led the boycott that ushered in the modern civil rights movement.

Were I to have telephoned *Talk of the Nation*, I would have embraced the 1960s as the century's most significant time for me. Although many racial barriers began to fall during the 1950s, the 1960s codified change and brought widespread hope.

In 1963, the year of King's "I Have a Dream" speech, I went away to college. For the first time in my life, I had white teachers and white classmates. And for the first time, I had white friends, male and female. We hitchhiked together across the country, slept in the same beds and sleeping bags, ate from the same plates and bowls, drank from the same liquor bottles, toked together, took turns urinating behind bushes and watching for cops.

Remarkably, nine of us—five blacks and four whites decked out in dirty bell bottoms and smelly sandals—traveled to Mississippi, Alabama and Florida to register black voters. I am still in awe of these white students for voluntarily putting their lives on the line.

They gave me hope. With Bob Dylan crooning a novel vision and Allen Ginsberg taking the imagination to new places, my white friends were motivated by outrage and a profound sense of justice. Even the death of our president, John F. Kennedy, did not extinguish their zeal for freedom and equality. Real or imagined, Camelot gave us, black and white, a desire to serve. Some volunteered for the Peace Corps; others, like me, the Marine Corps. The 1964 Civil Rights Act made me a legitimate stranger.

Then, of course, the folly of Vietnam spoiled the party forever. We went our separate ways. Malcolm X, King and Bobby Kennedy were gunned down. Kent State took life for granted. Charles Manson murdered the young and the beautiful. Black Panthers redefined revolution. Riots in Washington, Newark and Detroit scared white America and upped the ante for racial tolerance.

Many people, especially conservative Republicans, still believe that the 1960s ruined the nation. For me, the 1960s, even with the many contradictions and paradoxes, offered hope to the dispossessed. This was a pivotal moment during the American century—when blacks forced white America to reckon with them as real people for the first time.

Heavy past hangs over Groveland

FEBRUARY 7, 2001

Returning to this small Lake County town always unsettles me. Some of Florida's darkest moments unfolded here in 1949, and the years that immediately followed. Black History Month is a good time to look back.

In July of that year, reports circulated that four black men had raped a pretty blond. A white mob hunted down the suspects, severely beating them, killing one in a North Florida swamp. Law enforcement rescued the three survivors—Samuel Shepherd, Charles Greenlee and Walter Irvin—and threw them in jail.

There, the lawmen suspended the prisoners from pipes in the boiler room and beat them into unconsciousness. "One of them was so severely beaten that his testicles remained swollen for days," writes Juan Williams, in his biography of Supreme Court Justice Thurgood Marshall. "Another was injured so badly that his pants were still caked with dry blood days later when NAACP lawyers came to question him."

During the following nights, white-hooded night riders spread out across Groveland, Mascotte and other local communities and burned more than 200 black residences to the ground. As the blacks ran for their lives, mobs chased and beat some of them. Several hours later, state guardsmen marshalled and saved the lives of the blacks courageous enough to remain in the area.

Many of my relatives were victims of the mobs' violence. Some are still alive today. For example, my uncle Joe Maxwell, now in his 80s, was a prime target of the night riders. His crime? As a World War II veteran, he was suspected of sleeping with white women while on rest and recuperation in Europe. Many other black GIs who fought in Europe were attacked for the same reason.

My uncle, his wife Ruby, and their three small children were attacked in their home. Joe's white boss had warned him the day before that trouble was coming and offered to hide the family. Because he had a shotgun, Joe thought he could protect his family and decided to stay at home.

The next night, as he and Ruby prepared for bed, he heard the mob coming—the pickups, the rebel yells and the gunfire. The children were in their bed. Joe ran to their room, forced them beneath the bed and placed extra mattresses over them. He ran back to the window and heard a white man yell, "That's where that damned Joe Maxwell lives." Ruby begged him to get away from the window. A few seconds after he moved, a bullet shattered the glass, went through the wall and exploded a bag of crayons a few inches above the children's bed.

If Joe had not moved, he probably would have died. If the children had been in their bed and not under it, one of them might have died. The mob then shot up the house of one of my other uncles and several other houses belonging to my relatives. For the rest of that night, they hid and did not move.

Two days later, Joe and his family, accompanied by state militiamen, boarded a train in Wildwood and traveled to Fort Lauderdale where they stayed with my mother for a week. While they were there, the troops restored calm in Groveland, and many of the black families returned. Some came back to ashes, smoldering debris and empty lots. The families of the four men charged with rape faced the most danger as a mob gathered to lynch them. Again, the troops saved the day.

Back home, Joe's life was never the same. Before the violence, white men mostly ignored him and other blacks. Now, white men hurled insults and often threw bricks and bottles at black men from their vehicles. A semblance of normalcy did not return for several years.

Meanwhile, the three suspects were convicted of rape. The NAACP Legal Defense Fund, under the direction of Thurgood Marshall, defended the men. Shepherd and Irving were sentenced to the electric chair, and Greenlee, 16, was given life, and he did not appeal. Because the prosecution had no physical evidence of a rape, the high court overturned the convictions and ordered new trials for Shepherd and Irving.

While Lake County Sheriff Willis McCall was transferring Shepherd and Irving from Ocala to Tavares, he shot them, killing Shepherd. McCall said the men, handcuffed together, tried to escape. Irving said that McCall was lying, that he tried to kill them in cold blood. Florida Gov. LeRoy Collins pardoned the men.

Groveland's legacy of racism was set forever with the Groveland rape trial. The town has never come to terms with this ordeal and has not reached out to black residents—many of them victims. Until reconciliation is attempted, the shadows of Willis McCall and the mobs will hang over this place always.

Denial gets us nowhere when living with racism

FEBRUARY 11, 2001

Many people gain great comfort in pretending that racism is a thing of the past, a moot issue, something that only the "civil rights industry" wants to keep in the public eye.

Most white people want race simply to go away without having to do anything substantive about it. They want people like me to shut up. They do not realize that silence will sink us deeper into the mire.

From where I sit, a 55-year-old African American male with very dark skin, racism is alive and well and is not going anywhere soon.

Denial is the single biggest obstacle to discussing racism and doing something real about it. My dictionary says that denial is a refusal to admit the truth or reality, a refusal to acknowledge a person or a thing, disavowal, a negation of logic.

Indeed, when race is involved, we refuse to admit the truth or reality. We reject logic. What could be more dangerous, and cruel?

Some of the most honest words I have ever heard about race were uttered by Columbia University journalism professor and editor Sig Gissler: "Race, it is America's rawest nerve and most enduring dilemma. From birth to death, race is with us, defining, dividing, distorting."

Instead of being truthful like Gissler, most of us engage in stereotype and misinformation.

I refuse to play this game, ever.

Race defines my personal life and my professional life. Each day is a fight to maintain individual dignity. Each day is an experiment in getting along with white people. Each day is a struggle to subdue the desire to strike back with a vengeance.

Few days pass that I am not forced to confront a blatant or a subtle form of racism or racial insensitivity. These slights and indignities, although small on the surface and which may mean nothing to most white people, add up to a weight often too heavy for me to carry.

I know, for example, that real estate agents have steered me away from properties in upscale neighborhoods. One landlord once turned me down over the telephone because she said I sounded black.

Store security guards follow me, a gray-bearded grandfather, around as if I intend to steal some trinket and risk going to jail. These insults cut to the quick and ache like deep infections.

If a Martian were to spend a week earnestly assessing the relations between whites and blacks in America, I am certain that he would notice the deep separation between us. He would conclude that race and denial define our national character.

The awful truth is that the findings of the 1968 Kerner Commission report, stating that the United States was not one, but two societies, "one black, one white, separate and unequal," are mostly true in 2001.

Our schizophrenia on race remains much the same as it was in 1968. While we proclaim to be colorblind, we are race conscious in almost every way. Racial profiling, for example, is a despicable form of race consciousness and makes black males hate white people.

White people should not delude themselves about this fact.

I am a race-conscious African American. As such, I must take responsibility for myself and white people.

Let me explain with a simple example: I walk five miles five mornings a week, sometimes just before dawn. Whenever I approach a white woman on a sidewalk at an early hour, I cross to the other side so as not to scare her. I do not have to cross over. But I do so anyway. Why? Because I am not a fool. I know that many white women who are alone are afraid of black men. Not just any men per se. Black men.

Furthermore, I do not lose anything by crossing the street.

As a black man, a real victim of racism, someone who wants to survive physically, emotionally and psychologically intact, I am obligated to manage race for myself and for white people.

I must be smart. I must know what is occurring. More often than not, a white person, who has never been a victim of racism, will be unaware of an instance of racial insensitivity.

As an intelligent victim, however, I must be careful to read situations accurately. I should not label something racist when, in fact, it may be a simple case of congenital rudeness.

Are things hopeless?

Not at all, at least not to me. In my own life, I use each day as another reason to confront my own demons. Writing about race is part of that process. I consciously work at overcoming my racial prejudices. As such, I cultivate relationships with white people who care.

The real key, of course, is getting to know people intimately, being with one another after work and after school. Water cooler chats will not get it. I do not know about you, but I have a hard time hating people I get to know intimately, people with whom I have dinner and drinks.

Things are hopeful if we work hard at confronting racism honestly, if we stop denying racism's ugly reality and, if, motivated by goodwill, we get to know one another up close.

Jim Crow conflict clouded the point

FEBRUARY 14, 2001

In Florida, the ugly relationship between the races during Jim Crow produced human drama fraught with enough paradox and irony to give a young filmmaker sufficient material to shoot for the rest of his life.

Listen to the tale of Allan Platt, his wife and five children. In 1954, Platt, a fruit-picker, moved his family to Mount Dora, a tiny town in Lake County, from Holly Hill, S.C. When the Platts enrolled their children in school, the principal, D.D. Roseborough, knew immediately that trouble was coming.

Children complained to their parents that Denzell and Laura Belle Platt "looked like niggers." Their skin was "too dark," and they had "those noses."

Lake County's notorious sheriff, Willis McCall, heard about the family and wanted to see for himself. He drove to the Platts' home, lined the children up against a wall and photographed them. A desperate Allan Platt produced a marriage license and the children's birth certificates to prove that his brood was white. McCall did not budge.

Days later, he forced Roseborough to accompany him to the Platts' home to witness some real race science. Here is how a 1954 *Time* magazine article described the scene: "The principal tried to be polite, but the sheriff was in no mood for the amenities. He pointed to Denzell Platt, 17, and declared: "His features are Negro." Then he pointed to Laura Belle, 13, and said: "I don't like the shape of that one's nose." After the lesson in anthropology, Roseborough surrendered. The Platts, he said, would have to stay out of school "until the sheriff is satisfied."

Mabel Norris Reese, editor of *Topic*, Mount Dora's weekly newspaper, entered the fray. She visited the Platts, inspected their papers and determined the Platts were white.

In her column, according to *Time*, she wrote that the Platts were of Irish-Indian pedigree and were likely descendants of Sir Walter Raleigh's "lost colony" of Roanoke. "If you are a parent," she wrote, "look at your child and think what it would mean to you if an adult said: 'I do not like your child's nose' and thereby decreed that your child cannot associate with other children."

In the 1950s, Reese was courageous to challenge McCall. Over the years, she had been a thorn in the sheriff's side. She took on McCall even after he had poisoned her dog, painted "K.K.K." across her office windows, and placed a burning cross in her yard.

After the column ran, Bryant Bowles, founder of the racist National Association for the Advancement of White People, came to the area on a lecture tour. He joined McCall in harassing Reese. Bowles marched into the editor's office and swore to "get even" with her for condemning him. Soon afterward, the Platts' landlady was informed anonymously that her "house would burn down" if she did not evict "those niggers." The family was evicted.

Inspired by Reese, 65 students signed a petition supporting Denzell and Laura Belle and mailed it to *Time*.

"We care," the petition began. "The Constitution says that a person is innocent until proved guilty. We feel that the Platt children have had a raw deal. Their right to an education has been taken away because of the opinions and prejudice of one man. To be expelled for violation of Florida segregation law is one thing; to be expelled because of an unfounded suspicion is another. Therefore, we believe the Platt Children should be permitted to remain in school until the sheriff can prove they don't belong."

After the petition went public, a chalk line was drawn on a school sidewalk. One side was for "White People," the other for "Nigger Lovers." After standing on the "Nigger Lover" side, a boy was stoned. Two other children removed their names from the petition because they did not want to hurt their families' businesses.

Now, to the petition's paradox and irony: The students' first words are "we care." About what? They care that whites are being accused of being Negroes. When they write that the "Constitution says that a person is innocent until proved guilty," they are suggesting that to be a Negro is to have committed a crime against nature.

McCall is accused of "prejudice," but only because he is discriminating against white people. The ultimate irony is that if the Platt children were Negroes, everyone would agree that they deserved to be "expelled for violation of Florida's segregation law." Discriminating against whites, however, is unacceptable.

Time, along with Reese, also missed the paradox of the petition. Jim

Crow was like that: It caused a convenient loss of logic, even among smart people.

Serving ourselves in the name of King

JANUARY 20, 2002

I do not claim to have been a friend of the Rev. Martin Luther King Jr.

I worked for his organization, the Southern Christian Leadership Conference, when I was an undergraduate at Bethune-Cookman College in Daytona Beach, where, when not in class, I helped to organize the black hotel and garbage workers. I also wrote press releases.

My work let me meet King several times and march with him in Mississippi, Alabama and Florida. All who worked for him were impressed with his eloquence, charisma, drive, courage and sensitivity. Imagine how special we college kids, poorly paid and overworked, felt being in this famous man's orbit.

Those were heady days.

As we pay homage to King's life and work and as we approach the month that celebrates black history, I am reminded of a significant part of King's message many of us rarely pay attention to: While imploring white America to recognize its racism and heal itself, King asked black America to act on its own behalf, to help pull itself out of poverty and crime, to educate itself, to make a bright future for its children.

More than ever before, this part of King's vision needs to become reality for African Americans. All of the marches, parades, concerts, television documentaries and speeches in his honor during the next weeks will amount to nothing but confetti if black people do not act and dedicate themselves to service.

Although King's widow, Coretta, along with her four children, is embroiled in controversy over marketing her husband's name and image, she has not lost sight of how blacks should honor him.

"We have called for people to remember to celebrate, and, most importantly, to act," she said recently from her Atlanta office. "We like to say we celebrate the birthday (in January) and not memorialize it, as we do in April (when he was gunned down). Now we should ask people to really commemorate his life with some form of service and to give back to the community.

"Martin Luther King gave his life loving and serving others, and we think it's a very appropriate way to celebrate the day. People can come together in a spirit of cooperation, love and humanitarian service to help someone else."

The King Center for Nonviolent Social Change in Atlanta and *Ebony* magazine have developed tangible ways for blacks to personally continue King's legacy while, at the same time, transforming their communities, larger society and even the world:

Donate a day of service. Provide meals for the homeless, clean up the neighborhood or work with seniors.
Read and meditate on the writings of King.
Rededicate yourself to nonviolence in your personal relationships and work for the triumph of nonviolence in the world.
Work to eliminate racism and intolerance.
Conduct yourselves with dignity and discipline.
Get in touch with who you are and work in the community with others to renew the spirit of the black community.
Register to vote. Conduct a voter-registration drive.
Help rebuild the black family.
Work to end poverty at all levels.
Become a youth mentor.

Everywhere I travel in the United States, I see far too many black communities that do nothing or next to nothing to uplift themselves. Such inaction insults King's legacy.

I am often asked to identify the issues King would be working on if he were alive. Obviously, I have no real way of knowing. I do know, however, that he would be distressed by the blight that continues to sweep black America. He would wonder why black wealth is not returning to our communities. He would wonder why we are not investing in ourselves.

King, along with many others, gave his life getting laws on the books and persuading institutions to change, all moves that gave African Americans added mobility. Today, we, black people, need to take the next step: We should look inward and dedicate ourselves to uplifting ourselves.

Martin Luther King III captured the essence of his father's message to black America. "For us to be truly successful, we have to create an opportunity for those coming behind us. We have to pull others up and not abandon them, and that is truly part of the philosophy of my father."

Individual action is everything. Blame and recrimination hold us back. To honor King, we, African Americans, must first honor ourselves. We honor ourselves by doing for ourselves.

Blacks share a duty to one another

FEBRUARY 3, 2002

Daytona Beach

When I was an undergraduate here at Bethune-Cookman College during the 1969-1970 term, my friends and I used to joke that we would know we had "made it" when our alma mater invited us back to campus as a keynote speaker.

I have apparently made it because I have been invited back as keynoter for several events, most recently a few days ago. Bethune-Cookman, with an enrollment of 2,720, is a private, historically black college. Like other such colleges and universities, it serves as the only place where some African Americans can receive higher learning. Even today, a student can enroll with a grade point average of 2.25 on a 4.0 scale.

Because I believe African Americans are uniquely disadvantaged in a society where race and ethnicity matter more than most people acknowledge, my speech stressed the necessity of helping ourselves. The significance of Black History Month gives me a reason to share parts of my talk with Bethune-Cookman's students, most of them second-term freshmen.

Many black college students, like their white counterparts, believe they are "superior" when, in fact, they are merely privileged. Yes, to be born with a good mind, to have had fate assign you to a wholesome family life and to have responsible adults who make your early years safe and secure is to be privileged.

Privileged people have a moral and social obligation to serve others. This fact is highly salient for African Americans. As a class of real victims of racial discrimination, blacks share a special duty to do for one another. If we do not give back, we should not expect any other group to help us.

To give back, we must make a personal commitment to make a positive difference. We should help others because we want to, not because we merely want to fit in or because we want to be well liked.

Students, especially juniors and seniors, should actively seek out a black neighborhood and establish legal ways to uplift the residents.

Following are some specific things students can do:

Regularly read to a child or a group of children. The simple act of reading to children can make a world of difference in homes where reading is not valued.

Speak to black students in public schools. Inspire them to follow your example. Even better, bring children to your college campus and let them attend class with you. Such an experience can be life-changing.

Establish a tutoring program. The good news is that several groups at Bethune-Cookman are doing just that. I am especially impressed with the work of the Greek organizations whose members have official programs that have the blessings of the public schools.

In too many towns, students and local residents rarely spend quality time together. Students should actively find ways to form educational and social alliances with local black residents. Regularly meeting local residents for lunch or dinner, for example, creates long-lasting social capital. A Jacksonville senior has dinner each month with black men to help them write resumes and complete various applications.

When I was an undergraduate, my friends and I often found time to bring local children to the movies with us. To this day, I am amazed at the impact that simple act made in the kids' lives. For some, it meant the difference between fighting on the streets and having wholesome fun.

The personal commitment to make a positive difference should not stop with a college degree. In reality, the commitment should become stronger. Again, here are some specific ways to serve:

If you become a lawyer, perform regular pro bono work. One of the tragedies of our rich society is that poor people rarely get a fair day in court. They cannot afford it. Black lawyers have an obligation to help others get a fair shake.

If you become a doctor, sponsor free health clinics in low-income black communities where many working people cannot afford regular medical care. Over the years, I have visited many free health clinics for the purpose of seeing who donates services. Too often I am disappointed to see so few black professionals helping out. I commend those who serve, but we need many more to do so.

As a banker, you should try to find ways to make funds available to black applicants who may not qualify under traditional terms. I have a former classmate in Detroit who persuaded his bank to lend to a select group of small black businesses that have made a difference.

Black teachers have a special obligation to inspire black children. Each year, statistics show black children lagging behind most other groups in every academic measure. Black teachers should do whatever they must to reverse this trend. If visiting homes after school will help, then visit homes.

Blacks with the financial means should establish college scholarships for this and the next generation of black children. Education is the only real solution to the stubborn problems plaguing our communities.

If you have money, regularly write checks for good causes.

At the outset, I said that blacks are a class of real victims of racial discrimination. Indeed, we are victims. But we need not live as such.

We have to actively recognize that we must do for ourselves by loving ourselves, by serving others because we are committed to making a positive difference.

The white women who risked it all for civil rights

MARCH 3, 2002

A dear friend telephoned a few days ago and reminded me that I was letting another Black History Month pass without writing about one of the unsung groups of the civil rights movement of the 1960s. My friend is white. Although born financially well off, she has taught journalism at the same traditionally black college in Mississippi since 1972.

I met her during the summer of 1965 in Meadville, Miss., when I was a 19-year-old college student from Texas, and she a 19-year-old college student from Georgia. She was a pretty, petite member of the Student Nonviolent Coordinating Committee. I was a journalism intern for the Southern Christian Leadership Conference.

Her job was more important than mine, and her life was in much more danger than mine. I merely had to observe, report and write stories and shoot photographs. She put her life on the line.

She was one of thousands of white women who joined the black-led civil rights movement, who came of age during the era of the nation's greatest social, intellectual and political discontent and renewal. She is right: Hers is an unsung group of freedom fighters. She easily could have suffered the fate of Viola Gregg Luizzo, a mother of five, who traveled from her comfortable home in Michigan to the South to help us. On March 25, 1965, an Alabama Klansman fired a .38-caliber pistol through the window of her car, killing her instantly.

We knew the dangers of working in Meadville. A few months before our arrival, two black men, Henry Dee, 19, and Charles Moore, 20, had been murdered by Klansmen and their bodies dumped in the Mississippi River. Dee had been decapitated, and a piece of wire encircled his torso. Divers found only the lower half of Moore's body. His ankles were tied with a rope.

Yes, we knew that cops, Klansmen and ordinary racists were especially brutal when white women and black men, suggesting sexual intimacy, were caught together.

My friend lived in a shack with three other women in an all-black, remote section of the county. During the day, she taught in what we called the Freedom School, places where thousands of black children, underserved by the South's separate-but-equal school system, learned to read and write. During evening hours, she joined other activists in registering illiterate and near-illiterate blacks to vote.

One night, while accompanying her and three black workers to a home where they would help an old black couple complete a Social Security application, I asked her this question: "You're the daughter of a Southern Baptist preacher. Why're you risking your life for niggers?"

I remember her answer well (I wrote it in my journal): "Don't use that word in my presence. Racism is a sin. As a Christian, I've got to work, even die, to get rid of this sin."

"But you're white."

"Which makes me even more responsible."

I swore that night I would write about her and other white women who risked their lives for the cause of civil rights. Alas, I am just now getting around to it, nearly 40 years later.

To make my job easier, my friend sent me a copy of *Deep in Our Hearts: Nine White Women in the Freedom Movement*. Published in 2000 by the University of Georgia Press, it is a volume that anthologizes the memoirs of Constance Curry, Joan C. Browning, Dorothy Dawson Burlage, Penny Patch, Theresa Del Pozzo, Sue Thrasher, Elaine DeLott Baker, Emmie Schrader Adams, Casey Hayden.

I read it a few days ago, and all of the memories, the fears and the euphoria mostly, returned. I remember the late-night rides on deep-rutted roads through pine forests; steamy wooden churches in the middle of nowhere; white girls curled up under quilts on the floors of cars and the beds of pickups so that redneck cops would not spot them with niggers; black dudes scared they would be blamed if a white cop shoots a white woman; dank and stinking jail cells in towns with very long names; "doing your business" in bushes and behind trees; hastily written picket signs with misspelled words; delicious meals cooked by fat black women wearing feed-sack dresses and colorful aprons.

In their preface, the women list the questions they answer in the memoirs: "These are our stories of the costly times we wouldn't have missed for the world, and of the people and places and events that filled them. We speak to several questions: Why us? Why did we, of all the white women growing up in our hometowns, cross the color line in the days of segregation and join the Southern Freedom Movement of the sixties? How did we find our way? What happened to us there? How did we leave, and what did we take with us? And, especially, what was it like?"

The thing I admire most about these women, along with those I knew personally, was their selflessness, the devotion to doing right because right is right. I especially respected those like my friend, whose families openly treated African Americans as inferiors. More than one were disinherited by their parents because of their involvement with the movement.

But these women, mere teenagers, persevered at our side, holding to their heart-deep commitment to social justice. In their special way, they helped this nation at least acknowledge its promise of equality to all citizens. They showed white people that racism not only disfigures its black victims, it also disfigures white people. It turns some whites into grotesque creatures who don sheets and hoods, who burn crosses and murder in the name of God and their race.

Deep in Our Hearts dispels the myth that whites in the civil rights movement were a monolith, rich, East Coast, Ivy League brats with too much time on their hands.

Here is the truth, in the nine women's own words: "We are all different: Southern and northern; rural and urban; state university and Ivy League; middle class, working class, and poor. We moved to our radical activities in various ways: by Marxism, Christian existentialism, and immigrant folk wisdom; by our grandmothers and the Constitution; by

Thoreau and Dumas; by living on a kibbutz; by African freedom fighters; and a Deep South upbringing."

These nine white women, along with thousands of others, made our country a better place. The movement did not end in these women's personal lives after they went home for the last time.

Penny Patch speaks for her co-writers, and she speaks for me: "The experience remains at the core of who I am."

The reality of racism 40 years ago

OCTOBER 6, 2002

Two, four, six, eight, we will never integrate.

Chant of a white mob in Mississippi

As far as I could tell at the time, Sept. 30, 1962, was just another charmed day in the lives of happy teenagers.

My friends and I walked around the western edge of the black cemetery and through the woods on our way to school. This was our usual route. The morning was sunny, and we found a few juicy scuppernongs that had survived the summer and the busy fingers of the little kids. The five of us, all star football players, lollygagged along the path that led us to the deep-rutted dirt road alongside our football practice field.

We were excited because we were preparing for the biggest game in the history of our school, Crescent City's all-Negro Middleton High. We were playing mighty Central Academy in Palatka. We walked across the field and daydreamed of whipping C.A., the nickname of our cross-county rival.

As we settled into our homeroom and as Miss Howard called the roll, our principal, Mr. Burney, came on the intercom and ordered grades 10 through 12 into the cafetorium. After the three classes were seated, we noticed the television in the middle of the stage.

I could not imagine what was so important that Mr. Burney would let us watch television during a school day. The last time such a thing had happened, I was in seventh grade, when Jackie Robinson and the Brooklyn Dodgers, beloved by Negroes everywhere, were playing the Yankees in the seventh game of the 1956 World Series.

Mr. Burney's words are forever burnished in my memory: "You young people need to see what's going on in Oxford, Mississippi. Now pay attention."

He turned on the black-and-white set and sat in the rear of the room. First, we saw President John F. Kennedy's face and heard his familiar voice, a voice that inspired trust in Negroes. He had ordered federal troops to Oxford to help a little skinny Negro named James Meredith enroll in the University of Mississippi.

Meredith would be the first Negro to enroll in this bastion of Jim Crow.

Next, we saw the scowling face of Mississippi Gov. Ross Barnett, and then we heard his voice. He passionately declared himself a "segregationist," and he vowed that no Negro would ever attend Ole Miss.

My usually rambunctious schoolmates and I were stone silent as we watched dozens of outnumbered U.S. marshals try to push back a white mob of hundreds. Then, on the TV screen, we saw all hell break loose. Chants of "nigger" became action. Molotov cocktails, bottles and bricks rained down on the marshals.

We watched the scene in horror. These were white people fighting other white people because of Meredith, a Negro.

"Everybody pay attention!" Mr. Burney yelled in the semi-dark room. He did not have to remind us. We were transfixed.

Before calm was restored, after troops arrived from Fort Bragg's Company A 503 MP Battalion and the Mississippi National Guard, two rioters had been killed and 200 others injured.

We had seen angry whites in Crescent City, but the fury we witnessed that day on TV filled us with dread. Jim Crow suddenly was a real entity. He wore an evil face. And that face was white.

For the first time in my young life, I was afraid for the future. Within a year, many of my classmates and I would be going away to college. What would happen to us?

That afternoon, a pall fell over our football practice. C.A. was no longer our most important enemy.

The next day, Justice Department attorney John Doar and federal marshals escorted Meredith to Ole Miss, where he registered as the university's first Negro student.

I went away to college the next year but not with the hopefulness I had felt before witnessing the Meredith nightmare. Everything had changed. I had seen a side of America I had only read about or had heard my elders describe.

That experience probably led me to the civil rights movement and eventually to Mississippi, where I helped register blacks to vote. The events of that day showed me that America was a place of profound hatreds, a place capable of murder because of race.

Today, during the 40th anniversary of the Meredith/Ole Miss confrontation, I remind myself that racial harmony is a fragile thing, perhaps an illusion. I know that a Jasper, Texas, can happen at any time, that we have not seen the last of the dynamics that surrounded the O.J. Simpson trial, that many school boards nationwide have no African Americans, that the U.S. Senate remains lily-white.

Much has changed since my friends and I innocently walked to school on the morning of Sept. 30, 1962. Beneath the surface, however, much remains the same.

A disgrace to King's legacy

JANUARY 19, 2003

In San Angelo, Tex., I had, for the first time, the dubious honor of living on a roadway named for the Rev. Martin Luther King Jr. Mine was officially dubbed Martin Luther King Boulevard. I mention this fact to establish my bona fides for the discussion to follow.

As we celebrate King's birthday, more than 500 streets in the United States bear the civil rights leader's name. No other American enjoys such a distinction. Soon after King was assassinated on April 4, 1968, in Memphis, African Americans began a campaign to get a holiday named in his honor and to get streets and buildings named for him.

They have succeeded on that score, obviously. In fact, a school in Arequipa, Peru, has been named for the Nobel Peace Prize winner, and so has a library in Lusaka, Zambia. Even as I write, city governments and other organizations are considering ways to memorialize King by using his name.

That said, an ugly side of the King-name phenomenon is ignored during this season of celebration.

Black comedian Chris Rock tells a joke that goes something like this: When a white friend told Chris Rock that he was on a street called Martin Luther King and asked what he should do, Chris Rock answered, "Run!" At another time and on a more serious note, Rock said: "I don't care where you live in America, if you're on Martin Luther King Boulevard, there's some violence going on."

He is right.

But in our zeal to honor King, we forget to ask a few fundamental questions that would show us that most of the streets, boulevards and avenues named for King actually disgrace his great legacy.

Let me explain.

The black part of town that King Street passes through here in St. Petersburg, where I live and work, is a corridor of broad dilapidation, abandoned structures, vacant lots with junked vehicles and trash and debris, black-on-black violence, drug trafficking, public drinking, rudeness, indolence. Even worse, perhaps, most of the viable businesses on this stretch of MLK are owned by people other than blacks—a testament to black powerlessness.

The reasons for this state of affairs are many and complex. From the beginning, streets named for King—at least significant segments of them—were in poor black neighborhoods. From the beginning, these streets were themselves symbols of segregation and decay. From the beginning, streets named for King were a "black thing." African Americans happily settled for streets in these places because this was all they were going to get from whites who were under fire from fellow whites to resist change.

Listen to Martin Luther King III, head of the Southern Christian Leadership Conference, the organization his father co-founded: "Most of the streets are still located in areas where they have been neglected. Their (white leaders') intentions were honorable, but, unfortunately, what they didn't do in most cases was to create the kind of street or area that would be an appropriate tribute."

On the surface, King's words are correct. But he fails to see the real source of the "neglect." The fault does not lie with white people. It lies with black people.

Has everyone forgotten that Martin Luther King Jr. was born and reared on a clean, quiet, middle-class street in Atlanta, that he grew up with strict conservative values—values such as serving your community, protecting and respecting your neighbors, hard work, thrift, sobriety, cleanliness?

Martin Luther King III has fallen under the spell of blaming white people for the sorry state of streets honoring his father. We blacks have failed to rise to the level demanded of us to honor our slain leader.

If we do nothing else, we should resolve to transform all King roadways into clean, well-lighted places that will attract businesses of all stripes, that will entice tourists to spend time and money among us, that let local residents know that a visit to King Street is a chance to enjoy yet another part of their city.

For many black communities, the streets named for King are their main streets. In some places, such as St. Petersburg, many white people use King Street to travel to and from their homes each day, to and from work each day, to take their kids to and from school each day.

And what do these white people see?

In some parts of St. Petersburg, a wasteland.

Out of fear, they stop only when traffic lights or wrecks or other roadblocks stop them. Why else would they stop? For the same reason as whites—fear—many blacks also avoid the King streets in their cities.

Kimberley Wilson, a member of the African American Leadership Group, asked: "Why isn't black America outraged that (King's) name is attached to the crime-ridden ghettoes and schools where no one is learning? What kind of tribute is this to Dr. King's legacy?"

It is not a tribute to King's legacy. It is an outrage. It disgraces the memory of one of the greatest figures of the last century.

Jim Crow is given a new outfit

FEBRUARY 2, 2003

In 1949, Virgil Hawkins, an African American professor at historically black Bethune-Cookman College in Daytona Beach, applied for admission to the University of Florida College of Law. Hawkins' application was summarily rejected. And in quick order, the state Board of Regents, the state attorney general and the Florida Supreme Court agreed that Hawkins could not attend UF's law school.

In the court's last word on the matter—flouting a U.S. Supreme Court decision—Florida Supreme Court Justice Glenn Terrell, an unreconstructed racist, declared that racial segregation was God's wish for humankind: "When God created man, he created each race to his own continent according to color—Europe to the white man, Africa to the black man, and America to the red man."

For many African Americans, as the hypocritical debate over affirmative action rages today, Terrell's words still resonate. We hear his warped attitude reflected in much of the right-wing talk about the evil of affirmative action for black citizens, a group that has been systematically and institutionally denied admission into many mainstream arenas while many unqualified whites enjoy admission.

Hawkins and other aspiring black lawyers had nowhere to go if they wanted to learn their profession in their home state of Florida. Jim Crow ruled the day and was supported by segregationist readings of the Old Testament and racist interpretations of the Florida and U.S. constitutions. Later, without benefiting Hawkins and his generation, the U.S. Supreme Court outlawed discrimination based solely on skin color.

Suddenly, officials at UF would have to admit blacks into its flagship, lily-white law school. UF and its supporters in Tallahassee were not ready to commit such an act of justice. What happened next, as described in the 2002 summer issue of *The Journal of Blacks in Higher Education*, gave Florida officials a way to maintain de facto segregation at UF:

"Under the separate but equal principle of *Plessy v. Ferguson*, if the University of Florida was not willing to admit black students to its law school, the state would have to provide 'equal' facilities for blacks. So in 1951 a small law school was created on the campus of Florida A&M University in Tallahassee. It had a tiny 6,000-book library. Over the next 17 years, the law school graduated only 57 students, an average of less than four per year."

But change marched into the Sunshine State. When Hawkins withdrew his application in 1958, the state agreed to let other blacks into UF in 1962, and shrewd lawmakers immediately cut off funding to FAMU's law school. The 6,000-book collection was boxed up and carted off to the law library at Florida State University over the next hill.

During subsequent years, blacks attended UF's law school, but their relationship with the college has been rocky at best, and reports of discrimination never go away.

Now, with Republicans and their supporters demonizing affirmative action, Florida has fashioned a new, more benign, form of Jim Crow. And the precepts underpinning *Plessy v. Ferguson* have given legislators a way to play all sides of the issue.

Two years ago, Florida Gov. Jeb Bush issued an executive order banning race as a consideration in admission to the state's universities. He implemented the so-called One Florida plan, which was supposed to replace affirmative action. It admitted to the state university system the top 20 percent of the graduating class at each public high school. These otherwise qualified students, however, would have to compete for slots at the flagship UF campus. And, of course, race could not be a consideration.

With the then-2002 gubernatorial election fast approaching, with black anger fomenting over One Florida and with black and Hispanic demands for new law schools growing louder, Bush reached into the past and gave them what they wanted. He and the GOP-controlled Legislature established law schools for mostly black FAMU and predominantly Hispanic Florida International University in Miami.

Consider this contradictory language in the legislation authorizing FAMU's law school: "The College of Law at Florida A&M University shall be dedicated to providing opportunities for minorities to attain representation with the legal profession proportionate to their representation in the general population. However, the College of Law shall not include preferences in the admissions process for applicants on the basis of race, national origin, or sex."

Fancy language aside, everyone knows that the FAMU law school— a second-tier institution—will become a virtual ghetto, while UF's law school will become whiter.

Here is *The Journal of Blacks in Higher Education*'s assessment of what FAMU's law school means: "Segregationists . . . were delighted with the prospect of a new law school earmarked for blacks. The legislators necessarily knew that very few white students would want to attend a law school at a historically black university. Like it or not, in the minds of most whites a continuing stigma attaches to black educational institutions. Therefore, it was almost certain that blacks would take up most of the spaces at the new school."

Like many other Florida-based black journalists, I got to know Virgil Hawkins well. My sense is that even if FAMU's law school were created with the best of intentions, Hawkins would see it as a gussied-up version of Jim Crow.

The unflattering truth is that FAMU's law school would have been Hawkins' second or third choice. Remember, he applied to the University of Florida, not to one of the nation's black colleges of law. He wanted to attend the state's best.

Moral responsibility in matters of race

APRIL 9, 2003

Here we go again: affirmative action, this time involving the University of Michigan. And this time, even the president of the United States—himself not any teacher's brightest star—weighed in against using race as a factor in college admissions.

What gets me is that so many white people who benefit from being white want to ignore race—our rawest nerve and the most enduring, corrosive force in American social life. Everything about race still matters. Nothing else marks the individual or the group so immediately, so thoroughly, so permanently.

I must repeat one point: White people benefit from being white because being white is inherently an advantage in a society controlled in every way by whites.

Let me share a real-life experience: A white friend of mine is an attorney who was born wealthy. While a high school senior, he came home one day and complained that two of the approximately 10 black students on the prestigious campus planned to use affirmative action to get into the University of Florida Law School.

My friend still remembers his father's words, which went something to this effect: "Don't ever say anything like that in my presence again. No matter how many black kids get into law school through affirmative action, you, a white person, will always have every advantage."

That one lesson stayed with him. His firm works hard to find African American summer interns and attorneys fresh out of law school. His firm annually logs an exemplary record of pro bono work for the poor. He understands the U.S. Constitution as well as the next person. And he understands something else: As a white person with every advantage, he has certain moral responsibilities, one of which is to use no small amount of common sense in matters of race.

Affirmative action is what good people do instinctively. I first saw real affirmative action in 1963, as a freshman at Wiley College in Marshall, Texas, when Negro students could not set foot on most white campuses in the South without trouble.

For the first time, I had white teachers. My French, history, political science and math professors were white. Three of them were young

Woodrow Wilson Fellows who could have taught almost anywhere they wanted but who chose our tiny historically black college.

I asked Edward Carns, my history professor, why he had come to this intellectual outpost. Having been born and reared in Baltimore and having seen the ill effects of black poverty up close, he felt duty-bound to help Southern Negroes, he said. Because Negroes could not attend tax-supported white schools, white professors of good conscience had a moral obligation to travel to Negro schools and teach for a few years at least. Carns taught at two other historically black colleges before marrying and moving on to the Ivy League. His service to us was affirmative action. My schoolmates and I are eternally grateful.

Years later, after I left the military and attended historically black Bethune-Cookman College in Daytona Beach, I had other young white professors who understood how America had cheated us and who comprehended their moral duty to reach out to us. They understood affirmative action in its purest sense: doing what is morally right to redress past wrongs.

When I became a professor, I followed the example of my white professors. My resume looks like a Kerouacian itinerary. During my first eight years as a professor, I worked at four different schools—Kennedy-King College in Chicago; Northern Illinois University in DeKalb; the University of Illinois-Chicago; Governor's State University in Park Forest South, Ill.

On each campus, half of my courses were in the English department, the other half in the remediation program intended to help black students admitted under affirmative action. I wanted to work at places where I could be of use, where I could help black students learn skills and gain knowledge they had been denied in high school.

As an itinerant, I was practicing affirmative action, just as my white professors had taught me to do. Today, we need such affirmative action more than ever, an affirmative action of the heart and of good conscience.

In the upper reaches of the government, good will toward minorities has been replaced by the mean-spirited conservatism of Republican ideologues. Fortunately, though, many people of conscience remain. Fortune 500 companies and leaders of the military academies and services, for example, have written briefs to the U.S. Supreme Court on behalf of the University of Michigan not endorsing affirmative action.

Is Fannie Mae software biased against minority home buyers?

APRIL 4, 2004

Each day, on television and radio, Fannie Mae ads boast, "Our business is the American dream." This slogan, highlighted by a smiling family of four, also graces the top of Fannie Mae's website.

The American Dream, of course, is homeownership.

Congress established Fannie Mae in 1938 to "expand the flow of mortgage money by creating a secondary market." Decades later, after becoming a private company, Fannie Mae, along with its sibling Freddie Mac, began focusing on mortgages for minorities. On its website, the agency declares: "No company in America is more committed to expanding minority homeownership. Nobody is creating more innovative mortgage products and partnerships to break down the barriers. And nobody is more determined to lead the market in serving minority families."

The website further states that currently "more than 24-million American families live in homes Fannie Mae has helped finance. In 2003, Fannie Mae purchased or guaranteed $1.4-trillion of home mortgages from 1,000 lenders."

Most Americans who read or hear such promotions and statistics rarely think that anything could be amiss at Fannie Mae, a Fortune 500 giant. Who would complain about an agency that vows to "break down the barriers" for minorities?

Safiyyah Rahmaan does, and she does so vehemently. After having been denied a conventional mortgage, she learned the hard way that Fannie Mae's warm-and-fuzzy image in its ads and website is a far cry from how the company operates behind closed doors.

After several banks had turned down her loan applications, Rahmaan, 43, discovered that Fannie Mae had thoroughly investigated her financial life and had branded her without her knowledge.

"Fannie Mae isn't really helping the masses like the impression it gives," Rahmaan said.

Represented by the Tampa law firm of James, Hoyer, Newcomer & Smiljanich, Rahmaan is leading a class action lawsuit that aims to force Fannie Mae to treat minorities seeking home loans fairly. The firm is filing a similar suit against Freddie Mac. At issue in the suit is whether in its mission to computerize mortgage lending, Fannie Mae has wound up penalizing black and Hispanic home buyers, the very clients it is mandated to help.

The alleged culprit is Desktop Underwriter, the computer system Fannie Mae uses to make lending decisions. Freddie Mac uses a similar system called Loan Prospector. When a mortgage broker submits a customer's mortgage application to these systems, Fannie Mae or Freddie Mac pulls the customer's credit report and decides if the person is a good risk for the loan. But the agencies never talk to the customer.

Only the numbers matter in the decisions.

"A computer can't boil a person's character down to a number," said Christa Collins, one of Rahmaan's attorneys. "We believe these computer programs discriminate against minorities. There is a mountain of studies showing that in their rush to use these computerized lending models, Fannie Mae and Freddie Mac have left behind their core constituency of minority borrowers."

Collins argues that Fannie Mae and Freddie Mac operate much like the Great Oz: controlling choices of prospective home buyers from behind the curtains. Although most home buyers, especially first-time minority applicants, have only vaguely heard of Fannie Mae and Freddie Mac, these two conglomerates exercise vast control over the U.S. mortgage market. They can do so because they are the primary purchasers of home mortgages in the nation.

The companies do not issue mortgages directly but rather buy them from banks and neighborhood brokers, who originally help customers obtain loans. To stay in business, brokers have to sell the loans they generate by making their loans appealing to Fannie Mae and Freddie Mac.

When Fannie and Freddie introduced their computerized lending programs, the culture of home mortgage lending changed. Brokers learned in seconds if Fannie and Freddie would buy a loan they were offering the customer.

Although customers dealt with their brokers, Fannie or Freddie's computer program called the shots by producing a credit score, which is at the center of Rahmaan's complaint. Her attorneys are suing Fannie and Freddie for racial discrimination, arguing that the firms' "credit scoring" programs for rating mortgages violate the civil rights of minorities.

Credit scoring is the process of distilling a person's entire credit report into a single three-digit number. That number determines if an applicant gets the loan and at what interest rate. Credit scoring became popular in the late 1990s, when insurance companies began using it to price car and home insurance.

Collins, one of Rahmaan's attorneys, contends that credit scoring "is the latest proxy used by insurance companies to redline coverage areas and focus on wealthy white customers. Whether you're talking mortgages or insurance, we think the evidence will show credit scoring hurts minorities, single parents, renters, city dwellers, old people who like to pay in cash, people who've never bothered to create a credit history (so-called "thin files") and members of ethnic groups in which families tend to lend money to its own.

"Fannie Mae, therefore, slams the doors in the faces of minority home buyers and perpetuates the discrimination it is supposed to cure. Furthermore, Fannie Mae fails to give prospective homeowners notice of the adverse action Fannie Mae takes against them."

Rahmaan said Fannie Mae calculated her credit worthiness and circumscribed her life, without knowing her—without speaking with her, without meeting her, without informing her as to how the agency arrived at its verdict.

"It is hard to speculate how much lower an interest rate Ms. Rahmaan would have gotten had Fannie Mae approved her because the mortgage market is so fluid," Collins said. "However, it was not uncommon for the difference between conventional and subprime loans at the time to be several percentage points. On the residence in question, Ms. Rahmaan presently pays 10.25 percent interest. She is current with that obligation."

Rahmaan said that if Fannie Mae had met her personally, the agency would have experienced the ideal applicant. "If Fannie Mae had a poster child, it would be me," she said. "Besides being financially responsible, I'm a double minority. So, why did I get 'caution' and not 'approved' on my rating? Why am I forced to go and pay a higher interest rate? This is not helping me."

*   *   *

Indeed, Rahmaan, as a single mom, would seem to be an excellent risk for a Fannie Mae mortgage. All of her adult life, her top priority has been caring for her eight children. During the mid-1980s, she and her husband began their own business called Ocean Delight, a frozen fish delivery service in Rochester, N.Y. After her divorce, she supplemented the child support she received with a variety of full-time and part-time jobs, when she moved to Wilson, N.C., about 50 miles east of Raleigh.

Here, she established and operated a concession business, selling food and drink each day in front of the Wilson courthouse and during special local events. In 1997, she opened the Milk Store, a small neighborhood market providing items such as eggs, cereal and milk that are covered by the Federal Women, Infants and Children Program.

Rahmaan sold the Milk Store five years later and opened a similar business called the Baby Stop. Saving her money, she went into real estate investments, buying her first house through owner financing. She rehabilitated the house herself. All the while, she met her other monthly financial obligations.

In 2001, Rahmaan's steady progress hit a wall when she applied for a conventional loan at several institutions and was denied. After a few months of returning to the banks and getting the runaround, she learned that Fannie Mae's computer system, Desktop Underwriter, was behind the denials.

"I was forced to go and deal with mortgage brokers, and that forced me into a higher interest rate," she said. "Just knowing that my life had been fed into this computer, it rendered a decision that also altered my life. I'm a mother of eight. If anyone needed a lower interest rate, I needed it. But I had to go to a B lender. I didn't know and was not told what the decision was made on. Because of this lawsuit, I learned that my white counterpart with a similar background, with similar things on her credit report, was rendered a different decision."

Rahmaan is angry also because Fannie Mae ignored, or dismissed, her pride and work ethic.

"There were opportunities for me to go to the department of social services to seek aid because I was unemployed when I came to Wilson," she said. "But I didn't want or expect a handout. I want to build something that makes me independent and not have to rely on the system. Give me a level playing field, and I'll make something happen. I don't need for you to grease the tracks for me. Just don't hurt me.

"I feel like I've been raped because they went through my life, invaded my life, my privacy, and made decisions I didn't even know what they were making. They had this information on me that they withheld from me. If I had known I was going to be judged by them, I could've decided if I wanted to deal with them or not. As it was, I had no choice."

As the lawsuit moves forward, Rahmaan says she has to remember that Fannie Mae is not a charitable organization, as many people may believe after seeing the agency's upbeat ads.

"This is a business," she said. "A cutthroat business that discriminates."

On March 15, Fannie Mae filed a motion for summary judgment for dismissal in the federal district court in the District of Columbia, arguing that Rahmaan was denied various loans because "her credit history was very poor." The denials had nothing to do with Rahmaan's race, spokesman Chuck Greener wrote in an official statement.

Apathy feeds black-on-black violence

JULY 22, 2007

If St. Petersburg is a microcosm of black life in the United States, and I believe that it is, black America is in such dire straits because of violent black-on-black crime and apathy it may be doomed to second-class citizenship in perpetuity.

Just 10 days ago, another decent, family-oriented, hardworking, law-abiding black resident was shot and killed in one of St. Petersburg's predominantly black neighborhoods.

This time, the victim was 68-year-old Amuel Murph, a retired Postal Service employee who lived in middle-class Lake Maggiore Shores. Police say Murph was gunned down at close range in his driveway while taking out trash at about 5 a.m. Police believe that he may have chanced upon a group of robbers trying to break in or steal three vehicles. The killer used a heavy assault rifle.

When Murph's wife of 45 years, Mary Murph, came to the window to see what had happened, the killer fired at her several times but missed. Like her husband, Mary Murph, 64, has led an exemplary life. In 1972, she founded the Tampa Bay Area Sickle Disease Foundation, and she was a guidance counselor at Campbell Elementary School.

Although Amuel Murph's death is yet another statistic in the bloody tapestry of black life in America, I take his loss personally. I am angry. I knew Amuel Murph only casually, when we greeted each other at the post office on First Avenue N. He had a ready smile and a sincere "hello."

I met his wife several years ago at a health fair for black residents. Because of her, I became a supporter of sickle cell efforts. One of the couple's daughters, Tangela, owned the Reader's Choice Books and Gift Expression bookstore in Maximo Plaza on 34th Street S. Over the years, I bought several books there.

Sadly, another good man, a black man who fretted over the appearance of his house and his yard, has been murdered in a black neighborhood.

At this writing, the police are trying to gather clues as to who the killer is. I will bet a year's salary that several black people in the general Midtown area know the killer and his accomplices.

Thus far, however, no one has come forward with information. As a result of the code of silence prevalent in too many black areas nationwide, black criminals feel safe to carry out their remorseless work. A few years ago, a teenage thug in Bartlett Park—bragging that he had hijacked two cars and had robbed a drug dealer with a handgun—told me that he was "the freest nigga in the 'hood."

Why? Because he could do whatever he pleased and "nobody better say sh—," he said with cold confidence.

He frightened me. And he sickened me.

I told a police officer about him, but the officer said the department couldn't act because I hadn't witnessed the teen committing a crime. Several months later, though, the teen was arrested on a charge of armed robbery, only because the police had developed enough evidence on their own. They didn't get any help from the community.

Many blacks, along with some white liberals, complain that the police don't do enough to control violent crime in the black community. Such complaints are naive, and they wrongly blame the police.

Only when blacks take to their own streets, only when blacks start snitching and only when blacks declare that they are mad as hell and will not take it anymore will black-on-black crime decrease.

As long as black criminals feel safe to ply their evil trade in black neighborhoods, black-on-black horrors will proliferate.

We blacks have ourselves to blame.

To honor King, live up to him

JANUARY 17, 2010

Because Martin Luther King Jr. dedicated his life to fighting for civil rights and justice for America's black victims of de jure and de facto discrimination, blacks owe him more than parades, speeches and concerts. We should use the King holiday to commit ourselves to living up to his dreams and efforts.

If we are ever to enjoy the full benefits of the history-changing civil rights legislation passed during King's lifetime and afterward, we need to start holding up our end of the bargain. To enjoy these hard-earned benefits, we must be prepared to enjoy them. We must become introspective and accept responsibility for our lives as individuals. We must commit ourselves to serving our neighbors and improving our communities.

Education, as King knew, is essential for success in most areas of American life. Merely having the right to attend the nation's public schools is not enough. Hundreds of thousands of black children still lag behind their white and Asian classmates academically. Too many black students, especially males, are disruptive and wind up suspended or expelled. Legions simply drop out.

My detractors will accuse me of being insensitive, of letting the nation's school boards, principals and teachers off the hook. Not so. While the "system" always can do more for students, many black adults responsible for our children fail to hold up their end of the bargain. Teachers are most effective when students come to class prepared to learn. Being prepared to learn includes having a rested and nourished body, respect for authority and a positive attitude.

I will not recite the abysmal scores of our students on the ACT and SAT college entrances exams. Simply stated, we should be as concerned about the scores as we were 20 years ago. Our college graduation rates should scare us to death. We must commit ourselves to significantly raising these numbers if we want to give our children successful futures in a world where meritocracy matters more and more.

King Day also is the ideal time to commit ourselves to a serious effort to begin reversing the soaring incarceration rates of blacks in the nation's jails and prisons, a phenomenon some researchers trace to our lack of education. The Nation of Islam aptly refers to our high incarceration rates as "America's new slavery."

A 2008 Pew Center on the States report found that 1.6 million inmates were in U.S. prisons. One in 9 black men ages 20 to 34 was behind bars, compared with 1 in 30 for other men in the same age group. For black women ages 35 to 39, the number is 1 in 100, compared with 1 in 355 for white women in the same age group.

We urgently need to commit ourselves to rebuilding the two-parent family to lower the high number of black children born out of wedlock. Studies find that between 70 percent and 80 percent of black children are born to single mothers, many of them teenagers. Some black neighborhoods do not have any two-parent families. These trends must be reversed.

We also need to focus on our physical health. King Day is an excellent time to start. Life expectancy has steadily increased for whites and blacks since 1970, according to the U.S. Department of Health and Human Services. Between 1970 and 2006, white males' life expectancy increased from 68.0 to 75.7 years (11.3 percent), while white females' life expectancy increased from 75.6 to 80.6 years (6.6 percent). At the same time, life expectancy of black males increased from 60.0 to 69.7 years (16.2 percent), while life expectancy increased from 68.3 to 76.5 years for (11.7 percent) for black females.

Improved life expectancy for blacks, however, is tempered by some negative measures, according to *The Journal of the American Medical Association*: "The gap has narrowed in the past 10 years in part because of declining death rates from AIDS-related complications, homicide, accidental injury and other factors."

Were King alive, he would urge blacks to change their saving habits. Whether we are considering income, home ownership, household wealth or investing, the stark economic divide between whites and African Americans persists.

Unfortunately, as a Pew Research Center survey found, euphoria over President Barack Obama's election and a romantic longing for a "postracial" America have caused a majority of blacks to believe that the standard-of-living gap between whites and blacks has narrowed when, in fact, it has not. Although such a belief makes some of us feel good, it does not alter reality.

In the same unrealistic way, if our parades, speeches and concerts are not accompanied by earnest, long-term commitments to self-improvement and personal sacrifice for a better future, King Day is virtually meaningless.

The best way to honor King is to hold up our end of the bargain.

It's wrong to change 'Huck Finn'

JANUARY 16, 2011

That confounded book is making news again, and the controversy is the same one it has always been. The book I'm referring to, of course, is Mark Twain's novel *The Adventures of Huckleberry Finn*. This time, New-

South Books in Alabama is publishing an edition that elides the N-word all of its 219 times, changing it to "slave."

Over the years, I've had a special personal relationship with *Huck Finn*, published in 1884. A textual purist, I've always thought the enduring fuss has been much ado about nothing, tiresome nonsense over the generations.

One of my most precious literary possessions is a 1948 copy of *Huck Finn* published by Grosset & Dunlap for the Illustrated Junior Library (note the word "junior"). My grandmother gave me the novel when I was in sixth grade. A woman for whom she was a maid gave it to her; it had belonged to the woman's Army-drafted son.

I was drawn into the novel the moment I opened the front cover and saw the color illustration of Huck and Jim, the runaway slave, sitting under a tree on the bank of the Mississippi River. Huck and Jim are deep in conversation. Jim, who is fishing with a simple line, looks worried, and Huck appears relaxed as he smokes his pipe. A big catfish, which Jim has caught, lies on the ground between them, and Huck's musket and the rabbit he's killed rest against the tree. Steamboats ply the muddy water, and a lone fisherman in a skiff maneuvers for a good spot.

From the first sentence, Huck Finn captivated me. I liked the scruffy, pipe-smoking 13-year-old narrating the picaresque tale. And although I was black, a year younger than Huck and living in another century, I identified with his unruliness, his many exploits, the small-town ambience and the natural wonders along the Mississippi as it flows through Missouri and Arkansas.

When I first encountered the N-word, on Page 4, I took it in stride. It was a word I was accustomed to hearing uttered every day by blacks and whites. As an avid reader, I was accustomed to seeing the word in stories by white writers and black writers such as Zora Neale Hurston, Ralph Ellison and Richard Wright. I couldn't count the number of times I'd been called the N-word by fellow blacks, sometimes to diminish me, other times as a term of endearment. The word was part of the fabric of my life.

My 10th-grade English teacher, Gloria Bonaparte, assigned *Huck Finn* to us, and we read it without a second thought. Mrs. Bonaparte said it was one of the great American novels we should read, and she explained that Twain used the N-word because it was the most natural word for Huck to refer to blacks, given his time and place. We understood.

Years later, after I became a college English professor, I always assigned *Huck Finn*. I had a potentially career-ending experience when I taught at a state university in Illinois. I had six black students and 15 white students in a survey of American literature course. Five of the black students refused to read the novel, citing the N-word as the reason. I told them that they had to read the book or drop the course.

They went to my boss. He asked me if I would assign the students another novel. I said, "Absolutely not." In those days, professors still had some authority. Two of the students relented, read the novel and passed the course. The others dropped out, and I never saw them again.

I had another bad *Huck Finn* encounter when I wrote for the *Gainesville Sun*. A teacher at Gainesville's predominantly black Eastside High School assigned the novel and immediately faced a firestorm of criticism. I wrote a column defending her and, of course, was attacked.

During a roundtable discussion at a black church a week after the column was published, I again defended the teacher and the novel. I was denounced as an "Uncle Tom," "a fool," "a traitor" and several profane names. A man called me a "stupid n——." Realizing what he'd done, he smiled, sat and remained silent the rest of the evening.

I gave up long ago trying to convince others that the N-word belongs in *Huck Finn*, that removing it is like airbrushing Mona Lisa's expression to make the painting less ambiguous.

It is clear to me that as Twain employed the N-word, he ennobled Jim, the runaway slave. Jim is the moral center of the novel. He is superior to the whites, even Huck. As a textual purist, I wish we would let *The Adventures of Huckleberry Finn* be *The Adventures of Huckleberry Finn* just as Twain intended.

We don't have the right to alter an artist's work for any reason. Authorial intent is unalterable.

Breaking down stereotypes

AUGUST 7, 2011

When I first heard of the recent mass murders in Norway, I assumed, like millions of other people worldwide, that the killer was an outsider of some kind. Upon learning that the suspect is Anders Behring Breivik, I was surprised.

I had assumed that the killer, who detonated a car bomb and opened fire on a youth camp, was an outsider because, like most people everywhere, I am a prisoner of stereotypes. How could anyone except an outsider commit such a terrible act in peaceful Norway? But the suspect is not an outsider. Instead, he is a good-looking, blond Norwegian who apparently believes that Christian Europe would be better off without Muslims.

After Breivik's identity emerged and I realized how wrong I had been, I did some soul searching. As a black male in the United States, I am intimately familiar with the complexities of stereotypes, the fixed or conventional notions or conceptions about a person or a group, especially a group.

Stereotypes may convey the positive or the negative. Most, if not all, successful black people consciously combat negative stereotypes. Otherwise, they would not be successful. As children in Jim Crow schools, my schoolmates and I were taught that American society did not expect much of us, that to survive we needed to be keenly aware of what dominant groups thought of us. We would have to work three times as hard as our white counterparts for the same rewards. We would have to "prove" ourselves in every arena to overcome the debilitating effects of stereotypes.

I vividly recall when my seventh-grade homeroom teacher, Constance Howard, told my classmates and me that if we learned to speak and write well, we could "go far" because whites never expect a "Negro to speak and write well." She called it "the element of surprise." In fact, she taught us the meaning of the word "stereotype." She insisted that we "avoid playing into stereotypes." She said that "white people expect Negroes to be as dumb as rocks." She said we should "bust stereotypes."

Mrs. Howard greatly influenced me, and I took her advice, especially about writing. Good writers read voraciously and practiced the craft, she said. Each night, I read—Mark Twain, Flannery O'Connor, Shakespeare, H.G. Wells, Thomas Wolfe, James Baldwin, Eudora Welty, William Faulkner, Richard Wright, John Steinbeck, Jane Austen, Ernest Hemingway, Marjorie Kinnan Rawlings and many more—until my folks ordered me to turn out the light and go to bed.

I was determined to be smart, not stereotypically "dumb." And I was not the only one. Several of my classmates and I competed. Who, for example, had read the most books in a week's time? Who could recite an assigned poem?

When I became a college teacher, I would take my black students aside and tell them what I had learned from Mrs. Howard a generation earlier, busting stereotypes. Some eagerly took my advice of using the element of surprise of being smart.

Most, however, rejected my advice, accusing me of wanting them to "act white." My most disappointing experience came at historically black Stillman College in Tuscaloosa, Ala., where I taught for two years. I gave a speech imploring students to do what I had done as an undergraduate: read as much as possible, revise their essays as many times as needed, travel and surround themselves with smart people.

A colleague told me that several students complained immediately following the speech. One reportedly said, "Mr. Maxwell talks like he wants us to be scholars." Another reportedly said, "Nobody wants to go around acting white like him."

I asked the members of my English class this question: "If being smart is acting white, is being dumb acting black?"

Their responses were angry, one calling me an "Uncle Tom." I explained, unsuccessfully, that they were playing into a stereotype when they, black college students, were not seen as being intellectual. I explained that they gained power when they refused to play into negative stereotypes.

"Yes," I said, "I want you all to surprise the world by becoming scholars."

Black male attitudes feed crisis

MARCH 11, 2012

As a retiree, I have undergone two criminal background checks during the last two years. The first was to be cleared to become an adjunct professor at St. Petersburg College, and the second was to be accepted as a volunteer for Pinellas County's nature parks.

During the SPC process, I was with several other middle-aged to older people, black and white, seeking part- or full-time employment. All of us were well-groomed and appropriately dressed. At the sheriff's facility, I was with four young black males, one white female and two white males. The whites were appropriate in every manner. The black males were ill-groomed and sagging, totally inappropriate for that public space.

I listened as the two black males next to me complained that in addition to an interview, a criminal background check was required for the lowly jobs they were seeking. The youngest-looking one worried that a shoplifting conviction would block him from getting the job. His sentence had been 60 days in jail and a $500 fine. The other had been arrested but not convicted.

After being fingerprinted, I saw the two young black males still waiting for their turns. Although I have not seen them since that morning, I have not forgotten them, their inappropriateness and the perilous quest for employment they probably will face if they do not change their attitudes and behavior, if they do not learn to respect societal norms.

They and millions of other young black males nationwide are associated with crime, a stereotype referred to as "perceived criminality." Many Americans believe that black males commit violent crimes at a rate higher than other groups. Unfortunately, crime statistics consistently support this perception, and it is reinforced in popular culture. It is also true that African American males are overrepresented in the nation's prison system. According to the Justice Department, there are 3,408 black male inmates for every 100,000 black males in the country, compared to 417 white male inmates for every 100,000 white males.

As far as I know, the overwhelming majority of African Americans are aware of the grim statistics that produce the phenomenon of perceived criminality. They also are aware of its destructive consequences. The problem is that many blacks stay in a state of denial and blame everything and everybody else except themselves and their own practices for this crisis.

This crisis has to be repaired. And I am not naive. Although I know there are racial and structural barriers in U.S. society and in the economy that have contributed to many of the problems blacks face, I also know that blacks can change the direction of their lives and increase their opportunities of being successful.

Those arrogant young males I encountered at the sheriff's facility chose to be inappropriate. They chose to make everyone else in the room uncomfortable. They chose to commit their crimes and enter a justice system that dehumanizes. I see dozens of them every day in every city or town or black neighborhood I find myself in.

What must African Americans do about young males? I am not a social scientist, but I am certain that blacks cannot solve their problems until they become introspective and acknowledge their complicity in this predicament. They must muster the will, the courage and a plan to earnestly deal with the issue of perceived criminality and its destructive impact on black males.

Frankly, I do not see American society embracing young black males anytime soon. Blacks must do their own embracing: Parents must raise their boys properly. Churches, the most powerful force in black culture, must regularly preach the gospel of save-the-young-black-male. Leaders must stop trying to be well-liked by their fellow blacks and start telling the harsh truth and risk being called Uncle Toms and sellouts.

Young males must be steered away from crime and unsavory behavior and attitudes that will mark them for life. They must be taught to stay in school, to avoid suspensions and expulsions. According to a new U.S. Education Department report, black boys are more likely to be harshly disciplined in school than other students.

Blacks are facing a human rights crisis in their midst, and it is their responsibility to end this crisis. It is insanity to continue to blame white people for this crisis while expecting to get a different result. It is up to blacks to stop the insanity of losing young black males.

Race is so familiar, we ignore its harm

APRIL 8, 2012

If nothing else, the killing of Trayvon Martin has many Americans openly talking about race and racism again. That is good, even though some of our talk is harsh.

But then, racism is harsh.

Many white people simply want the topic to go away. Trust me when I say that most blacks also want it to disappear—but for other reasons. Trayvon Martin's killing shows that the time has come for all decent Americans to commit to earnestly acknowledging the ugly truth about race and racism and banishing the sophistry of denial.

The most powerful acknowledgment of the ugliness of race I have read comes from Sig Gissler, administrator of the Pulitzer prizes, Columbia University journalism professor and specialist in race and media ethics. He wrote: "Race—it is America's rawest nerve and most enduring dilemma. From birth to death, race is with us, defining, dividing, distorting."

I add the following to Gissler's insight: From birth to death, race is one of the most painfully personal of all human experiences.

As a black person, I live race. I am acutely aware that my race constitutes what is referred as a "master status." That is, in the eyes of whites and other nonblacks, my skin color, my most visible characteristic, is the most important piece of information about me.

This condition is inescapable. The consequences of race can be profoundly hurtful, each encounter robbing you of a piece of dignity, the degree depending on your sense of self-worth.

I vividly recall an experience of 34 years ago when as a professional I became intellectually aware of the degrading effect of my skin color. I was an English professor at Florida Keys Community College in Key West. Wearing new khakis and a crisp button-down shirt on the first night of class, I carried my textbook, a notepad and the class roster as I walked to my classroom.

A white student walked toward me and told me I needed to "mop up the water" under the air conditioner in her classroom. I asked for the room number. It was my room. Not saying anything to her, I found the janitor's station and placed a note on the door. When I walked into my classroom, I recognized the student. She sat in the second row. Based on her startled reaction, she knew she had wrongly assumed her teacher was the janitor.

As I wrote my name on the blackboard, she walked out. I learned a few days later she had enrolled in another section of the course. Her new teacher, a white man, was one of my spearfishing buddies. Over time, we had uneasy laughs about the incident.

I was certain that if I had been white, the student would not have assumed I was a janitor. My colleague agreed. Her mistake was grounded in race. How else could she have overlooked my attire, my textbook and notepad?

No scholar has definitively theorized about race, at least not to my satisfaction. Fancy language cannot explain it. And the voguish genetic and anthropological reports of late—arguments that humankind is one big family—have not generated useful clarity and better race relations.

Race produces racism, and racism naturally enables discrimination from the benign to the horrific. Paradoxically, race appears to be so familiar to us as groups and individuals, we mistakenly assume that we understand it. Therefore, we take it for granted, seeing it as too tiresome a subject to discuss.

The truth, I believe, is that race confounds our understanding precisely because, besides being ever-present, it is subconsciously lived by the victim and by the perpetrator, making it a complex mix of conflicting sentiments and degrading actions, equally degrading reactions and crass evasions. Race is so familiar that many of us fail to see that just as it harms the perpetrator and the victim alike, it indicts us in the same way.

In the United States, race is inevitable, a reality that explains in part why when race comes up, even very smart people begin to either smirk, roll their eyes, sigh, protest or leave the room. Please, not race again.

While most of us view ourselves as being decent and honorable and ethical, the acknowledgment of race shames many of us, reminding us that for all of our laws and claims of believing in equality, we are creatures of racial exclusionism and abusiveness.

Like Sig Gissler, we should have the courage and honesty to acknowledge the ugly truth that race is our "rawest nerve." Only then can we begin to find answers.

Medical racism's high cost

DECEMBER 9, 2012

In his new book, *Black & Blue: The Origins and Consequences of Medical Racism*, John Hoberman shows how racial bias among doctors negatively affects diagnosis and treatment for black patients.

The book comes at a perfect time, during the implementation of the Affordable Care Act, President Barack Obama's biggest domestic accomplishment.

In an email message, Hoberman, professor of Germanic studies at the University of Texas at Austin, wrote that the legislation "serves the medical needs of countless African Americans by making medical care available to millions of people who have not been able to afford it. It is well known that poverty and lack of access to care do more to cause illness and premature death than any other factors."

While access to care for African Americans is important, quality of care is crucial. But all too often and in too many medical offices and facilities nationwide, the quality of care patients receive depends on the color of their skin.

This moral shortcoming should be earnestly discussed at the highest levels of medicine, but it rarely is, Hoberman writes. It definitely is not part of medical schools' curricula.

Many studies have documented racial discrimination in U.S. medicine. As far back as 1979, for example, a team of medical authors wrote in *The Journal of the American Medical Association* that "it is an open secret that physicians dislike certain patients." The open secret was that African Americans sat at the top of the list of disliked patients.

Black & Blue goes where previous studies have not. It is an unapologetic and systematic analysis of how American doctors perceive racial differences and how their opinions determine diagnoses and treatment of their black patients.

Like others who have written about medical racism, Hoberman traces the history of medical abuses of black people. But unlike others, he explores the racially driven thinking and behaviors of today's physicians, revealing the physician's private world, where racial biases and misinformation distort diagnoses and treatments.

Although many people believe that doctors are paragons of reason and are members of a unique moral community, Hoberman writes that doctors have the same racial stereotypes, believe the same tales and hold the same beliefs about racial differences in the general population.

Racial folklore is part of all "medical subdisciplines," from cardiology to gynecology to psychiatry, Hoberman argues. And doctors have placed racial identities on "every organ system of the human body, along with racial interpretations of black children, the black elderly, the black athlete, black musicality, black pain thresholds, and other aspects of black minds and bodies."

He writes that blacks are fully aware of their diminished value and mistreatment, learning long ago to distrust the white medical establishment. And they know something else: The medical profession refuses to examine itself seriously.

The relationship between blacks and the mostly white medical profession is dysfunctional, and that dysfunction has caused great medical harm to blacks, Hoberman writes. Studies regularly show that blacks in general are not as healthy as whites, but these same studies fail to reveal underlying causes of the disparities. We read about the large numbers of blacks who lack insurance, and we know that few primary care doctors practice in black communities. We rarely read, however, about the negative impact of the bias, prejudice and stereotyping by health care providers that may directly contribute to the poor health of blacks.

Many blacks hesitate to enter offices where they know their skin color alone will mark them as being unworthy of the best care.

African American patients are not the only victims of racism, Hoberman writes. Many black doctors face the same discrimination and slights blacks seeking treatment face.

The cure for medical racism, Hoberman argues, will come only when medical schools abandon their "race-aversive curricula" and start including "real race relations training."

He also argues that black leaders outside what he refers to as the "vulnerable black medical community" should take up the cause of demanding changes in the nation's medical schools. The ugly truth, he wrote in an email message, is that "most white people are not interested in black people's problems."

For conservatives, it's all about race

APRIL 19, 2013

When I was a journalism professor in 2005 at Stillman College in Tuscaloosa, a white student from the University of Alabama came to my campus and handed me a bullet-ridden sheet of standard copy paper.

It was a target that had been used at a local shooting range.

The image on the target was an enlargement of my photograph published in the *Tuscaloosa News* with my weekly column. Most of my forehead was shot out, and my eyes and nose were gone. The student said many whites in Tuscaloosa hated me and advised me to be "extra careful."

I was reminded of that experience after reading about Sgt. Ron King, the white firearms instructor recently fired from the Port Canaveral Police Department. He allegedly offered fellow officers shooting targets with a silhouette resembling Trayvon Martin, the unarmed black 17-year-old shot and killed last year in nearby Sanford by neighborhood watchman George Zimmerman.

King said that race was not his motivation in attempting to get others to use the targets, which had images of Skittles candy and a bottle of tea, items Trayvon Martin was carrying. I don't believe King. Neither did his boss and those who refused to accept the targets.

I suggest that the racial animus that motivated King represents a major current of the American zeitgeist in 2013.

Look no further than Republican sentiments and spiteful rhetoric surrounding Barack Obama and his presidency. From the beginning,

Republicans made it clear that they were going to give the nation's first black president a hard time. Senate Minority Leader Mitch McConnell stated publicly that his No. 1 goal was to make Obama a "one-term president."

In his study *The Persistence of the Color Line: Racial Politics and the Obama Presidency*, Randall Kennedy, a professor of law at Harvard Law School, points out that Obama faces pressures his predecessors never faced.

Most of the president's words and many of his actions and policies are interpreted through the prism of race. After Trayvon Martin was killed, for example, Obama lamented the tragedy in part by saying that if he had a son, "He'd look like Trayvon." Many conservatives pounced, accusing Obama of playing the "race card."

Not so. The president's words reflected the heartfelt sadness of a loving father.

Many of Obama's domestic policies and proposals, including on the economy and affordable health care, are described as the work of a black man determined to establish socialism, redistributing wealth from rich people to blacks and other undeserving groups.

On foreign policy, especially related to the Middle East, the president is seen as the "other," someone who is not truly American even though he was born in the United States. He is accused of weakening the country's image abroad, even endangering our very existence.

The social and cultural lives of the president and the first lady are under a microscope. I don't think we've ever had so much criticism of the first family's vacation spots, modes of travel and entertainment. I cannot help but conclude that it is all about race.

The irony is that Obama was America's best hope of finally improving race relations and perhaps having some honest dialogue. That hope has been squandered. From the beginning, Obama has done his best to avoid racial issues. In fact, he's angered and disappointed many blacks precisely because he hasn't given them special attention.

In her book *The Obamas*, Jodi Kantor writes that a close friend of Obama told her this: "The first black president doesn't want to give any insight into being the first black president."

That friend was right. Obama has tried to govern as an American. Conservatives are the ones who play the race card. In his dignified way, Obama is serving as the president of all the people.

Why blacks need to vote

SEPTEMBER 5, 2014

I'm really angry at the black residents of Ferguson, Mo., where a white police officer shot and killed unarmed black teenager Michael Brown and set off days of protests and disturbances.

The tragic events in Ferguson underscore the failures of the police department and magnify the city's dangerous racial divide between whites and blacks. But they also reveal how Ferguson's black residents failed to exercise their most precious right as citizens: the right to vote, the power of the ballot.

That betrayal is the source of my anger. (And, by the way, although I'm writing about Ferguson, the betrayal of the franchise can be found in many cities.)

For a long time, Ferguson's population was majority white. During the last 25 years, the population, now 21,000, has become 67 percent black. But being the majority for some two decades has done nothing to give blacks any power where it matters most: local government.

Some stark facts: The city has never had a black mayor, and it has had only one black City Council member. Only three of the police department's 53 officers are black, and the city's other departments and agencies have mostly white staffs.

Why? The overwhelming majority of blacks there aren't registered to vote. Untold numbers have criminal backgrounds that bar them from voting, and others just don't bother. Most alarming, many don't participate in the political process out of ignorance.

You don't have to believe me. Here's what Shiron Hagens, a 41-year-old black mother who was in Ferguson to initiate a voter registration drive, told the *New York Times* about local blacks: "A lot of people just didn't realize that the people who impact their lives every day are directly elected. The prosecutor—he's elected. People didn't know that. The City Council—they're elected. These are the sorts of people who make decisions about hiring police chiefs. People didn't know."

How can anyone born and reared in this country not know about local elections and their far-reaching consequences?

During a speech about events in Ferguson at historically black Bethune-Cookman University in Daytona Beach, Florida Supreme

Court Justice James E.C. Perry, one of two black justices on the court, said: "Voting affects everything. Politics are local; all politics are local. . . . Voting determines who is mayor, who makes the decisions, who makes the rules. It is a sacred responsibility. It is your obligation to make sure you vote. Vote for people who have your interests at heart. Look at what they do when they come before you. If you don't see them any other time, you won't see them then. But when you vote, at least they know they have to pay attention to you."

Perry, an active participant in the civil rights movement during the early 1960s, discussed the bloody struggle to get blacks to take full advantage of their right to vote. I also was part of that struggle, and I'm angry that too many of today's blacks, especially the young, are apathetic about the political process. As a 17-year-old college freshman, I joined thousands of other students in standing up to white mobs to register black voters in the South. We often had our tables overturned, our literature and documents destroyed and our vehicles disabled. We were attacked with fists, clubbed, kicked, spat on, attacked by dogs, water-hosed and chased out of town. When the mobs didn't get us, local law enforcement invented reasons to detain or arrest us.

Many of us still carry the physical and psychological scars of that violent era. To us, securing the right to vote—and voting—was a key to becoming full citizens of the United States of America.

When we trample our right to vote, especially at the local level, we relinquish our right to viable representation in our government, becoming virtual noncitizens.

Demarkus Madyun, 26, of St. Louis, who spoke to the *New York Times* during a voter registration effort in Ferguson, clearly understands the vital need to vote.

"If we're going to try to say that the system has to be corrected for us to receive justice, we have to do everything that we can to be part of the system," he said. "Until we have people in office, it will never be better. Not just presidents—mayors, county executives, the governor."

A generation of brave people fought and died for the right to vote. So, when I see today's blacks throwing away this right, I become angry. No, raging mad.

Growing up in the era of the Florida School for Boys

DECEMBER 12, 2014

As researchers continue to unearth remains in Marianna at the closed Florida School for Boys, also known as the Arthur G. Dozier School for Boys, I'm transported back to the fear I experienced as a boy in Florida during Jim Crow.

The notorious reform school had two campuses, one for whites and one for blacks. We referred to it simply as "Marianna." We knew many of the horror stories about boys who went there and never saw the free world again. Our parents and other guardians used Marianna to keep us in line and out of trouble with "the law."

The fear of a brutal, racist legal system scared many of us, forcing us to seriously weigh the consequences of our behavior. We were too afraid, for example, to make any kind of move if a law enforcement officer confronted us. We never displayed anger when hassled; anger wasn't an option for black males.

When I lived in Lake County, the racial atrocities of Sheriff Willis "Caboose" McCall were our major sources of fear. One of my uncles used to say, "A black man's life ain't worth maggot puke with Sheriff McCall."

Many black men would hide at the sight of McCall's trademark Stetson hat and Western tie. We boys learned to do the same. In addition to many years of unjust arrests and beatings of black men, McCall is perhaps best remembered for the 1951 shooting of two black men—one died—who he claimed attempted to escape from the backseat of his car as he was taking them to the Lake County jail. They were two of four black men accused of raping a white woman in Groveland. In the end, all four were exonerated.

McCall's exploits were so legendary that adults merely had to say his name in our presence to convince us to stay out of trouble. I recall nights when McCall drove through the "Negro Quarters" where I lived. If word got out ahead of time, we stayed behind closed doors.

Although McCall's terror was frightening, it paled alongside that of the Emmett Till tragedy. Emmett, a Chicago resident, was the 14-year-old boy who was lynched by white men in Money, Miss., in 1955 for allegedly whistling at a white woman. Emmett was spending the summer in Mississippi with relatives. News of the murder traveled worldwide, and photos of Emmett's mutilated body gave new meaning to America's racial cruelty.

Although my contemporaries and I were more than 500 miles from Money, we were afraid. The specter of being lynched, shot in the head and mutilated for insulting a white woman never left our imaginations.

After Mamie Till, Emmett's mother, permitted her son's body to be viewed in an open casket, the entire nation was reminded that Americans, especially Southern white men, were capable of heinous race-related crimes. Emmett's face was bludgeoned beyond recognition, and a bullet hole was in his head. Having been under water for several days, the body was badly decomposed.

Jet magazine published photos of Emmett's body. For our survival, the adults in our lives used those photos to scare us, to teach us to avert our eyes in the presence of white women and to step off the sidewalk whenever one approached. We were to be obsequious, polite, unassuming—and silent. We were.

Ironically, Mamie Till knew that the South was a dangerous place for black males. *Jet* and *Ebony* magazines reported that while putting Emmett on the bus in Chicago for the trip to Mississippi, Mamie Till warned: "Be careful, Emmett. If you have to get down on your knees and bow when a white person goes past, do it willingly."

Apparently, Emmett had too much youthful pride to follow his mother's advice.

Everything I've cited occurred years before the self-esteem and "black pride" era, before the civil rights movement began in earnest and long before hip-hop's ego-centered culture was created. Make no mistake: Today's young black males reject my generation's obsequiousness, politeness and silence. They reject my generation's tolerance of abuse, and they should reject it. But if they fight back violently, they still risk dying.

Making black lives matter

JANUARY 31, 2015

In the wake of the killings of unarmed African American males by white police officers, a new mantra for black life in the United States has emerged: "Black Lives Matter."

It's appearing on placards, billboards, handbills, T-shirts and elsewhere. While it has powerful emotional appeal to us, we need to ask ourselves this: How is our new mantra being perceived by people who aren't African American? What are they thinking?

We are, after all, trying to convince them that our lives matter.

A white man who's read my column for many years was brutally honest in a letter to me a few weeks ago: "Bill, you people live like animals. You don't care about your own lives. I'll start caring about you when you show me you care about yourself. I don't care about you people. A lot of white people feel this way. Think about it, Bill. Write about it."

Initially, I was angry. But I reread the letter several times and got the message. And, yes, I've thought about it a lot, and I must conclude that evidence in many areas suggests that we don't care enough about ourselves.

Take black-on-black murders. According to the Violence Policy Center, a Washington think tank, although we're only 13 percent of the nation's population we account for half of all homicide victims. More precisely, black males are 6 percent of the U.S. population but we represent nearly 40 percent of those murdered.

Whites aren't murdering us. We're murdering one another, which strongly suggests that we don't care about one another and that our own lives don't matter to us. People who care about one another don't murder one another. My letter writer is right: We need to show the rest of society that we care about our own lives. We aren't doing that.

I've lived in several major cities, including New York, Chicago, Fort Lauderdale and St. Petersburg, and I've lived in rural areas. No matter where I've been, I've seen too many African Americans who don't care about the physical conditions of their homes and neighborhoods. Trash and filth abound. Buildings are allowed to deteriorate, all indicating that black lives don't matter. In many instances, a simple coat of paint could make all the difference. Clearing debris could give a street a sense of safety.

But all too often matters remain the same or get worse. Why? It's because too many of our communities lack social capital—that sense of communal bonding and reciprocity. Aside from the church and Greek organizations, we don't have healthy community networks in which good things are shared, in which positive behavior is seen as a strength, in which friendship is nurtured as a source of future well-being.

Where social capital exists, people care about one another. They do good things for one another, not bad things to one another.

I've concluded that aside from stopping the epidemic of black-on-black murders, the best way for us to show that black lives matter is for us to prove that we value education, the great ennobling force.

Let's face it. Too many black children rank at the bottom of every measure of academic excellence, and this poor performance follows most of them throughout their lives. Teachers can't do it all. Valuing learning must start in the home.

Unfortunately, far too many black parents see our schools as places of abuse and bondage. But they're wrong. Our schools are places that foster freedom through knowledge.

In praising her school experience, Pulitzer Prize-winning author Alice Walker said: "Just knowing has meant everything to me. Knowing has pushed me out into the world, into college, into places, into people."

And "just knowing"—education—changes behavior.

If we want the rest of society to acknowledge that black lives matter, we have to change. We're not going to alter the attitudes and opinions of others if we don't change, if we continue in our refusal to see the consequences of our behavior.

Education is the key.

Honest talk needed about race

JULY, 31, 2015

Racism always will exist in the United States. Too many of us, white and black, refuse to stop the pretense about race and reconsider the national myth of "equality for all." By pretending that we are equal, we never need to confront the harsh reality of race and inequality.

Let me say at the outset that when I speak of race, I am referring to white people and black people only, especially black descendants of U.S. slaves.

A damning reality of racism, which most of us are wary of acknowledging, is that it has created separation that is ingrained in our national character. Separation has harmed blacks both in degree and manner more than it has harmed whites. After all, blacks are the minority. Whites are the majority.

But separation hurts everyone equally in that it has created a nation of strangers, forcing us to obsess over unwholesome differentness that may be real, perceived or manufactured for the sake of advantage.

Although it will seem counterintuitive to many whites, large numbers of blacks embrace separation, even if it is to their detriment.

Many have cast aside the old romanticism of the Land of the Free. No matter what conventional wisdom holds, insightful blacks know that they are permanent strangers in the place of their birth. They view themselves as being separate, having experienced perpetual disconnectedness, alienation and otherness. The result is unavoidable resentment that defines their existence as a diaspora transported to the New World in putrid holds of slave ships.

Because the legacy of slavery and its racism are so corrosive, we need the dispassionate eyes of foreigners to help us understand ourselves, to help us dare a little introspection.

In 1997, South African Nobel Prize-winning novelist Nadine Gordimer gave Americans a clear view of themselves in "Separate," an essay she wrote for *New York Times Magazine*. I wrote about her observations at the time and return to some of those observations now.

As a white woman born into privilege and as an outspoken opponent of apartheid, Gordimer did what few American whites will ever do: Without defensiveness or denial, she expressed the raw truth about race.

She wrote that while traveling in the United States from the 1950s to the early 1990s, she mixed freely among ordinary and famous American blacks in their homes and in public places. But after 1994, she met few American-born blacks because, as she wrote, they "do not want to mix with whites, however much potential compatibility is beckoning to be recognized. The old, old answer I think not only survives but seems to have grown in bitterness, for reasons (of economics and opportunity) Americans know best: When you have been so long rejected, your collective consciousness tells you that the open-door, open-arms invitation has come too late. You gain your self-respect by saying 'no.'"

Gordimer was prescient. Today, large numbers of young blacks and jaded older blacks have made saying "no" their identity.

Hip-hop artists are prime examples. Their music, attire and other attributes are declaring "no." Hip-hop virtually has rejected all that is white and all that is American. Even performers who don business suits off stage and in boardrooms do so with black distinction. It truly can be called Hip-hop Nation.

In many cities, black parents are rejecting desegregated public schools as eagerly as whites have rejected them. More and more, they are opt-ing for charter, private and parochial schools. These schools are their versions of white segregation academies that mushroomed during Jim Crow and that remain strong today.

Blacks attend their own churches where their style of worship and sermons assuage the indignities of daily racial encounters. The institution of Historically Black Colleges and Universities refuses to die. Some schools, in fact, are gaining in popularity because increasing numbers of black students choose the "black experience" over the hostility they may encounter on majority-white campuses.

Centuries-long rejection has caused black resentment that has grown into a willing embrace of America's racial separateness.

So what are we to do about race, some 300 years since the first dehumanized black slaves were dragged ashore in manacles?

I do not know. But I suppose a rational beginning would be to encourage white opinion leaders in all sectors to follow the lead of Nadine Gordimer: Cast off denial and boldly speak or write the unvarnished truth about race.

And while speaking or writing, remember that truth-telling about race is not the exclusive job of black people.

What Black Lives Matter is really about

JULY 29, 2016

Few acts are more loathsome than intentional misrepresentation of an inconvenient or unpopular truth. In this instance, most Americans have witnessed Republicans intentionally misrepresenting Black Lives Matter, both as a movement and as a slogan.

Honest and knowledgeable people know what Black Lives Matter means. And I suspect that deep down, Republicans know, too, but they must pretend otherwise to carry out their nefarious agenda.

Aside from GOP presidential nominee Donald Trump, former New York Mayor Rudy Giuliani has been one of the most prominent Republicans to publicly misrepresent Black Lives Matter. At the party's convention in Cleveland, he claimed that Black Lives Matter is "inherently racist . . . because it divides us. . . . All lives matter: white lives, black lives, all lives."

Well, of course, all lives matter.

This is precisely the truth that Black Lives Matter is struggling to bring to America's attention: For too long, blacks have been, and still are, the "other" in the Land of the Free, the nation of their birth. The "other," by the way, is defined as a person or group of people who are treated as intrinsically different from dominant populations. The "other" are easily diminished or ostracized.

The philosophical essence of Black Lives Matter is the plea to fully include black people in the fabric of American life.

Well-meaning people acknowledge the unwritten variations of the Black Lives Matter slogan: Black Lives Matter, Too; Black Lives Matter Also; Like Other Lives, Black Lives Matter.

The movement is an apolitical call for inclusiveness, a call to acknowledge the unique challenges of the black experience and the enduring harm of institutionalized racism.

After Black Lives Matter leaders were forced to defend the movement's goals following the deaths of police officers in Dallas and Baton Rouge, La., President Barack Obama weighed in.

"The phrase 'Black Lives Matter' simply refers to the notion that there's a specific vulnerability for African Americans that needs to be addressed," he said in a town-hall-style meeting. "It's not meant to suggest that other lives don't matter; it's to suggest that other folks aren't experiencing this particular vulnerability."

Obama was alluding to ugly milestones in black history. Blacks are the only group shipped to this country as slaves in large numbers, more than 10 million. Slavery lasted for nearly 250 years.

The Emancipation Proclamation of 1863 officially freed slaves, but Reconstruction, meant to rebuild the South, saw defeated whites punish former slaves. Freedom morphed into the Black Codes and the Jim Crow era, ushering in the legal separation of the races and making it impossible for blacks to become full citizens.

Over time, it took a string of federal acts and U.S. Supreme Court decisions to give blacks a modicum of full citizenship. Notable acts and decisions include *Brown v. Board of Education* in 1954; President John F. Kennedy's 1961 executive order to ensure that government contractors "take affirmative action to ensure that applicants are employed, and employees are treated during employment, without regard to their race"; the Civil Rights Act of 1964; and the Voting Rights Act of 1965.

Just think: White Americans had to be forced by the government to treat black citizens equitably. And the struggle for equality continues.

Too many conservatives routinely discredit black people and matters associated with black identity. They engage in, among other tactics, blaming the victim, crass denial and appropriation and distortion of black ideas and expressions.

How often have we heard Republicans claim that unarmed black males would not get killed by the police if they did not break the law or simply kept their mouths shut?

How about this one? To respectably oppose affirmative action, whites appropriated select words of the Rev. Martin Luther King Jr.: "I have a dream that my four little children will one day live in a nation where they will not be judged by the color of their skin, but by the content of their character."

Many conservatives say that affirmative action gives preference to less-qualified blacks over more-qualified whites because it relies on skin color and not on the "content of character," which, they eagerly claim, King would oppose.

How about America's hyphenated names of nationality? From the beginning, we have been a hyphenated people. We have always had, among many other names, English-American, French-American, Italian-American, Irish-American, Jewish-American, Japanese-American, German-American, Scandinavian-American, Cuban-American, Russian-American.

But when the Census Bureau decided to drop "Negro" and replace it with "black" and "African-American" in surveys, many white conservatives protested. Why? I am not sure. I wager, though, that it had a lot to do with pairing Africa with America. Imagine: African-American.

Like the examples above, the Black Lives Matter movement is being demonized because the word "black" is in its name.

Hate crimes are part of America

NOVEMBER 4, 2018

Many Americans are stunned by the recent pipe bombs mailed to President Donald Trump's critics and by the 11 murders of Jews at the synagogue in Pittsburgh. The hateful social media posts by the accused men have caused no small amount of introspection for many Americans.

Many elected officials have opined that "we are better than this as a nation" and that "this is not who we are."

I disagree. We have a long history of such violence. It is quintessentially who we are.

As a black man born in Fort Lauderdale in 1945, having come of age during Jim Crow's racist "separate-but-equal" era, I know that Americans are capable of unspeakable atrocities. Some of these atrocities are violent, while others are social, psychological and economic practices that have the power to determine the very quality of our lives.

While the United States polices and judges the human rights behavior of other nations, we are hardly the exemplar of valuing human worth and dignity. The old instinct to discount and dehumanize non-whites remains at the core of the American character.

Consider the shameful history of how blacks have been treated. We were brought to the colonies in the holds of ships in 1619 as slaves. We were not officially given full citizenship until 1865, with passage of the 13th Amendment. Many whites, mostly Southerners, immediately sought to dismantle black citizenship by suppressing our ability to vote. Without the vote, second-class citizenship was, and is, assured.

I remember as a kid that almost every facet of life was stacked against us. We were powerless to do anything about our under-financed and poorly equipped "Negro schools." Home loan rejections and auto loan discrimination were a given. We could not enter certain buildings or swim in designated areas of public beaches. Black mothers could not give birth at local hospitals.

I learned at a young age that persistent injustice is never arbitrary. It is organized to harm specific people.

I recall the evening in July 1959, when my mother, father and I drove to the Greyhound Bus station in Fort Lauderdale to pick up three of my young cousins from Virginia.

They had not come for summer vacation. The public schools in Prince Edward County where my cousins were students had been shuttered. Whites would not let their children attend school with blacks.

A few black churches opened their doors and used untrained teachers. Some kids, like my cousins, found schools out of state where relatives lived.

Whites used the tax dollars from the school closures to establish private segregation academies for white children. In 1964, the courts overturned the policy, and public schools reopened to everyone. By then, however, severe damage had been done. Research shows the illiteracy rate of blacks in Prince Edward County ages 5 to 22 went from 3 percent to 23 percent.

This kind of inhumanity, although it did not involve guns, ruined many lives forever.

When I first heard about the Pittsburgh shootings, I was reminded again that violence is a way of life in America.

I immediately thought of historically black Emanuel A.M.E. Church in Charleston, S.C., where, in 2015, white racist Dylann Roof gunned down nine African Americans even as some invited him to worship with them.

I also thought of the 1963 bombing of the 16th Street Baptist Church in Birmingham. KKK members killed four black girls with dynamite. The girls were preparing for Sunday morning services.

The heinousness of the Pittsburgh synagogue murders also reminded me of Harry and Harriette Moore of Mims, Fla. Harry was an outspoken educator and president of the Florida chapter of the NAACP. His activism for black teachers angered local whites. On Christmas night 1951, when the couple had gone to bed after celebrating their 25th wedding anniversary, a bomb planted by the KKK blew up their house. Harry died en route to the black hospital in Sanford. Harriette died nine days later in that black hospital.

Hate-inspired practices and tragedies will continue. They may be increasing. Despite what politicians and others claim, this is who we are as a people.

Farmworkers

Hiring illegals creates enslavement

AUGUST 2, 2000

It was a scene made for the movies: Last Thursday in Gainesville, armored personnel carriers deployed sharpshooters at 1707 Williston Road, home of Chang Qin Zheng, his wife Jin Shuang Zheng and his brother Zheng Zheng.

When the action stopped, federal and local authorities had arrested the Zhengs, shackled and hauled away as many as 20 other Asian and Hispanic illegal aliens. Several others ran away. After the initial arrests, more than 30 other workers remained in the house, which has barracks-style facilities—cots, pallets and bunk beds.

The Zhengs, charged with conspiracy to harbor illegal aliens for commercial gain, own two local restaurants—China Super Buffet at 1900 SW 13th St., and the New China restaurant at 3423 Archer Road. Using vans and cars, the Zhengs would ferry their workers to and from the restaurants to keep them out of public view.

One man said that he and others were virtual slaves, working 12 to 14 hours a day, seven days a week—for inadequate pay and no benefits.

They live in fear of law enforcement and their ruthless employers driven by the profit motive. Both restaurants, by the way, were back in business the next day.

Several immigration officials I spoke with said that the Gainesville case is typical of many others elsewhere, and it shows the length to which owners will go to get reliable scut-work employees. The case also shows that immigration officials cannot rein in the illegal trafficking of human cargo until employers cooperate.

"Unfortunately, from knowing other federal investigations around the country, this is clearly a growing problem," said Michael Patterson, U.S. Attorney for the Northern District of Florida. "One can suspect that, like other criminal enterprises, when they reach communities in North Florida, they are probably everywhere."

The Immigration and Naturalization Service estimates that 5-million undocumented workers reside in the United States, with the hospitality industry employing many in an underworld that cheats taxpayers and potential native workers. Florida, which has 350,000 illegal aliens, trails only California with 2-million and Texas with 700,000.

As smugglers, called snakeheads, in Mexico, Eastern Europe and China become bolder, their contacts in this country seem more willing to flout INS scrutiny. Zheng Zheng, one of the owners of the Gainesville restaurants, is himself an illegal alien. In 1997, INS authorities in New York ordered him deported.

Hotel and restaurant owners argue that because so many Americans refuse to work in the industry, they must seek employees abroad. On any given day, according to the Gulf Beaches of Tampa Bay Chamber of Commerce, as many as 1,000 jobs in hotels and restaurants go unfilled. Employers are desperate, and some will break the law to stay in business.

Some Tampa Bay area hoteliers say that they can find workers in the former Soviet Union more easily than here. Indeed, help wanted signs dot the area, especially businesses along Gulf Boulevard in Pinellas. Last year, the St. Pete Beach Commission passed a measure supporting a plan to recruit employees from abroad.

The *St. Petersburg Times* reported last year that INS arrested 47 illegal aliens, all Eastern Europeans, working in local hotels. During the arrests, officials discovered an elaborate scheme to hire illegal immigrants and conceal their identities with false documents.

Hoteliers played dumb, of course.

Hospitality industry officials are a tight-lipped bunch because huge sums of money are involved. The wrong move at the wrong time could shut down a profitable establishment. The Gainesville raids were the result of a seven-month investigation prompted by an anonymous letter to the Gainesville FBI. INS and FBI officials staked out the Zhengs' house and sent agents to eat in the two restaurants to verify the identities of the workers.

Authorities say that they do not know if other Chinese restaurants in Gainesville employ illegal aliens, but they are investigating.

Hiring illegals may save hoteliers and restaurateurs money in the short run. But it breaks the law and perpetuates the enslavement of tens of thousands of people, many of them children, who could easily obtain documents that permit them to work legally.

And that is the rub: Legal workers are irksome. They demand higher wages and benefits, such as insurance, and amenities—weekends off, vacation—the rest of America takes for granted.

Farmworkers get short shrift over fair wages

OCTOBER 29, 2000

The newspaper headline reads: "Farmworkers threaten strike for better pay."

Here is an excerpt from the article: "About 250 migrant farmworkers and crew leaders in the impoverished vegetable belt of southwest Florida (Immokalee) have banded to demand better pay. The workers are prepared to strike to get their demands and may form a union, the Rev. Bill Talty said in a telephone interview Thursday. Talty, who is leading a migrant workers' movement, said tomato pickers were demanding a one-third increase in piece-work rates, from 30 cents to 40 cents per bushel."

About 100 miles to the south in Florida City, the Associated Press reports another tomato pickers' strike. An excerpt: "The strike began last Thursday as pickers demanded 45 cents a bucket—about 32 pounds of tomatoes. This was five cents over the going wage at the close of last year's harvest."

These articles could have been written yesterday, but they were not. The first was published in 1976, the second, 1978. Incredibly, the dozens of workers gathered in front of the old Capitol building this weekend for two days of prayer and fasting, say that conditions have barely changed for Florida tomato pickers nearly 25 years later.

Most field laborers still earn between 40 cents and 45 cents per bucket. If inflation and cost-of-living expenses are factored in, tomato pickers are financially worse off in 2000 than they were in 1976. According to latest U.S. Department of Labor statistics, 3 out of 5 farmworker households live in poverty. Half of all farmworkers earn wages of less than $7,500 a year.

Everyone—including growers, consumers, news outlets, the governor and other politicians—should be ashamed. Here we are in 2000 still openly discounting the worth of one of our most important work forces.

Representing five of the state's major farmworker organizations, participants came to Tallahassee to ask Gov. Jeb Bush to help them secure regional meetings with the state's major tomato growers. And they are requesting that Bush attends one of the meetings.

In a formal petition, the United Community of Florida Farm Workers requested that after the regional summits, the governor produces a "report with his recommendations for a practical mechanism for fair and appropriate resolution of labor conflicts in agriculture in the future."

On the surface, the pickers' request is simple. Not so, however, when the interests of farmworkers and the arrogance and greed of growers collide. Only one grower, the Gargiulo company, has negotiated a wage settlement with pickers. Two years ago, the company agreed to increase per bucket wage from 40 to 50 cents. Because Gargiulo officials negotiated with the pickers, theirs is the highest wage for tomato picking in the state. And the company is not going broke, the excuse other companies use to justify their stinginess.

Those companies outright refuse to speak with their pickers. In letters to the Coalition of Immokalee Workers in Immokalee, Bush washed his hands of the effort to get the pickers and growers together at the same table. No report will be produced, of course. In one letter ladened with sarcasm, innuendo and dismissiveness, Bush wrote that "a number of growers were contacted to gauge their interest in a farmworker summit. There was no interest among the growers contacted. As I mentioned in my initial response, I cannot compel Florida's growers, as I would not compel any of Florida's private sector businesses or workers, to enter into labor and management negotiations."

The pickers did not ask Bush to "compel" the growers. They requested that he "encourage" them.

In another letter, Bush wrote: "To involve the Office of the Governor in private sector wage and labor disputes would set a precedent without boundaries."

The governor is being disingenuous. If he or someone in his office spoke with growers, they should have known that the growers would refuse to sit down with pickers. Growers have utter contempt for their field crews. Here is where the governor's moral suasion could possibly make a difference. What law prevents a governor from intervening in private sector situations where great abuses occur?

The governor simply is not telling the truth. Consider: A few days after being elected, Bush telephoned an old friend, Luis Rodriguez of Fort Lauderdale, and asked him to meet with selected tomato growers to request that they raise the piece rate for a bucket of tomatoes from 40 to 45 cents.

The growers gave Bush his wish.

The governor took credit for the raise. Now, however, he says that he has no right to intervene in the private sector. Bush cannot have it both ways. Either he can intervene—as he did—or he cannot.

Since that historic meeting with the growers, moreover, Rodriguez has, without presenting any evidence, demonized the coalition as being a shill for the so-called Mexican lobby. He has, in effect, helped to destroy any goodwill that Bush had built with farmworkers. Rodriguez has said that he will not meet with coalition members because growers do not consider the organization a legitimate farmworker representative. Growers reject all farmworker advocacy groups. Like Bush, Rodriguez is being disingenuous.

This is a sorry turn of events, because Bush's initial contact with farmworkers offered, in his own words, a "new way."

"My hope is that everyone here today and all residents of Florida can earn a decent wage and be able to provide for their kids, be able to get adequate health care," he said in Immokalee. "Part of the reason that I aspire to serve is to create the best possible climate for the greatest number of people, so that they can pursue their dreams independently. And part of that is getting a good wage."

Apparently, Bush has had second thoughts about using his considerable weight in helping farmworkers "earn good wage." Yes, he has garnered some modest gains in less controversial areas, such as housing and health care. But the lack of a living wage is at the core of farmworkers' problems.

Bottom line: Farmworkers will never earn a living wage until they can bargain collectively, until they can sit down with the growers. But growers—protected by winks and nods from Tallahassee and Washington—do not want farmworkers to organize.

To enable growers to keep their workers powerless, Congress excluded farmworkers from the Wagner Act, the National Labor Relations Act, the National Labor Relations Board, the Fair Labor Standards Act and other labor legislation and panels. Farmworkers have been regularly fired, quarantined and physically attacked for trying to organize. Firing farmworkers for union activity is not illegal. These workers need someone to fight for them.

In addition to problems with Gov. Bush, more trouble for Florida farmworkers may come out of Washington. As of this writing, a bill sponsored by Florida Sen. Bob Graham and Oregon Sen. Gordon Smith is being debated. It may be voted on this week. Supporters are trying to hide it in an omnibus bill. Or, as a Graham spokeswoman lightheartedly said in a telephone interview, they are trying to attach it to "any moving vehicle."

Called the Agricultural Job Opportunity Benefits and Security Act, the proposal would replace H-2A, the nation's current foreign guest-worker program. The goal of the bill, Graham said last year, is to transform a heavily illegal work force into one that is legal. Under the new system, illegal workers could earn legal status if they satisfy specific requirements. Undocumented workers would need to spend five more years in the fields to qualify for permanent legal status.

Those who can show that they worked at least 150 days as farm hands within the last year could immediately receive legal status as temporary non-immigrants. Pickers who work a minimum of 180 days annually in five of the next seven years would qualify to apply for a permanent residency. The proposal also contains modified standards for housing, transportation and wages. Graham claims that the bill will improve the plight of both domestic and foreign workers.

But farmworker advocates disagree, arguing that the proposal will widen the gulf between workers and management. Greg Schell, managing attorney for the Migrant Justice Project in Belle Glade, said: "This bill represents an enormous step backwards for America's workers. Florida's farmers would be guaranteed a limitless supply of cheap foreign labor at bargain basement prices. If this bill is adopted, all competitive incentives will be removed for Florida growers to improve wages and benefits for farmworkers."

If the bill passes, Gov. Bush will have even more reason to reaffirm the "new way" he touted while a gubernatorial candidate on the stump. He and other politicians should realize now that they are dealing with intelligent, hard-working people who deserve to be treated better, who, according to demographers, will become a powerful voting bloc in the very near future.

Migrant farmworker abuse continues

NOVEMBER 28, 2001

The outpouring of good will following the terrorist attacks on the World Trade Center and the Pentagon has not trickled down to the tens of thousands of laborers who plant, tend and harvest our bounty.

For them, mostly Hispanics, the lack of caring on the part of the rest of the nation is nothing new. Time has stood still for this population.

On Thanksgiving Day 1960, Edward R. Murrow stunned the nation with his *Harvest of Shame*, the landmark documentary that highlighted the conditions under which Palm Beach County migrants lived and worked. More than 40 years later, farmworkers labor and live under many of the same oppressive and dehumanizing conditions.

And as matters were in 1960, growers and their powerful friends in the seats of power—governors and the president of the United States included—continue to ignore the pleas of farmworkers.

With the support of legal aid lawyers, a handful of private citizens and clergy, farmworkers struggle to get an uncaring nation to listen. Most recently, eight migrant and seasonal farmworkers filed a class-action lawsuit two days before Thanksgiving in the U.S. District Court in West Palm Beach.

The field hands accuse Mecca Farms Inc. of systematically underpaying them for picking tomatoes and other crops. Specifically, the workers, who represent at least 400 others, argue that Mecca Farms failed to pay the federal minimum wage, maintain accurate payroll records, ensure that the transportation provided to the workers complied with federal safety standards and pay or ensure payment of Social Security (FICA) taxes.

The suit seeks unspecified damages, but attorneys for the farmworkers estimate that unpaid wages alone total hundreds of thousands of dollars. Mecca Farms, based in Lantana, is one of Florida's largest tomato growers. Mecca Farms' labor contractors Rogerio Rodriguez, Maria T. Sanchez and M. Sanchez & Son Inc. also are defendants in the suit.

The abuses of growers and their contractors result not only in workers being underpaid for back-breaking work but also in physical injuries and death.

Last April, for example, a van driven by a farm labor contractor hired by Mecca Farms crashed into another vehicle on Interstate 95. Two workers were taken to nearby hospitals. The severity of the injuries was increased by the conditions of the vehicle, which lacked seat belts.

"The April accident is an all too common event," says Cathleen Caron, one of the plaintiffs' attorneys. "Farmworkers are at risk across the state because the agricultural community turns a blind eye to unsafe conditions under which its workers are brought to labor in its fields every day."

Two of the plaintiffs named in the case were injured in the accident.

The suit is not the first time Mecca Farms has come under pressure for violating federal standards protecting farmworkers. In 1995, the U.S. Department of Labor levied a $15,000 civil penalty against the company for violations similar to the ones alleged in the current suit. One of its contractors, Rogerio Rodriguez, also has been the subject of several Department of Labor investigations. Each time, though, he is slapped on the hand. His worst punishment was a $1,000 fine in 1991.

Growers skirt all responsibility for their workers by hiring labor contractors, unscrupulous middlemen who handle the workers' daily welfare. Two Florida lawmakers, black Democrats, introduced a bill last year that would have corrected some of the problems, but the effort was shot down by the GOP-led Legislature. This contractor arrangement is at the heart of the blatant abuses farmworkers suffer. American growers, especially those in Florida, claim that because of their generosity, Mexican workers live the "life of Riley" in the United States.

"A Mecca Farms spokesman is the champion of saying that the Mexicans treat their workers so poorly on Mexican farms, while we treat our workers so much better here," said Caron, who is with the Migrant Farmworker Justice of Lake Worth. "But when you look, American growers' immediate reaction is 'We're not their employer.'"

"At the same time that they're willing to say bad labor standards exist in Mexico, they're refusing to even look to see if they're complying with the labor standards here. They flatly refuse to accept responsibility. They pretend that their contractors are following the law, which is not happening. It's hypocritical. No one is listening to us. The agricultural lobby is strong. We're very frustrated."

No date for the trial has been set. Meanwhile, the vicious cycle of farmworker abuse in Florida and the rest of the nation continues.

Slavery alive in Florida agriculture industry

JULY 3, 2002

With more regularity, federal officials who monitor farm labor issues are digging out the 13th Amendment to the U.S. Constitution. Written in 1865, it officially ended slavery in America. Again, the 13th Amendment "officially" ended slavery.

In reality, 137 years later, "modern-day slavery" is alive and well in the nation's agricultural states, and Florida is a leader in the exploitation of human chattel, with five slavery cases having gone through the courts in as many years.

Most recently, on June 27, brothers Juan and Ramiro Ramos, along with their cousin, Jose Ramos, were convicted in U.S. District Court in Fort Pierce on federal charges of conspiring to hold as many as 700 migrant laborers as slaves, threatening them with violence and holding them as hostages over alleged debts of $1,000. The men will be sentenced in November. They could face up to 25 years in prison and lose more than $3-million in property.

They would charge desperate, undocumented workers $1,000 to smuggle them by trailer from Arizona to the citrus groves of Lake Placid in Okeechobee County. The migrants could gain their freedom only after paying the $1,000.

Trouble was, many workers could never pay the money because of the other expenses the Ramoses tacked on. To prevent the workers from escaping, the crew leaders kept them under surveillance and threatened them with physical violence or death. Over the years, many workers have been severely beaten for trying to escape.

The Ramos abuses came to light because of the Coalition of Immokalee Workers—the same farmworker advocacy group that Gov. Jeb Bush's personal farm labor emissary claims is part of the so-called "Mexican lobby." Officials with the FBI and the Border Patrol in West Palm Beach said they had investigated the case for two years before moving in.

But the viciousness of the Ramos case pales alongside that of Michael Allen Lee of Fort Pierce. Last year, he was sentenced to four years in prison and three years of supervised release. For years, Lee, an African American, recruited homeless black men off the streets of Central Florida with promises of high wages and the comforts of home.

The harsh reality is that Lee, now 44, himself a descendant of slaves, was a scary slave master. On average, a fruit picker in Florida can earn between $35 to $50 a day. But Lee's pickers rarely brought home more than $10. He forced workers to live in houses that he owned, where he sometimes put 15 to 20 men together in four bedrooms and charged each $30 apiece a week. They would sleep on floor mats.

Closely guarded, the men awoke before 5 each morning, rode in crammed vans to convenience stores, where Lee would give them $3 to $5 for breakfast and lunch. They worked in the groves until 6 in the evening, or later, and were driven back to their living quarters.

Lee provided a mandatory, cheap evening meal. In a secret ledger, he charged his workers for rent, food, transportation, drinks and drugs and whatever else he could get away with. A man who earned $500 week, for example, could wind up keeping only $150 after Lee's deductions.

The workers were forced to remain silent. Those who complained or tried to escape were dealt with harshly. Take the case of George Williams, who died before Lee was convicted. When Williams complained too much, Lee had him held down while he beat him within an inch of his life, federal officials said.

These are just two cases of farmworker enslavement. Lillian Hirales, an attorney with the Migrant Farmworker Justice Project in Lake Worth, said that thousands of undocumented workers, mostly Mexicans, are being enslaved in Florida each year. She, like other advocates, cite lax enforcement of regulations and the grower-labor contractor (crew boss) system.

Under this system, growers hire contractors, who then hire the pickers, keep track of them, house them and pay them. Everyone, including the governor and his emissary, knows that this egregious loophole lets farmers off the hook. Sure, Lee is behind bars, and the Ramoses may be on their way there. But rest assured, the farmers who hired them have replaced them with crew leaders.

Laura Germino, a representative of the Coalition of Immokalee Workers, identifies the root of the problem: "It's time now that the agriculture industry take a look at itself and decide that it's not going to operate under the rules of the past and continue beating and holding workers by force."

The time has come for Gov. Jeb Bush to step up and put his moral weight behind this worthy crusade.

A tradition of abuse in the fields of Florida

MARCH 26, 2003

Lake Wales

Now that Hispanics have become the nation's most populous ethnic minority, a handful of Florida elected officials are paying grudging attention to how inhumanely we treat our state's tens of thousands of migrant
farmworkers.

I grew up as a migrant worker and have been writing about the plight
of this group for more than 15 years. I can say from experience and study
that our state—its ordinary residents and its leaders—does not give a
damn about farmworkers. I even have a few colleagues at the *St. Petersburg Times* and, of course, dozens of regular readers, who ask why I write
about "migrants so much"?

One reader admonished me: "Why don't you tell those wet backs to
get real jobs and quit complaining or go back to Mexico?" I advised him
to plant his own veggies and harvest them for his family and friends. His
reply is unprintable in this newspaper.

His is the typical attitude of Floridians toward migrant farmworkers.
We see their outlines in our fields, groves and orchards, but we rarely see
their faces up close. Others of us live such insulated lives that we never
see these laborers at all.

During the last legislative session, Rep. Frank Peterman, D-St. Petersburg, filed a bill on behalf of farmworkers. It failed. Watching the latest census report showing the growing number of Hispanics in Florida,
other legislators, including a few Republicans, have joined Peterman and
farmworker advocates in trying to bring fairness to these laborers.

Specifically, the new state law would require employers to better train
and inform workers to protect them from the pesticides they work in.
Peterman, along with state House Majority Leader Marco Rubio, R-Miami, also wants lawmakers to have authority to go after growers when
the contractors they hire cheat field hands out of wages.

Florida's GOP-controlled Legislature is going to be a hard sell for
Peterman and Rubio. During his second gubernatorial race, Gov. Jeb
Bush promised farmworkers represented by the Coalition of Immokalee
Workers that he would listen to their concerns. He apparently had a

memory lapse after the election. The governor's farm-labor emissary even portrays the coalition as a front for the so-called "Mexican lobby."

As a result, one of farm labor's most vocal support groups does not have an effective voice in Tallahassee. Peterman's legislation is needed now more than ever.

Severe dermatitis, for example, remains a problem for farmworkers because many workers, including children, do not seek medical attention because they are afraid of being fired or punished in some other way. They rely on home remedies. Instances of slavery and forced prostitution continue to surface because growers and their crew chiefs do not have to worry about being punished. A few courageous judges have sent a handful of these racketeers to prison, even as the governor and others remain silent.

But crew chiefs are bottom-rung criminals. The growers themselves—those who use the crew chiefs and who have ample knowledge of what is going on—should be tried in court. Far too many of them have elected and unelected officials in their pockets. Florida agribusiness dumps huge sums into the campaigns of many politicians. No small number of lawmakers are themselves growers or hail from farm-owning families.

These merchants of greed are in no mind to approve legislation that will force them to treat migrant farmworkers fairly and decently. And they are ethically incapable of policing themselves. As a result, Florida has a tradition of abuse in the fields and a system of winking and nodding with the gang in Tallahassee.

But politicians, growers and their subcontractors do not deserve all the blame for the abuse of farmworkers in the Sunshine State. Florida consumers are no better. We would not tolerate such mistreatment of any other group. We become self-righteously outraged when we hear of sweatshops in faraway Third World countries.

Well, a simple trip a few miles inland from any of our major roadways will reveal a world of harsh treatment and criminal practices. If you do not believe me, come to Polk County, where I am as I write. Go to western Palm Beach County. Go to Immokalee. Look around Hillsborough and Manatee counties.

The *Orlando Sentinel* reports that the U.S. Department of Labor set a national priority to crack down on wage abuses in the agriculture industry and other industries that exploit immigrants. During 2002, officials closed 2,177 cases and collected about $2.1-million in back wages owed to farmworkers. Although promising, these figures represent a drop in the bucket.

Who is for the farmworker?

MARCH 14, 2004

Florida Gov. Jeb Bush is touting legislation to improve the lives of Florida's 300,000-plus farmworkers, who endure institutional and systemic injustices each day in our fields and groves and their personal lives.

Bush suddenly got religion during this presidential election season and decided to back laws that would make employers guilty of a felony if they jeopardize workers' health. The legislation also would bring back a neglected labor review board, require employers to inform workers of the dangers of pesticides and encourage workers to report violations on a toll-free telephone line.

These long-overdue measures sound reasonable until I see who joined Bush as he announced the legislation: three state lawmakers who are growers in their home districts. And I was disappointed that Bush intoned that "the vast majority of Florida's farm labor contractors, or crew chiefs as they're known, operate well within the law. The legislation we're announcing today targets those who don't."

In essence, Bush's proposal is a cleaned-up red herring, outlining an anemic effort to go after crew chiefs, the middlemen. It does not go after the true culprits in this unethical system: the big shots who own the farms, the wealthy movers and shakers who control Florida's agribusiness.

Remember, agriculture is the state's second largest industry, hauling in annual sales of $7-billion. We are talking raw power—huge campaign contributions, quid pro quo, kingmaking.

Few farmworker advocates, strike organizers, lawyers or clergy agree with Bush when he claims that most crew chiefs operate legally.

When a crew operates illegally, the grower who hired him is responsible. The crew chief system is nothing but sleight of hand. Rich growers hire subcontractors to handle the day-to-day matters related to the laborers—pay (including income taxes and Social Security), housing, transportation to and from the fields, insurance and medical care.

As practiced in Florida, it is a vicious system that absolves the growers of any responsibility for the plight of their field hands. Bush's legislation would merely increase from $1,000 to $2,500 the maximum penalty levied against abusers. As far as I am concerned, the crew boss system is immoral primarily because it practices intentional cruelty.

Several companies have been sued, for example, for cheating workers by "doctoring" their hours, a scheme that lets growers avoid paying minimum wage. Growers also save money by not informing their workers about the dangerous pesticides they are exposed to. Underaged children still work in some fields. Crew leaders are permitted to pack as many as 25 workers into tiny trailers, charging each worker as much as $50 a week. Most farmworkers do not have health insurance, and vacation is virtually nonexistent. Many of the vehicles that transport farmworkers are unsafe and uninsured.

In short, it is a system that abuses the weak—the disenfranchised—for profit.

Levying fines against a handful of crew chiefs and holding well-publicized news conferences will not fix this system of human exploitation.

The ugly truth is that moral arguments carry little, if any, weight with Florida's anti-labor politicians and consumers who demand inexpensive, fresh, unblemished produce.

The time has come for earnest, politically unencumbered legislation that deals with the root cause of migrant farmworker poverty in Florida and other parts of the nation. Florida's farm labor problems are the nation's farm labor problems because migrants travel from state to state to survive, and they suffer the same abuses wherever they work.

What is the root cause of perpetual poverty among farmworkers?

In her book *The Fruits of Their Labor*, Cindy Hahamovitch, a professor at the College of William and Mary, writes: "Conditions remain dismal . . . not because poverty is an inevitable feature of modern agriculture or because crew leaders trap migrants into a new sort of debt peonage. They are dismal because the federal government intervened on behalf of growers, undermining farmworkers' bargaining power and relieving growers of the need to recruit labor by improving wages and conditions."

The federal government and the states can improve the plight of farmworkers by not automatically intervening for growers when labor problems need to be fixed or when such fixes will cost growers money.

Lawmakers can transform the lives of farmworkers overnight by committing the ultimate act of legislative decency and common sense: Give farmworkers the right to bargain collectively, without being harassed or terrorized.

But growers do not want farmworkers to organize. To assist growers in keeping their workers powerless, Congress excluded farmworkers from the Wagner Act, the National Labor Relations Act, the National Labor Relations Board, the Fair Labor Standards Act and other labor legislation and panels.

Gov. Bush should start the process of getting Florida out of the business of abuse and put the state on the high road on behalf of farmworkers by establishing a labor relations act that spells out the specific rights of farmworkers and the duties of growers. At the same time, a viable labor relations board that includes farmworker representatives—chosen by farmworkers—should be established. The board would report directly to the governor. It would not be a rubber-stamping panel in bed with the growers. It would be one that recommends real, even unpopular, remedies.

Such a board is necessary in Florida because the state Department of Labor and the Department of Agriculture protect growers. No government department champions the rights of farmworkers. Everything is done for management.

Again, a cornerstone of Florida's labor relations act for farmworkers would be the right to bargain collectively. Without the ability to organize, farmworkers cannot galvanize their interests and demand a seat at the negotiating table. Name another labor force that lacks the right to talk directly to management. As matters stand, farmworkers rarely see management face-to-face.

I suspect that Florida growers are winking and nodding as Gov. Bush announces measures ostensibly intended to help farmworkers. But regulations alone are not enough. The state also must allocate enough money to put independent inspectors in the fields and groves. And here is the bottom line: Growers must be held legally accountable for the treatment of their laborers.

Eating that tomato can put you in moral peril

JULY 13, 2008

Some deeds and practices define our individual and shared morality. When, for example, we turn our backs on the cruel treatment of farmworkers, we are complicit in inhumanity and are acting immorally.

Tens of thousands of Floridians read about the case of *U.S. v. Ronald Evans* without blinking an eye. To me, everyone who eats fruits and vegetables should be outraged and should be, in some manner, advocating for farmworker justice.

A review: In 2007, farm labor contractor Ronald Evans, his wife Jequita Evans and their son Ron Evans Jr. were sentenced to federal prison for enslaving farmworkers and for other labor-related crimes in Florida and North Carolina. They were sentenced to 30, 20 and 10 years respectively.

Ronald Evans recruited homeless U.S. citizens from shelters across the Southeast, including in Tampa, Miami and New Orleans, with promises of decent jobs and housing. After the farmworkers arrived at the labor camps in Palatka and New Grove, N.C., Ronald Evans deducted the price of rent, food, crack cocaine and alcohol from the workers' pay, keeping the workers "perpetually indebted" in what the U.S. Justice Department referred to as "a form of servitude morally and legally reprehensible."

Justice Department records show that the Palatka labor camp was enclosed by a chain-link fence topped with barbed wire. A "No Trespassing" sign warned outsiders.

The Evans family worked for grower Frank Johns, then-chairman of the Florida Fruit & Vegetable Association, the powerful lobby of the state's agricultural industry. As a grower, Johns was not charged with a crime.

This is not an isolated case. Since 1997, through efforts of the Coalition of Immokalee Workers, six other labor outfits have been prosecuted for servitude. The cases involved more than a dozen employers and more than 1,000 workers, who testified to being locked in their compounds at night, beaten, raped, pistol-whipped and shot.

Remember, the average U.S. farmworker earns a little more than $10,000 a year. They are excluded from the protections of the nation's employment laws, and they are prevented from legally organizing.

As a result of such inhumanity and exploitation, American consumers can enjoy cheap, fresh and attractive produce. Companies such as Tropicana, Minute Maid, Taco Bell, Wendy's, Burger King, McDonald's, Kroger and Walmart profit from so-called "everyday low prices" made possible on the backs of abused workers.

As individuals, we are morally obligated to demand economic justice for those who harvest our food. George Orwell, who wrote extensively about poverty in England, said: "Economic injustice will stop the moment we want to stop it, and no sooner, and if we genuinely want it to stop the method adopted hardly matters."

One person I know who is trying to get consumers to see that their buying habits directly contribute to the hardships of farmworkers is the Rev. Aaron McEmrys, a Unitarian Universalist minister in Santa Barbara, Calif. I recently met McEmrys, a former union organizer, when he participated in a farmworker seminar in Fort Lauderdale.

I quote him at length: "The things we do and the ways we live affect our fellow beings in ways that are often hard to see. Sometimes, even things that seem small and innocent to us can do terrible damage to others in the wider world. As long as we remain blissfully ignorant, we might be passively complicit in the suffering of others, but we are not knowing, willing participants. We are just ignorant.

"Once we know, however, really know, about how our choices or our lifestyles can hurt and oppress others, we have some real choices to make. We can either change our ways to stop hurting people or we can go on as we always have. But with one big difference: We aren't innocent anymore. We are still complicit, but now actively so. We have chosen to live in such a way that pushes people down instead of lifting them up, that strips away our humanity and theirs instead of celebrating our shared humanity.

"We all agree that slavery is an abomination—a sin—a crime against humanity. And yet this kind of oppression is exactly what the people who pick our tomatoes have to live with every day. The tomatoes that nourish our bodies and add flavor to so many of our meals come with a price tag. They come at the cost of human dignity, human freedom. Once we know this, we have some real choices to make: We can either change our ways or we can go on eating those cheap tomatoes knowing that we have chosen, by default, to be fed by the suffering of other human beings—human beings just like us.

"It's not a question of whether we should get involved. If we eat tomatoes, then we are already involved. The only real questions are: What are we going to do about it? How will we be involved from here on out?

"Here is a real truth: When we do the right thing, when we change our ways, even just a little, to live in such a way as to lift up the best in ourselves and others, the tomatoes will taste better. I guarantee it."

American consumers have a moral duty to stop the exploitation of farmworkers. If we do not, as McEmrys argues, we enable servitude and are guilty of the "sin of complicity."

It was no isolated tragedy

DECEMBER 6, 2009

On Nov. 28, the Hillsborough County Sheriff's Office called Dover-based Bingham On Site Sewers Inc. to the Silver Lane Mobile Home Park in Valrico. Luis Martinez, 2, had been missing almost 24 hours. A few volunteer searchers had discovered an 11-by-13-inch opening in the ground the night before. That opening was where the cap to the underground septic tank should have been.

Investigators asked On Site Sewers to pump out the septic tank's five feet of raw sewage. At the bottom of the tank, about 50 yards from where Luis had lived with his parents, who are strawberry pickers, and 2-month-old sister, workers found the boy's body and the missing lid. Reportedly, the tank had overflowed a month earlier.

At first glance, Luis' death may appear to be just another isolated tragedy in an out-of-the-way mobile home park for low-income people. But it is not an isolated event. The circumstances surrounding the tragedy illustrate the dangers that migrant farmworkers and their children face each day.

Most ordinary Americans and government officials ignore the stark living conditions and mistreatment of farmworkers who plant and harvest our produce.

Hours after Luis' body was recovered, Hillsborough County code enforcement inspectors came to Silver Lane and found several violations, including a second septic tank without a lid. Later, they reported that the park, owned by Kenneth Winter, was an illegal migrant labor camp. It is on an unpaved road that ends at a cul-de-sac. Winter also owns a second mobile home park nearby that operates as an illegal migrant labor camp.

Code enforcement officials have given Winter 30 days to fix the violations in the two parks and to get the proper permit to operate them as migrant camps. He has not been charged with a crime.

After being forced by Luis' death to come to two mobile home parks, code, health and law enforcement officials claimed that they were unaware of the living conditions out there. Ignorance, especially institutionalized ignorance, is no excuse. Given the availability of information with the click of a mouse or a phone call, to be ignorant is to be guilty of moral negligence and culpability.

Who do officials think live in those shacks and dilapidated mobile homes in Hillsborough's farming areas?

The conditions in Hillsborough are typical. Tens of thousands of the nation's approximately 3.5 million farmworkers and their children face a combination of physical injuries and health problems, some fatal, directly related to their living conditions. Not surprisingly, Florida ranks annually as one of the nation's most negligent and exploitative states.

According to the nonprofit Housing Assistance Council, funded by the Department of Housing and Urban Development to support low-income housing in rural areas, more than 52 percent of farmworker housing units nationwide are crowded. Seventy-four percent of the households in crowded units have children. A council survey shows that crowded housing often lacks toilets, showers, bathtubs, stoves and refrigerators that work, making it impossible to store food safely, prepare warm meals or shower after long days in fields.

Farmworkers routinely come in direct contact with pesticides. The lack of laundry facilities in their housing exposes them to high levels of pesticide poisoning. More than a quarter of the places the council surveyed were directly adjacent to pesticide-treated fields. Many had broken windows and windows missing screens.

"Crowded conditions are associated with increased incidence of infectious diseases such as tuberculosis and influenza," council researchers wrote. "Lack of sanitary facilities, sanitary facilities located in sleeping areas, and broken cooking appliances can contribute to the contraction of hepatitis, gastroenteritis, and other conditions. . . . Water leakage and broken windows expose residents to irritants such as dust and mold, which can complicate respiratory problems such as asthma."

Further, some problems, such as sagging structural features, exposed electrical wiring, lead paint, broken steps and holes in floors, threaten the safety of farmworkers, especially young children. An uncapped septic tank is inexcusable.

My hope is that Luis' death will not be forgotten after it no longer generates vigils and headlines. I want the tragedy to put a human face on a group that remains invisible to most of us.

I cannot make the case for the rights of Florida farmworkers better than it was made in a 2005 joint letter by nine respected human rights groups to the Inter-American Commission on Human Rights: "The United States government should fulfill its responsibilities to protect agricultural workers in Florida from human rights violations and take steps to prevent further violations. The private sector, in particular the corporate sector, should comply with the law as well as recognize its role in ensuring that the human rights of its workers are respected."

Luis' death and the fact that two illegal migrant camps could operate in plain sight near State Road 60 tell me we have a long way to go.

Decades of hard work for low pay

OCTOBER 24, 2010

Like everyone else who cares about the plight of farmworkers, I am encouraged that Pacific Tomato Growers, one of the nation's largest producers of tomatoes, recently made peace with the Coalition of Immokalee Workers.

During a news conference on Oct. 13, Pacific's operating partner, Jon Esformes, pledged to upgrade the company's working conditions and pay its pickers a penny more per pound for tomatoes. One penny will do wonders for many workers, raising their yearly wages from about $10,000 to roughly $17,000. The increase took effect the next day.

Other benefits are part of the agreement: worker education and health and safety programs, a process for handling complaints and shade in the fields. The CIW had been fighting for these and other amenities for more than a decade.

Rather than speak as a wonky businessman, Esformes quoted words of atonement by philosopher Abraham Joshua Heschel: "Few are guilty, but all are responsible. . . . The transgressions that took place are totally unacceptable today and they were totally unacceptable yesterday."

Many of today's consumers have no knowledge of yesterday and, therefore, have no historical perspective as to why our produce always has been some of the freshest and least expensive in the world.

The harsh truth is that America's bounty always has been planted, tended and harvested by abused minorities who have remained, and still remain, mostly invisible and powerless. As I watch the CIW's efforts, I recall my childhood, when I often worked alongside my father in these same Collier County fields. In those days and before, Florida farmworkers were predominantly black. Hardly any Mexican or other Hispanic workers could be found east of the Mississippi.

My father and I lived with about 80 other pickers in a camp about 6 miles south of Immokalee. Conditions in the camp, like those in others from Belle Glade to Long Island, N.Y., were filthy and violent. Our living quarters were a tin-roofed, wooden, windowless bull pen where 10 to 15 men and boys slept on pallets. Families with children and single women slept in shacks across the compound from the men.

Everyone used the same fly-infested, two-holed outhouses. Real toilet paper was scarce. Most of us used newspaper and brown grocery bags. Privacy and quiet were next to impossible. The crew leader's girlfriend prepared meals for the single men. Families with children cooked their own meals. For some men, especially the physically weak or hot-tempered, life was violent and often short. The knife was the weapon of choice. The sense of manhood, even for young boys like me, framed male relationships.

Hard work—stooping, sweating and lifting all day—was at the center of our lives. We literally were the property of the crew chief and the grower. We rode from field to field on the beds of trucks and in old school buses that regularly broke down.

My father and the other men who sent money back home complained about the low wages. Those without women back home used their wages to buy physical pleasure. Venereal disease was rampant. Alcoholism was normal. We did not have doctors on the road, so if you were injured or became ill, good luck.

Paradoxically, everyone, including children, worked hard. You could not survive as a farmworker if you did not work hard. Life was tough for us back then, and it is tough for today's workers because the genesis of injustice in the fields flows from on high, from Congress.

The 1938 Fair Labor Standards Act that guaranteed, among other protections, minimum wage for each hour worked, overtime and accurate record-keeping, did not apply to farmworkers, especially migrants. Working conditions, housing and the right to know about environmental hazards such as pesticides did not apply to field hands, either. Agriculture, small farms in particular, is still exempt from many FLSA rules.

In light of history, Pacific Tomato Growers' pact with the CIW is a giant step toward bringing justice to the fields. The hope now is that other companies and organizations, such as Publix and the Florida Tomato Growers Exchange, do the right thing. Everyone benefits when farmworkers are treated fairly.

Pesticides put workers at risk

JANUARY 15, 2012

We hear a lot about farmworkers' low wages, their poor housing and the anti-immigrant movement that has frightened many. But we rarely hear about another serious problem farmworkers face: widespread exposure to pesticides on the job.

Jeannie Economos, the pesticide coordinator for the Farmworker Association of Florida in Apopka, sees this problem firsthand every day. She told me about a Mexican woman who walked into the association's office one recent afternoon. Her entire face was swollen, her eyes almost shut. The woman was certain she had been exposed to pesticides in the plant nursery where she worked.

She said a doctor had prescribed a steroid-based cream for her face, but she did not want to use a steroid for what she believed was pesticide exposure. Economos, who has handled such cases for 11 years, asked the woman to file an official complaint about the incident with the Florida Department of Agriculture and Consumer Services.

The woman did not file the complaint because she was afraid of being labeled a troublemaker and losing her job even though she was a legal U.S. resident. Instead, she bought an over-the-counter cream that gave some relief. She returned to work without receiving proper medical treatment.

Her predicament is all too familiar to farmworker advocates in Florida, which has a year-round average of 300,000 agricultural workers.

"There are significant and very disturbing problems related to farmworkers and pesticide exposure," Economos said. "One problem is that the current harsh and ugly anti-immigrant sentiment around the country and the severe anti-immigrant laws recently enacted in Georgia and Alabama have made farmworkers more afraid than ever to come forward when there are violations of regulations in the workplace and/or when they are experiencing symptoms of pesticide exposure."

Economos said Florida's heavy use of certain toxic chemicals puts farmworkers at high risk of exposure. The state's hot and humid climate and the long nine-month growing season make working conditions in the fields and greenhouses especially dangerous. Several studies have linked specific pesticides to thyroid cancer, ADHD in children and birth defects.

In 2002 and 2003, for example, three children of farmworkers were born with severe birth defects in Immokalee. The births occurred about six weeks apart and in the same area. Evidence showed the parents had been exposed to newly sprayed pesticides. Plant City-based Ag-Mart, the employer involved, settled out of court with the couple whose baby was born with no limbs. The amount was said to be in the millions. Few such dramatic cases have been in the news since, but the dangers have not gone away.

Florida's lax enforcement of federal pesticide regulations greatly concerns farmworker advocates. "By last count, there were over 40,000 agricultural operations in Florida and only 40 inspectors statewide to monitor and enforce regulations on all the agricultural operations in the state," Economos said. "More inspectors are needed to do better monitoring, inspection and enforcement. Even on farms where there is enforcement when violations are found, the penalty is often just a warning."

Another problem is that few laborers are trained to understand the effects of the pesticides in their workplaces. The major reason: Farmworkers are not covered under the National Labor Relations Act. And because Florida is a right-to-work state, farmworkers have difficulty forming unions to protect their interests. As such, they lack a legal right to know which pesticides they come in contact with.

"The Worker Protection Standards require that workers receive a pesticide training every five years," Economos said. "We feel that workers should be trained every year to impress upon them the seriousness of the conditions in which they work. We have had workers tell us that a crew leader will ask them to sign or initial a paper to show that they had received the training without actually giving the training to them."

Growers also are required to train workers within the first five days of beginning the job. This is a dangerous practice, because laborers can be on the job for up to five days before learning how to protect themselves from pesticide exposure, Economos said. Workers should be trained before ever going into fields or greenhouses.

Advocates argue that because farmworkers do not have political and economic clout in statehouses and the nation's capital, they remain invisible in spite of the essential work they do—work that no one else will do.

"Unless you are able to be totally self-sufficient and grow your own food, you are probably dependent on farmworkers for the food you eat," Economos said. "How many people realize that? Farmworkers need to be treated like the skilled workers they are, and they deserve the same rights and protections the rest of us take for granted."

Fighting for penny a pound

MARCH 4, 2012

Like many other consumers in Florida and the rest of the Southeast, I have made Publix supermarkets an essential part of my life by buying most of my food at one of their conveniently located stores.

But each time I buy tomatoes at a Publix, I am mindful of the backbreaking toil of the laborers who picked them and lugged them to a truck. I also am aware that for each 32-pound bucket of tomatoes picked, a worker gets on average 50 cents, a rate unchanged since 1980. Most workers earn roughly $10,000 a year. Besides low wages, they have no right to overtime pay, no health insurance, no sick leave, no paid vacation and no right to organize to change these conditions.

To raise workers' pay, the Coalition of Immokalee Workers, a community-based organization of mainly Latino, Mayan Indian and Haitian immigrants, has been trying to persuade the $25 billion Publix chain to join the organization's Campaign for Fair Food. Publix has flatly refused to join.

Beginning Monday, the CIW and its supporters will begin a hunger strike at Publix headquarters in Lakeland in another attempt to get the company to come aboard. The fast will end March 10.

The purpose of the Campaign for Fair Food, which began in 2001, is to get the nation's food retailers that sell tomatoes to pay an extra penny per pound for each bucket of tomatoes picked. Growers pass the penny on to farmworkers. A major reason for farmworkers' low wages is that companies such as Publix do high-volume, low-cost purchasing.

To initiate the campaign more than 10 years ago, the CIW asked Taco Bell to pay the extra penny. When the company balked, the CIW called a nationwide boycott of the chain. In March 2005, Taco Bell, a division of Yum! Brands, which includes Pizza Hut and KFC, agreed to pay the extra penny to its suppliers of Florida tomatoes.

Since then, other companies have joined the campaign, including McDonald's, Burger King, Subway, Whole Foods Market, Trader Joe's and food service providers Compass Group, Bon Appetit, Aramark and Sodexo. Many Florida growers are now supporters.

CIW leaders said the extra penny is making a positive impact. Still, Publix continues to hold out. I asked Shannon Patten, the company's media and community relations manager, why. In an email, she wrote that Publix pays market value for tomatoes and would pay an extra penny if growers and packers would put it in the price, but the company will not pay employees of other companies directly for their labor.

"The CIW is seeking to negotiate wages and working conditions of employment with the growers and the CIW is trying to drag Publix into these negotiations," she said. "This is a labor dispute and we simply aren't involved. As you know, tomatoes are just one example of the more than 35,000 products sold in our stores. With so many products available for sale to customers, the reality is that there is the potential for countless ongoing disputes between suppliers and their employees at any given time. Publix has a long history of nonintervention in such disputes."

As much as I appreciate Publix's response to my questions, I believe the company is disingenuous when it accuses the CIW of asking it to pay the employees of other employers directly.

Gerardo Reyes, the CIW's spokesman, said more than $4 million has been distributed to workers since Jan. 11 through the Fair Food program, and none of the money has been paid in any transaction between retail purchasers and the workers. He said Publix officials know that.

"Not only does the Fair Food program not require what Publix is claiming, it does not allow it," Reyes said. The Fair Food premium works like a fair trade premium does. And Publix pays and promotes that on every bag of its Greenwise Fair Trade Coffee. Tomato retail buyers pay a small premium to the grower on every pound of tomatoes they buy through the Fair Food program. The growers then distribute that money to their workers through their regular payroll as a line item on each worker's paycheck.

"Publix says they would pay the Fair Food premium if the growers would only 'put it in the price.' Well, they should consider their bluff called. The growers will put the premium in the price for any retailer who wants that, and we would sign a Fair Food agreement today with Publix stating they can pay that way if that is what they want."

If Publix joins the campaign, CIW leaders believe other giants such as Walmart, Kroger and Ahold will start to listen.

College spares a young man from modern-day slavery

MAY 20, 2012

On a Saturday morning in the spring of 1963, my life changed forever. It was the day my grandparents drove me from Crescent City to Jacksonville, where I caught the train to Wiley College in Marshall, Texas.

Inexplicably, at least to me, my grandfather took St. Johns County Road 207 through Hastings and Spuds. I wondered why he did not stay on U.S. 17, the best route to Jacksonville.

As we approached the first potato field, I understood. A few days before, I had worked in that very field. Dozens of migrants crawled or stooped as they gathered potatoes and tossed them into wire baskets. Others were dumping the contents of their baskets into burlap sacks.

I peered out my window and recognized several of my schoolmates in the field, boys I often had labored alongside over the years.

The simple words of my grandfather, a fruit picker, ring in my ears today: "If you go to college, you won't have to be a slave in these fields."

Ben Montgomery's superb story on May 13, "Drugs, debt bind laborers in slavery," in the *Tampa Bay Times* transported me back to my childhood years as a migrant farmworker. At age 6, I had joined my father and a crew of about 50 other laborers in the migrant stream, traveling from bean fields in Broward County to potato fields in Riverhead, N.Y., with several harvesting jobs in between.

We always lived in labor camps far from town. Long distances enabled abuse and peonage—out of sight, out of mind. Up and down the East Coast, the camps were dark, filthy and brutish. In some camps, our living quarters were leaky, windowless bull pens where 10 to 15 single men and boys slept on pallets. The handful of married couples and their children slept in separate quarters.

Single men were the preferred workers because they were easier to control. Families were "messy," as a crew chief said.

We had fly-infested outhouses everywhere we went. During summer months, mosquitoes attacked us inside these stinking places, forcing many of us to relieve ourselves outside.

Store-bought toilet paper was like gold. The majority of us used newspaper that we softened by vigorously rubbing it between our hands. In some Florida camps, we used Spanish moss if we did not have newspaper. Red bugs were a problem. We never had showers or bathtubs, making cleanliness next to impossible.

A few crew chiefs were relatively humane, but I vividly remember the crooked and vicious ones. My father and I could escape much of the abuse because, besides standing well over 6 feet and weighing at least 230 pounds, he had a bad temper. He also owned a pickup, giving us the freedom to drive away when things became unbearable.

Most other workers, the alcoholics and drug addicts who did not own vehicles, were trapped. They were recruited, some shanghaied, from flophouses with promises of living wages. Crew chiefs extended credit on everything—food, soft drinks, booze, narcotics, bail, whores. The trade-off was that all loans had to be repaid with 100 percent interest or higher. Many workers had debts they could never pay off, and they could not leave. Fear and threats of bodily harm kept them enslaved. The bosses had goons who would hunt down errant workers and drag them back, whole or broken.

We had no allies, not even among local black preachers. Life outside the camps was as demoralizing as it was inside. As transients, we dared not tell local police or other authorities about the abuse. We could not rent rooms or apartments in town and were barred from some shops.

Whites despised us and were openly contemptuous. Blacks were worse. They often came to our camps to woo the women with promises of good times, to overcharge us for cheap merchandise and to otherwise get what they could for nothing.

Whenever we went to town, we traveled in groups for protection, some of the men carrying pocketknives or straight razors.

The reality of being perpetual outsiders weighed heavily on us, especially on the children. We did not fit in at school: Our clothes were odd, and some of us had body odor.

I survived it all, and I must acknowledge that the lives of migrants have improved in many ways. In some parts of the nation, however, especially in the Sunshine State, where agriculture is king and conservative politics rule, modern-day slavery thrives.

For a sane policy on farmwork

JULY 22, 2012

I dislike the use of cliches and truisms, but I accept some that nicely encapsulate the truth of a matter, like the one attributed to Albert Einstein that "insanity is doing the same thing over and over again and expecting different results."

That captures the insanity of U.S. immigration policy related to migrant and seasonal agricultural workers going back to the disastrous Bracero Program that began in the 1940s. The program brought thousands of Mexican laborers to the United States as a way to eliminate illegal immigration. It was officially shut down in 1964.

Our current policy is the same old hodgepodge of conflicting federal and state regulations. It is crafted by cynical politicians cheered on by ill-informed voters professing to believe in the mythical American/Protestant work ethic, the belief that Americans work harder than anyone else, will do any kind of work—even seasonal farmwork—and are fairly rewarded for their sweat and loyalty.

Many years before the economic downturn that began in 2007, conservatives in many agricultural states, especially in the South and Southwest, were promoting harsh crackdowns on undocumented farm laborers. The federal government joined in by establishing tough controls along the U.S.-Mexican border and by implementing equally tough lockup and deportation procedures.

Saner heads, including researchers, farmers and migrant/seasonal worker advocates, warned that such draconian rules would create labor shortages on many farms. But as the economic crisis deepened during 2008 through 2010 and as tea party politics gained traction, several states, including Arizona, Alabama and Georgia, ignored the warnings and passed "show-me-your-papers" laws.

At the same time, several less publicized trends were emerging that also affect the supply of available farm labor. Immigration experts report that along with Border Patrol agents who stop Mexicans from crossing the U.S. border illegally, human traffickers and drug cartels are preying on would-be border-crossers, forcing many to stay in Mexico. An improving Mexican economy is also keeping many workers home.

As predicted, these factors and new state laws have produced severe worker shortages coast to coast. American Farm Bureau officials say the U.S. produce industry will lose $5 billion to $9 billion in annual income because of labor shortages. In many places, fruits and vegetables are left to rot, and some growers plan to cut back on the acreage they plant next season. Others are shifting to crops such as peanuts, corn, soybeans and cotton that require far less stoop labor.

What are we doing to fix the problems?

Officials are tweaking the H-2A temporary worker visa program that was started in 1943. It gave Florida's sugarcane industry permission to hire thousands of Caribbean workers after growers claimed they could not find Americans to do the nasty, low-wage, dangerous work. The new version of H-2A is a bureaucratic nightmare for many growers, especially those who hire fewer than 10 employees.

Believing the false notion that Americans will do farmwork and motivated by their desire to reduce unemployment, federal and local officials are forcing farmers to document the need for foreign-born workers to be eligible for H-2A. They must prove they cannot find enough unskilled, unemployed locals to do the work, which can take months. Those who have what is known as "productivity standards" are seeing their applications for workers with "skills" and "experience" denied. This makes no sense.

And therein lies a major part of the insanity of our immigration policy related to migrant/seasonal workers: The majority of Americans falsely believe that anyone can and will do this backbreaking work. But many agricultural jobs, such as tending livestock and transplanting onions, require background skills in addition to a pair of hands and a strong back. Smart growers hesitate to simply grab people off the street.

Labor experts and farmers have been arguing for years, using empirical evidence, that average Americans lack the skills and toughness to do farmwork. But we persist in lying to ourselves time and again and expecting different results.

Migrant and seasonal workers are unique. In addition to being outdoors from sunup to sundown, they often work seven days a week for short periods before packing their belongings and moving on to the next job hundreds or thousands of miles away. They enjoy none of the benefits, such as health insurance, the rest of us expect.

Instead of passing laws that punish those who do the thankless work the rest of us will not do, we should use the increasing labor shortage and crop losses as the opportunity to stop the insanity. We have a moral obligation to establish immigration legislation that permanently and fairly rewards the invisible people who harvest our bounty.

150 years later, human slavery persists

SEPTEMBER 16, 2012

This year is the 150th anniversary of the Emancipation Proclamation. President Abraham Lincoln announced on Sept. 22, 1862, in a preliminary proclamation that slaves in any regions still in rebellion on Jan. 1, 1863, would be freed.

Many of those slaves were not freed. Ironically, in 2012, the United States still has millions of slaves. They are not of African descent on Southern plantations but from all points of the globe: prostitutes, domestic cleaners, restaurant and hotel workers, agricultural laborers and drug and gun carriers.

The United States, of course, is not alone in human trafficking, which is defined as denying a person the freedom to leave, the inability to obtain another job and being held through some type of coercive force.

Last spring, the International Labor Organization released a study estimating that at least 21 million people are in bondage worldwide. Other estimates put the number at 27 million.

This is no small matter. The study shows that the total world market value of human trafficking is in excess of $32 billion. A lot of that money flows to U.S. companies and individuals.

Fortunately, many individuals, nonprofit organizations and government agencies have worked tirelessly for many years to curb human slavery in the United States and the rest of the world. Their efforts are bringing long-overdue attention to this enduring tragedy.

Gary Haugen, president and CEO of International Justice Mission, a U.S.-based nonprofit human rights organization, is a leader in the effort to stamp out human slavery. Secretary of State Hillary Clinton honored Haugen in June for successes in 15 communities in developing countries in Asia, Africa and Latin America.

Haugen told me that traffickers always exploit the most vulnerable, those who are in the shadows of society. People trying to stay below the radar are lured by traffickers with promises of a better future. He said migrant farmworkers are especially vulnerable to enslavement because they move around and lack ties to the communities where they briefly work and live.

"Americans at all levels need to be aware that human trafficking is a real problem," he said. "We need to raise awareness amongst commercial enterprises that are making money off of trafficking without perhaps even knowing it. Consumers need to make sure that grocery stores that we shop at and large food supply and commercial enterprises know that consumers are going to be asking questions and requiring good citizenship and make sure that our food supply chain has no scent of any forced labor or labor abuses.

"We also need to make sure that the chief of police, the sheriff and local attorney understand that slavery is an issue across communities and that they need to prioritize proactive law enforcement to address this critical issue."

On the U.S. government side, Luis CdeBaca, ambassador-at-large to monitor and combat trafficking in persons at the State Department, is unequivocal about the scourge of trafficking.

He believes the campaign to stop trafficking has been strengthened because this year, for the first time, the United States includes itself in its own annual Trafficking in Persons Report, our principal diplomatic tool to interact with foreign governments on human trafficking.

Until now, many nations have scorned the report as being a tool for America to punish governments it dislikes. During a National Public Radio interview, CdeBaca said: "We included the United States because we realized the Obama administration was looking at where are the things that we're telling other countries that they need to do? And it wasn't a matter of simply saying, well, it would be only fair for us to analyze ourselves. It's also that we have a matrix of how we look at a country to see whether it's fighting trafficking effectively or not. And it was really kind of unfair to not apply that to the United States.

"There were trafficking victims in the U.S. who might not have been getting what they needed if we didn't apply that same diagnosis to ourselves. In some ways it's like having a doctor that had spent eight years not giving himself a blood pressure test while telling every one of his patients they needed to have their blood pressure checked."

Haugen, CdeBaca and others are leading what is being referred to as the "modern abolitionist movement." The shameful irony is that on the 150th anniversary of the Emancipation Proclamation, millions of people, many of them teenage girls, are enslaved in America.

Education

Worrisome gap in education for black men

JULY 30, 2000

The National Urban League's annual report on the state of black America is ready for shipping. As it does each year, the survey contains sobering observations and much positive news showing that African Americans, as a group, are increasingly enjoying the nation's broad wealth.

The overview also draws conclusions, as it does each year, that should make most of the nation's black leaders at all levels re-evaluate their priorities and begin an era of tough introspection. These leaders should be greatly concerned about the vast education attainment gap between black men and black women, and they should be concerned about the long-term implications of this disparity.

Specifically, according to the report, from 1977 to 1997, the number of bachelor's degrees earned by black men increased by 30 percent. During the same period, the number earned by black women rose by 77 percent. The picture for the master's degree is just as dismal: Increases for black men were 8 percent; for black women, 39 percent.

Another study, conducted by the *Journal of Blacks in Higher Education*, corroborates the Urban League's findings. It shows that in 1997, 454,000 black women had master's degrees. Black men had 222,000.

Why such a large gap in education attainment?

An easy explanation, one often repeated in the press, is that a disproportionately high number of black men are behind bars. University of

Michigan education professor Michael Nettles told the Associated Press, however, that the explanations are more complex.

He said that black men have more employment paths to follow after high school and that many simply bypass college altogether. More black men than women, for example, go from high school into the military. Another explanation is that the financially strapped black family depends on men more than women for essential income, the professor said.

Academic and social options and how black males are treated in public school also help determine who does and who does not attend college. Nettles argues that too many black males are in low-achieving and disciplinary environments, and too few are in advanced placement classes, a pipeline to college. Almost everyone agrees, off the record, that teachers and school officials generally have lower expectations for black males.

Hugh B. Price, the league's president, is correct when he says that the education attainment gap threatens the future of the black family as an institution. Average black women increasingly are having trouble finding black mates with comparable years of schooling and professional experience.

Studies show that a college degree is universally the surest path to a good job and financial security. Black women are graduating from college and getting good jobs, positions in corporate board rooms, partnerships in law firms and other high places.

So, as the education gap grows between black men and black women, the economic chasm widens just as fast or faster. "As the economic gap widens, questions of whether black women will find black men who can carry their share in the household will become evident," Price told AP.

As I said at the outset, the time has come for black leaders to initiate an unapologetic process of introspection in the black home. Yes, many public school systems shortchange black children, especially males. But the black family itself has the responsibility of reassessing how it treats the male. Most of what ails the male starts in the home and is perpetuated in the home.

A black man, father, grandfather and former teacher and one whose job is to think about such matters, I am aware of differences in how we rear our girls and our boys.

Denial will not save the day. Truth can, though. And here is some of that awful truth, offered by novelist, playwright and essayist James

Baldwin, a black man, in his 1985 book *The Evidence of Things Not Seen* (a nonfiction work about the Wayne Williams murders in Atlanta):

"There is, according to Andy (Young), a disease peculiar to the Black community, called 'sorriness.' I am not a Southerner, and I had never heard this term before. It is a disease that attacks Black males. It is transmitted by Mama, whose instinct, and it is not hard to see why, is to protect the Black male from the devastation that threatens him the moment he declares himself a man.

"All of our mothers, and all of our women, live with this small, doom-laden bell in the skull, silent, waiting, or resounding, every hour of every day. Mama lays this burden on Sister, from whom she expects (or indicates she expects) far more than she expects from Brother; but one of the results of this too comprehensible dynamic is that Brother may never grow up...."

To put Baldwin's view another way, we had a saying in the black community when I was a child that went like this: "We raise our girls and love our boys to death."

This is a scary scenario. Baldwin's comments do not explain all that affects the plight of the black male, but they establish a solid starting point. Here are a few of the basic questions we must answer: What does the individual black family expect of the male? Do we demand from him the same that we demand from our females? How can we eliminate this double standard?

The way that we answer these questions will determine the education and economic health of black America.

As understated as it sounds, the Urban League's conclusion is ominous and is worth repeating: "The numerical status of African American men in higher education is a cause for concern."

No-nonsense school gives second chance

MARCH 20, 2002

They got in trouble. They all did something bad, that we know. Some of their offenses were minor. Some offenses were serious enough, however, to have landed them in jail under ordinary circumstances. Their ages are 12 to 15, and they are in sixth through eighth grade.

They are the 73 students attending Safety Harbor Secondary School. This is no ordinary school.

No, this is a place where young people are sent to redeem themselves, to prove that they can get along in a regular school setting, and in society at large, where trouble is the exception and not the rule.

I was here because Philip Wirth, the principal, asked me to speak to the students and staff, to observe, to hang out.

I spoke to two separate groups. When each entered the room, I sat to the side and observed. The first thing I noticed was their uniformity in dress. Yes, the school (a public school!) has a strict dress code. All shirts and blouses (plain white) were neatly tucked into either black or navy blue pants or jeans. No one wore shorts. I saw only waist-located logos on pants and jeans. Shirts and blouses were logo-free.

The dress code is important because it is emblematic of the school's purpose, as expressed in its mission statement: "To create opportunities for personal growth and continuous social and academic improvement. We will accomplish this in an atmosphere of trust and cooperation."

Yes, kids are wont to compete, but at Safety Harbor Middle, the real competition is between the students' old self and the new one they are trying to create, between the old forces that caused their problems and the new ones that will rescue them and help them return to their schools and perhaps to new lives.

The school's anchor is its no-nonsense view of its students and why they are here. Who is responsible for the child's problems? The child is. Period.

Here is what the school's official assignment document states: "Students are reassigned to the program because they have chosen behavior(s) in the traditional school setting that interfere with their education and the education of others." Students choose their behaviors, good or bad.

The key, of course, is convincing young people that they play a role in determining their fates, that they play a leading role in how others treat them. One point I made was that all of us, no matter how young or old, give people clues as to how we want to be treated. Many young black males, for example, believe that "being smart" is "acting white." I pointed out that if that is true, then being the opposite, "being dumb," is being black.

The simple point is that black males can change the way teachers and others treat them by changing how they view intellectuality. Another point, meant for all students, is that simple politeness will open more doors of opportunity than rudeness. These are behaviors we choose. The school teaches this valuable lesson.

Indeed, in addition to the academic areas of English, reading and math, the school enforces zero tolerance for violent behavior and profanity. Each morning, students pledge to avoid violence and profanity, often the problems that landed them in hot water.

Another key to the school's success is its requirement that parents must be involved in their children's school lives. They must attend conferences with teachers and their children. Parents and their children must complete community projects that show the importance of living wholesomely with their neighbors.

Philip Wirth, the principal, is the driving force behind the school's success. He and his staff are on a mission: to work hard to save every child who comes to them.

I have personal experience with schools such as this. My son attended one. No matter how hard I preached good behavior, he chose something else. Fortunately, he had people like Wirth, who believed in him, who were forgiving and willing to give him a second chance.

The students at Safety Harbor Secondary are children who made mistakes. Too many of us, including school board policymakers, forget that we are dealing with children too immature, both physiologically and emotionally, to make adult decisions. Yet we shun them and condemn them.

Visiting this school reminded me that when children from certain backgrounds are at issue, we tend to be unforgiving. Wirth and his staff are giving kids who committed youthful indiscretions a second chance to redeem themselves.

Gov. Bush, why can't you support the Florida Center for Teachers?

JUNE 9, 2002

Dear Gov. Jeb Bush:

I will not waste your valuable time with a lot of detail. We know the story.

"Like many other Florida residents who support our public schools and real learning, I am disappointed you vetoed the $275,000 allocation for the Florida Center for Teachers."

The above words were the lead of a column I wrote this time last year about your vetoes following the end of the annual ordeal we call the legislative budget process.

Well, here you go again. On Wednesday, you vetoed this year's $275,000 allocation for the nonprofit Florida Center for Teachers.

"I fear for the future of the program," said Fran Cary, executive director of the St. Petersburg-based Florida Humanities Council, which manages the center.

I was hoping—I did not bet, of course—that since you had snubbed the center last year, you would approve 2002's allocation. No such luck. I also wrote these words last year, and they have just as much meaning now: "Myopic and arrogant, Bush has no good reason to take away the (center's) funding."

I need to say at this point, Governor, that the major reason the center means nothing to you is that you have not found a way to empirically establish its benefits. The center's programs do not—like expensive courses on how to take standardized tests—guarantee, or even suggest, that Florida children will score higher on the FCAT or other required examinations.

So, exactly what is the Florida Center for Teachers' function? What makes it valuable to hundreds of Florida teachers and their thousands of students? (If I had the power, Governor, I would force you to attend one of the center's weeklong institutes).

Ten years old, the center operates the only statewide staff development programs in the humanities for Florida's K-12 teachers. Its various seminars, planned and moderated by some of the state's best scholars, inspire teachers and enhance their knowledge of the state's history, literature, folklore, social issues and other topics.

Ann Simas Schoenacher, a Humanities Council program coordinator, assessed the center's efforts: "What teachers get in our seminars is a chance to be learners again. The enthusiasm for learning that is generated in a classroom by a teacher who has been renewed and has been allowed the freedom to think about 'big picture' issues cannot be measured yet by the FCAT."

Governor, your veto dismisses the intangibles of good teaching. Last year, you said you wanted teacher training to focus on school safety, data analysis, assessment, subject content, teaching methods and classroom assessment.

As far as I can tell, nothing has changed. You are right to insist on these areas, but you are wrong to dismiss teacher enrichment. Why do you ignore teacher enrichment? I am talking about special nurturing that celebrates excellence. Do you see any value in the professional support that sustains and reinvigorates love of the classroom?

"Year after year, veteran teachers tell us after they have returned to their classrooms that the center's renewal seminars are the best professional development programs they have attended," Schoenacher said. "More teachers than I can count have told me that they had made concrete plans to retire in six months or a year. But after they had the intellectual stimulation they experienced in our seminars, they decided to hold on and stay in the classroom."

The center is not a remedial program. It is, in fact, quite the opposite. It recognizes and rewards excellent teachers—those who inspire our children to learn more than test taking.

Governor, when Florida, like most other states, faces a critical teacher shortage, you and your conservative, from-somewhere-else supporters give us education on the cheap. And you continue to ignore the concerns of our most important resource: our inspired, competent teachers.

As a black man educated in Jim Crow's evil system of racial segregation, I learned that when my teachers feel good about themselves and their profession, children are the real winners.

Today, Governor, too many of our good teachers feel humiliated because of you. As far as they are concerned, you are not on their side.

Governor, let me say this: Instead of discounting the value of our public school teachers through stinginess and crass politics, you need to help us celebrate these underpaid public servants.

In closing, I invite you to telephone the Florida Center for Teachers and arrange to participate in at least two of this summer's teacher seminars.

Failing schools have dedicated teachers

JUNE 19, 2002

FCAT has spoken, and school grades have been posted.

The purpose of this column is not to minimize the importance of FCAT and the governor's A+ Plan. As a Florida parent and grandparent, I hope the governor's initiatives yield results that truly benefit our students over a lifetime.

My purpose is to put a human face on a process that discounts the hard work of teachers whose schools did not perform well on FCAT. The best way to put a human face on this problem is to let teachers speak for themselves.

Listen to this impassioned plea for understanding to Gov. Jeb Bush in a letter published in the *St. Petersburg Times*. It is from Sarah J. Robinson, an English teacher at Leto High School in Tampa:

"As a classroom teacher in a school not earning a high grade under Gov. Jeb Bush's grading system, I take great offense at his statements about high-performing schools having committed teachers. While I do not doubt . . . the commitment of the teachers in those other schools, to suggest that my colleagues and I are less so is a slap in the face and lacking in common sense.

"Does the governor think our jobs are easier teaching students whose families are poorer and less-educated in schools that are older and less-equipped than those 'high-performing' schools where our colleagues get bonuses each year? Who would have to be more dedicated to go to work each day?"

I do not know who has to be more dedicated to go to work each day, teachers at A schools or teachers at F schools. But I do personally know one of the most dedicated teachers in Florida. Her school, Dillard High in Fort Lauderdale, received an F. I know her as a former 10th grade classmate at Dillard in 1961.

My former classmate, a straight-A student, matriculated to Columbia University, where she became an honor student. Even during the bad old days of the late 1960s, she was offered teaching jobs from school districts in many parts of the country. Several private sector companies also wanted her.

But she followed her dream of becoming a teacher and returned to South Florida, eventually working her way back to Dillard 12 years ago. She taught one of my nephews and a niece and the kids of many of my former schoolmates and friends.

Let me tell you what I know about her: She knows her subject, and she spends her own money and time staying academically current. She is a natural-born reader and a salty traveler. But all that is to be taken for granted when one is a teacher. Proof of her commitment and dedication lies elsewhere.

"I know who I am, and I know who I chose to dedicate my life to," she said. "I came back to Dillard because I believed I could make a difference. Many of these kids have one parent, and a lot of time that one parent doesn't appreciate the importance of education. Think about it: If a parent doesn't give a damn about education and the family is poor on top of that, the teacher is looking at some major-league problems.

"Now, imagine a class with 25 kids and 20 of those kids come from the type of family I just described. I've been there. I refuse to give up on them. I do all I can for them."

Doing all she can for her students includes using her own money to buy classroom necessities. More significantly, at least to me, is that she spends two nights a week of her own time visiting students and parents in their homes. She also shows up at students' churches on Sunday to let her charges know that she cares about them. She persuaded her husband to accompany her sometimes.

"My colleagues and I do all we can with what we have," she said. "Our kids have a lot of real-life crises that undercut learning. We struggle each day. And I'm not blaming the kids, either."

Faced with the same problems, Robinson wrote in the *Times:* "And while I take some responsibility for how my students perform on that test, there are other factors that the governor ignores: parental support and responsibility. Less than 10 percent of my students' parents have ever come to a parent night, for example, but the governor would rather blame school personnel. . . . Instead of demanding that parents be more accountable or instead of taking responsibility for our state ranking 49th in the nation in spending on education, Gov. Bush continues to blame us for not being able to perform miracles."

These two teachers, like hundreds of others in failing schools, confront the stubborn problems of poverty. They need to be recognized for the difficult, thankless work they do. In many ways, they do perform miracles.

A valuable life lesson learned in school

JUNE 26, 2002

You know you are getting old when a former student writes to thank you for teaching her a valuable lesson that helps her rear her children.

Last week, I received such a letter from Janice Anderson, an African American, now 49, who took an honors English course I taught at Broward Community College in 1984. She was an excellent student—but not always so. At midterm, she made an F on her examination and a D on her essay. She stormed into my office and demanded to know "the real deal" with me.

I informed her that "the real deal" was her lack of academic discipline. I detected from the poor quality of her work that she was not reading the texts closely, that she was not writing her essays thoughtfully and that she was not revising her work critically. She had the wrong attitude toward learning and education to succeed in the academy.

She went to the dean, a 44-year-old white man, who called me into his office and demanded that I explain myself. I agreed to do so but only with the student present. I wanted the two of them to hear me at the same time.

This is the gist of my explanation: Janice was intelligent, but she did not appreciate the inherent value of learning, the complex process of lively inquiry, of using reason and logic to question everything and anything.

But she had a bigger problem, which I detected in the way she interacted with other blacks on campus: Janice was afraid to be smart because she feared what other blacks would say. I knew she was smart because I heard all of those sharp, subtle observations she muttered under her breath. I explained that I could not be blamed for her academic failure. She, Janice, had to do the hard work away from school, in her home.

"Real learning—learning that matters for a lifetime—is lonely," I told her.

I knew where she lived, a few blocks from where I was born in northwest Fort Lauderdale. The area was an anti-intellectual drug haven, where being a "down brother" or a "down sister" was the litmus test for "belonging."

I was surprised when she acknowledged that I was right. Indeed, she was embarrassed to let her friends see her reading a book or trying to type an essay. She did not want to seem different; she wanted to fit in with her longtime friends.

I will never forget her last words that day: "Being dumb is too high a price to pay just to fit in."

Here, I would love to avoid a happy ending and do the cynical journalist routine. But that would be a lie. The raw, real-life truth is that Janice transformed her relationship with school. I know because she wrote about it. The quality of her work and her grades improved considerably.

She stopped working full time and took a part-time job. She applied for a student loan and received it. She gave her friends strict orders to leave her alone, which included telephone calls only during certain hours. Reading, typing and sounding smart became points of pride rather than signs of "betraying the race" or "selling out."

Her boyfriend—"my old man," as she called him—felt neglected. He complained, beat her several times, moved out and found a new uneducated love to dominate.

Here is the real point of this column: That meeting with the dean and me changed Janice's life and made her an exemplary mother who reared two children alone.

"I make a good living as a nurse because I stopped worrying about what the people around me are saying," she wrote. "You made me realize that only I can help me. Only I can read for me. Only I can study for me. Only I can think for me. The real beauty is your challenge. You challenged me to teach my children to go against the grain. You challenged me to make them study. You told me to teach them to take pride in being smart. You told me that being dumb is just that—being dumb.

"That was a valuable lesson. Both of my kids attend Dillard. As you know, Dillard made an F on the FCAT. But my kids passed easily. They passed because I work with them at home. They play like other kids, but I make them do their school work. This summer, we're doing math and vocabulary sessions at home. They actually like it.

"I'm taking them to plays and concerts, like you recommended years ago. My kids will attend college. You can bet on it. It really boils down to what goes on in the home. You always said that in class. You said it didn't matter where you went to school so long as you study hard. Dillard may flunk FCAT, but my kids won't flunk. Thanks for being mean to me at BCC."

Let's do more to help the poor get a college education

JUNE 30, 2002

The rich keep getting richer, and poor keep getting poorer—and left out.

One group that feels poorer and more left out is the nation's thousands of qualified high school graduates who will be prevented from enjoying the benefits of a full college education.

A new report, "Empty Promises," released by the Advisory Committee on Student Financial Assistance, found that for this year alone, 406,000 academically acceptable high school graduates will not have the means to attend a four-year college. Another 168,000 will not be able to attend a college of any kind because they simply are broke.

Congress established the committee in 1986 to analyze financial aid policy.

How can this sorry condition exist in the world's richest industrialized nation, where the likes of WorldCom, Enron, Tyco, Rite Aid, Adelphia Communications, Dynergy, ImClone Systems, Arthur Andersen, Martha Stewart and others can play games with millions to billions of dollars, where CEOs are routinely paid millions and handed huge stock option packages even when their companies perform so-so?

Broadly speaking, greed, wrong-headed values and our deepening, conservative dismissal of low-income families have created a climate that permits this trend.

Reporting to Congress last Wednesday, the advisory committee and the secretary of education warned that if the federal government and the states do not increase need-based grants, millions of qualified students will be denied a college education during the next decade. In addition to facing a severe shortage of grants and scholarships, needy students, like others, face sharply rising tuition costs.

"Empty Promises" studied high school graduates whose families earned less than $50,000 a year. Republicans like to blame the victim, arguing that low- to moderate-income students do not attend four-year colleges in large numbers because they are poorly educated and are unmotivated before reaching college age. But the report, requested by Congress, looked at students who took college preparatory courses, passed them and held grade point averages of B-minus or higher.

The report clearly shows the students in question are not throwaway losers but high school graduates whose parents happen to be poor and who lack political clout. The findings are to be used in the 2003 congressional debate over the reauthorization of the Higher Education Act.

These are some of the specific findings: A qualified student from a low-income family (less than $25,000 annually) still needs up to $3,800 a year after loans, grants and work-study employment. Working and borrowing, parents of low-income students struggle to pay an average of $7,500 a year at a four-year state college, which is nearly one-third of their salary.

Juliet V. Garcia, the committee's chairwoman, said during the next 10 years, 4.4-million qualified students will not be able to afford a four-year college education, and 2-million will not be able to attend any college.

Garcia said mere statistics do not reflect the daily hardship low-income students confront. To attend college full time, they assume excessive debt and work long hours that prevent them from attending classes, studying and entertaining themselves as they should.

Although the government increased Pell grants, the nation's largest grant funder, by $3.3-billion over two years, low-income students are still being shunted.

Why? Because the rate of college tuition hikes is outpacing inflation. "No other sector of the economy is increasing at twice the rate of inflation," said Jeff Andrade, deputy assistant secretary for postsecondary education at the U.S. Department of Education.

States have been hard hit by the current economic slowdown, and most took the path of least resistance to cover red ink: They automatically increased tuition. Another cause for the tuition increase is that endowment-giving has dipped lower than it has been in years.

"Empty Promises" also indicates that although low-income students and their parents are more likely than their upper-income counterparts to read financial aid information, many (43 percent) do not personally speak with financial aid counselors.

In other words, out of ignorance, many do not take advantage of aid officially available to them. Because so much is at stake—the loss of college-qualified students—high school counselors and college financial aid representatives should become more proactive and encourage low-income clients to talk with advisers.

Everyone would benefit from such a move. Low-income students may not get rich as a result, but at least they will not be left out of opportunities.

A renewed joy and love of teaching

SEPTEMBER 22, 2002

When an official at Angelo State University telephoned me more than a year ago and asked if I had interest in being a visiting professor during the fall semester of 2002, I told him I would have to think about the proposition and would get back to him.

I was not interested in teaching.

After all, I had quit college teaching in 1994 to join the *St. Petersburg Times* editorial board because I no longer could muster the energy to face another group of unsmiling undergraduates who hated being forced to take required English courses.

I had had enough of trying to convince grown-ups, many of them rich brats, that reading was good for them, that learning writing skills would give them advantages they would appreciate in later years.

The joy had gone out of teaching, and I had to leave the profession.

When I did not respond within a few weeks, the Angelo State professor telephoned again. This time, he shared ample details about the job. I accepted, contingent, of course, upon the *Times'* approval. I accepted because university officials and faculty liked my work enough to invite me to be their colleague for a semester. To turn them down would have been disrespectful and arrogant.

My *Times'* bosses gave me the go ahead, and here I am in West Texas. I am happy that I came.

Spending more than eight years writing full time has given me a renewed love of teaching. Doing what I teach, writing, makes all the difference. Instead of using the work of other writers as prose models in my journalism class, for instance, I now lead students through my process of crafting columns, editorials and essays.

The students do not have to guess: The author sits in front of them.

My enthusiasm shows, and the students respond positively. But my enthusiasm alone would not matter if the students were not talented, ready learners. And they are. Nearly all had published at least one article or column before we met. Some are on the university newspaper staff; others write for the local daily, the *Standard-Times*.

They are engaged. They are uninhibited. I do not have to prod them into participating in class. They are talking before I enter the classroom, and they continue talking up to the moment I begin to lecture.

Best of all, a few boldly attempt creative ways of making the potentially stodgy opinion piece an entertaining experience both for themselves and for their reader, me.

Their first writing assignment was an editorial about recent police killings of civilians here in San Angelo. I am impressed with their efforts. Some of the editorials could be published in the state's best newspapers. In short, this is the best group of journalism students I have had anywhere.

My literature course, Ethnic Contributions to American Literature, is as rewarding as the opinion writing course. We are reading African American authors and studying African American films. The works, such as Alice Walker's novel *The Color Purple* and Spike Lee's film *Bamboozled*, take inward looks at black culture.

These works are not attacks against whites. They represent unapologetic introspection. *The Color Purple* is a graphic portrayal of black men's cruelty toward black women. Lawrence Otis Graham's memoir *Our Kind of People* describes the ugly skin-color caste system among African Americans.

Most of the students are white, and many have told me that a new world has been opened to them. Until now, they had not given a thought to exposing themselves to black culture.

"I'm ashamed to say black stuff didn't exist to me before taking this course," a student said. "It was another world. I was born and raised in West Texas. We don't have many blacks out here."

As a teacher, I am experiencing the pure enjoyment of facilitating real learning, introducing students to information and conversation they otherwise would shun. I watch some suddenly sit back in their chairs in wonder.

Imagine my delight when a student uttered these words to me in my office: "I'm becoming less judgmental of black people. I guess I'm learning some things. Believe it or not, Mr. Maxwell, you're my first black teacher. I never had one in public school, either."

For the first time in many years, I feel useful. I have rediscovered the value and the joy of teaching.

Immigrant students deserve a chance at college

MAY 25, 2004

I will not use these students' names because of the politics involved in their plight. I simply will refer to them as Student A and Student B. Both are Latino, both live in Hillsborough County and both lack resident immigrant status. They are graduating from high school this term.

Detractors of their causes often refer to them, among other names, as "illegal immigrants" and "illegal aliens."

Student A is a young man whose parents brought him to the United States from Mexico three years ago. He attended English-language classes for one semester, but he soon qualified for honors classes, including advanced placement English.

Student B is a young woman whose parents brought her to the United

States from Mexico five years ago. She completed advanced placement courses in English, English literature, biology, chemistry, physics, American history, French and European history. She will graduate No. 4 out of more than 450 students in her class.

Both students desperately want to attend college. But neither may get the opportunity if Florida's conservative lawmakers do not soften their contemptible attitude toward immigrant students and do not implement a law that grants these graduating seniors the same low in-state tuition rates their peers with resident status enjoy—discounts amounting to a fourth of full tuition at many colleges.

Last year, the bill that would have given undocumented immigrant students in-state tuition discounts died before reaching the House floor, thanks mainly to Speaker Johnnie Byrd, even though Gov. Jeb Bush supported the bill and even though it had passed the Florida Senate.

On Friday, House Bill 119, which gives immigrant students in-state discounts, came closer to reaching the House floor with approval in the Appropriations Committee. The fate of the bill again lies with Byrd because he has the power to bring it to the floor for a vote.

Byrd's spokesman, Tom Denham, said his boss—whose agricultural district depends on and quietly employs a large number of undocumented workers—opposes the bill and has philosophical difficulty giving benefits to people who are in the country illegally.

But Rep. Juan Carlos Zapata, R-Miami, the bill's sponsor, offered the *South Florida Sun-Sentinel* this common-sense observation: "It's a fairness issue, something that takes Florida demographic realities into account. We have a large undocumented immigrant population. For us to hold back kids that have done nothing wrong, and have gone through the system and performed, and then put this roadblock in their path doesn't make sense. And it doesn't seem like good public policy to me."

To encourage fellow Republicans to permit a committee vote, according to the *Sun-Sentinel*, Zapata dropped proposals to grant undocumented students access to state financial aid and scholarships.

Once again, as it often is when immigrant laborers and their children are involved, the Sunshine State is in the darkness. All of the other states with working immigrant populations, including California, Illinois, Oklahoma, New York, Texas, Utah and Washington, have passed similar legislation benefiting such residents.

Donna Perrino, executive director of Engaging Latino Communities for Education at the University of South Florida, a community-focused program sponsored by the W.K. Kellogg Foundation to increase the number of Latinos attending college, said that the overwhelming majority of undocumented immigrant students are innocent victims.

These young people did not have a say in coming to America, and they should not be held fully responsible for an immigration status they inherited from their parents. They should not be precluded from the opportunities they deserve from their talents and hard work. Common sense suggests that when immigrant children believe that college is a financially realistic possibility, they will not drop out of school and will become viable members of society.

"Allowing immigrant students to pay in-state tuition will not decrease opportunities for other students," states a position paper by the Florida Immigrant Coalition. "The most qualified students will still be admitted. This bill would give immigrant students the same opportunity as their classmates—no more and no less."

What Byrd decides will greatly influence the fates of Student A and Student B and others to follow. My hope is that he remembers that these students have been absorbed into the fabric of U.S. society. They had nothing to do with their parents' decisions.

They will become taxpayers and may become leaders, like so many other immigrants before them, if they are treated fairly.

A landmark revisited // *Brown v. Board of Education,* May 17, 1954

MAY 16, 2004

Crescent City

For the 50th anniversary of the landmark *Brown v. Board of Education* case that outlawed segregation in the nation's public schools, I returned to Crescent City, where I graduated from high school in 1963. With a population of nearly 2,000, Crescent City is in southern Putnam County, on U.S. Highway 17 between DeLand and Palatka.

I wanted to see how the place, especially its public schools, had changed since I was here, when white and black children were legally forced to attend separate schools.

On opposite sides of town, our schools mirrored life beyond the campuses, where everything else was separate, too. "Whites Only" and "Colored Only" signs told us where we could and could not go. Even the simple act of drinking water from a public fountain was governed by warnings. White and black children rarely had physical contact of any kind. While all of us, black and white, knew our places, we blacks grudgingly accepted the ill-conceived wisdom of segregation.

As I drove into the student parking lot of Crescent City Jr./Sr. High School, to keep a 1 o'clock appointment, I was surprised to see dozens of students of various ethnicities milling about and chatting in the shadow of the main building.

I was most struck by the basketball goal near the cafeteria and the six boys, three white and three black, who were shooting hoops. Such an activity—the races playing together—would have been unimaginable in 1963. I watched the game and cheering spectators for about 10 minutes, sensing an easygoing camaraderie I could not have anticipated.

Then I met Joe Warren, the 48-year-old African American principal. My first questions concerned the basketball game I had just seen in the middle of the day. I was impressed with how well the white and black kids interacted.

"I think it just starts with me," Warren said in the no-nonsense manner that his staff expects. "You, the leader, have to set an example. You have to go out and build a rapport with all of your kids. I can name three-fourths of my kids, and I have almost 900 of them. I think the rapport I have built with the kids over the years has spread. I treat them all the same—all of them. It's a relaxed atmosphere. They don't feel threatened. And they know that if someone steps across the line, we will take care of them regardless of who they are or what color they are."

Warren said that he came by his devotion to fairness the hard way. Instead of making him bitter, the racism he experienced during childhood influenced him to make a positive difference. He was born in Charleston, S.C., in 1956, to migrant farmworking parents. The family moved to Hastings, Fla., where he grew up and attended a segregated school until the ninth grade, when St. Johns County ended its separate-but-equal system. The year was 1970, 16 years after the *Brown* decision was to have killed Jim Crow.

Initially, racial tensions flared, and a few physical confrontations occurred, Warren said. But he soon learned a lesson in racial sensitivity and cooperation that remains with him to this day.

"After our schools integrated, the football team soldered our community together," Warren said. "We had 15 to 20 white kids on the team. We were surprised at the level of their play. We held the more skilled positions—quarterback, running back, receiver—but they had these big guys up front who could block. The coach pulled us together, and that's when we won our first state championship. Initially, when you looked in the stands, white people would be on one end, and black people would be on the other end. But as the season went along and we started to win, you started to notice the crowds started to mix. After we won the state championship, everything was fine."

Warren attended historically black South Carolina State University on a football scholarship. He majored in physical education and minored in biology. After graduating in 1979, he was hired as a biology teacher and football coach at Crescent City. Several years later, he became the school's principal—the county's first black principal in the post-Jim Crow era. Now, he is the district's only black male principal.

Warren believes that the degree of a principal's personal commitment to racial and ethnic diversity can make a campus a place where students, teachers and other staff members want to be, or it can make it a place they hate. His is a viable philosophy given the diversity of the students. When he first came to Crescent City, the student population was 65 percent white and 35 percent African American. Now, whites comprise 56 percent and Hispanics slightly outnumber blacks.

Listen to 25-year veteran language teacher Muriel Kuhn: "To say our school has diversity is an understatement. For such a small student body, our demographics encompass Caucasian, African American, Laotian, Latino, Philippine, Indian and Nigerian. Through our foreign exchange program, we have, or have had, students from Thailand, China, Russia, Brazil, Sweden and Germany. During my years at CCJSHS, I have not felt that the various groups had difficulty getting along. Our faculty and staff have worked diligently to encourage each culture to know about other cultures. We celebrate our differences."

Before leaving campus, I wanted to hear what some students had to say about the ethnic and racial dynamics of their school:

Ruth Chappell, 17, white, senior: "In my opinion, integration works at CCJSHS. There are rarely any fights between the races, and as you walk through the halls, you see friends of different races mixing and mingling as if they were siblings."
Danny Senoboboutavongnorat, 16, immigrated from Laos, junior:

"To me, integration is working okay here at school. I feel welcomed and not left out. A lot of people of different races know me. Everyone treats me well, and I've never had any problems with anyone. I am also able to work in groups and understand other people without arguing. We are a team."

Ramonda Johnson, 16, African American, junior: "I feel that for the most part, integration is working here. We have a mixture of many races. At times, we don't see eye to eye and may have disagreements, but we manage to work it out and learn to get along with each other."

Jonathan Gomez, 18, immigrated from Mexico, senior: "I think that the school should try harder to promote integration. The students try to integrate themselves, but much of it is just for a while. We need more help from the adults."

Although CCJSHS received a grade of "C" from the Florida Department of Education, many district officials believe that, given the campus' unique demographics, Warren and his staff perform extraordinarily. In addition to the town of Crescent City, the school draws students from the tiny working-class communities of Lake Como, Satsuma, San Mateo, Fruitland Park, Georgetown, Welaka, Pomona Park and Hoot Owl Ridge.

"We have the highest reduced-lunch rate in the county, the highest minority population among the high schools, and we have the highest ESOL (English for Speakers of Other Languages) population, and we have the highest poverty level," Warren said. "And I house grades 7-12. On the FCAT, we have to test seventh, eighth, ninth and 10th grades to get a school grade. The other two high schools only have ninth and 10th grades. Last year, we were at a 3.70, 10 points from a 'B' school. We're a 'C' school with our population."

An important part of the school's success can be attributed to its student-centered approach. "We make a big deal out of the kids," Warren said. "We pump the kids up. They're not afraid to approach any of the staff or me about their problems. It all starts with the kids. We try to get them excited about school. You have to be a fan of the kids. No color. Just kids."

Warren, an unequivocal integrationist, believes that a diverse student population needs a diverse faculty. But he believes that quality must come with diversity.

"Our students deserve the best, and I'm held accountable," he said. "I have to put the best teachers I can in the classroom, and I can't afford to see color. That would be taboo. You've got to be straight for the kids' sake."

Crescent City integrated its two high schools without incident in 1968, and the segregation academies that sprang up in many other Southern towns never took root here. Crescent City is one of the *Brown* decision's success stories.

Parents, not schools, failed these children

JUNE 3, 2007

Who's responsible for educating a child?

On its face, this is a simple question. But when we factor in the race of the child, the question becomes one mired in, among other forces, blame, anger, recrimination, self-aggrandizement, history, myth, politics and, of course, litigation.

All of these forces are converging in Pinellas County as the School Board and its attorneys prepare to do battle with Guy Burns, the attorney representing a plaintiff class composed of 20,000 black children currently attending and who will attend Pinellas schools.

The plaintiffs claim the schools failed to adequately educate black students in violation of Florida law and the state Constitution. Indeed, black students in Pinellas schools consistently score below all other groups on all standardized measures, dubbed the achievement gap, and they have the highest suspension and expulsion rates.

Popularly known as the "*Crowley* case," this class-action lawsuit is named for black parent William Crowley. It was filed in August 2000 by Crowley on behalf of his son, Akwete Osoka, then a 7-year-old student at Sawgrass Elementary School in St. Petersburg.

According to the lawsuit, the boy faced academic problems "typical of those difficulties commonly faced by students of African descent." The lawsuit was filed during the time the People's Democratic Uhuru Movement faced obstacles in trying to establish its all-black Marcus Garvey Academy charter school. Crowley had enrolled his son in the Uhuru after-school tutoring program, and he claimed the boy had begun reading above grade level as a result.

I have no doubt that this is a bogus lawsuit, and the judges who have permitted the case to go forward are patronizing and wrongheaded. They are blaming the wrong side for black children's failure to get a "high-quality" education.

Burns, now supported by a broad group of blacks that includes veteran educators, is blaming the schools for black students' abysmal academic performance. However, a 2005 study by University of Florida professor David N. Figlio and Princeton University professor Cecilia Elena Rouse argues that the moment black children in Pinellas come to kindergarten, they are not as prepared for learning as their peers. The study was commissioned by the Pinellas School District.

The researchers based their findings on precise data the district had collected as it tracked the 8,400 students who entered kindergarten in 1989 through high school graduation.

Michael W. Kirk, a Washington, D.C.-based attorney for Pinellas schools, summarizes the study's major finding: "Whatever is causing the gap, it, by definition, is something that happened to these children before they set foot in a Pinellas County school."

Everything I know as a teacher and as a parent forces me to agree. Every classroom teacher I know agrees, and every mature, responsible parent I know agrees.

Too many blacks have relinquished their parental duties, a shameful neglect that forces public school teachers and administrators to become surrogate parents to children who have full-blown lives beyond the schoolhouse door.

A few days ago, a white middle school teacher told me that when she tried to speak with black parents about their children's unruly behavior, she faced hostility.

"I can't get through to the kids, and I can't get through to the parents," she said. "What am I supposed to do?"

I did not have an answer. But I know this much: For sure, the courthouse is not the answer.

I have seen many children born and reared in poor, single-parent households who perform well academically and who do not get suspended or expelled from school. More often than not, these children have caring adults who participate in their intellectual and social lives.

Such adults know the home is life's anchor. They do not wait for strangers to do their job.

Last week, I went to the *St. Petersburg Times*' archives and read everything that has been written about the *Crowley* case since it started in

2000. The best thing I read is the eloquent letter from Margy Kincaid, a high school teacher in Palm Harbor, published this March 28. She discusses the achievement gap in Pinellas schools:

"The achievement gap is bridged in early childhood by the parents, by how cherished the children were, how their questions were answered or how often they were read to at night. It is bridged by how committed the parents are to their education and the value it holds. The children's behavior control starts in early childhood with the way their discipline has been handled by the parents.

"Public school teachers, and administrators and guidance counselors, for the most part, jump through hoops to help these children catch up and learn anger-management and see to it that they get food, clothing or even basic hygiene products. But without the backing of parents the job is next to impossible.

"Graduation rates will not improve, school violence and vandalism will not decrease, the gap will not be bridged until we get the parents to buy into the 24/7 responsibility that began when they created the special and unique individual who is their child."

Guy Burns, the *Crowley* case attorney, needs to listen to Margy Kincaid and her colleagues instead of listening to parents who fail their own children long before the children enter kindergarten.

FSU's tough love gets results

NOVEMBER 25, 2007

While so-called meritocracy is shutting the doors to higher education to black students in many states nationwide, Florida State University in Tallahassee is quietly paving a way for highly motivated black students to achieve who otherwise would be unable to attend a first-rate university.

The *St. Petersburg Times* reported on Monday that FSU has the highest black student six-year graduation rate in the nation. To wit: About 71 percent of FSU's black students graduate within six years, exceeding the state average by 17 percent and the national average by 30 percent. In fact, mostly white FSU graduates more black students than historically black Florida A&M University across town.

Those of us who have been following such trends and keeping track of the programs being implemented nationwide to recruit and retain black students are not surprised. Through its Center for Academic Retention and Enhancement, FSU has been doing almost everything right to nurture black students for several years.

Even before former Gov. Jeb Bush implemented One Florida in 1999, which ended affirmative action in college admissions, FSU was quietly finding ways to attract and keep black students through CARE.

Using real-life criteria, CARE accepts students from low-income families who are the first to attend college. Students are judged on traits such as their character, study habits, willingness to succeed and the motivation they showed in high school. Scores on the SAT are secondary.

Satisfying these criteria will get you into FSU, but they will not keep you there. Indeed, getting in is the easy part. After students are admitted, they must, for example, attend a six-week summer program on campus that introduces them to the rigors of academia. Counselors, mentors and administrators ferry the students around the city, and they try to obtain adequate financial aid for the students so they will not have to work too many hours.

Then the hard part starts: CARE students are required to study in the student union lab a minimum of eight hours a week. If their grades fall, they must put in more hours and improve. To assist them, they are given tutors and technicians who always are on duty and eager to serve.

History professor Fabian Tata coordinates the lab and, according to the *Times*, he meticulously tracks every hour students spend there. The payoff is that the retention rate for CARE students, 92 percent, is higher than that of other FSU freshmen, 88 percent.

The source of Tata's success with his students is simple, as he told the *Times*: "We are hard on them. We make sure they realize what an opportunity this is."

I spoke with two CARE students by telephone. One, a sophomore with a B grade-point average, said: "They gave me a chance to study at FSU, even though I made 961 on the SAT. The University of Florida wouldn't even talk to me, and I didn't want to go to FAMU. I'd stay in the lab 24-7 if they'd let me. This is the best thing that ever happened to me. I can't let my family down."

The other, a junior with a B+ grade-point average, said: "I'm tired all the time because I have to study so hard. I want to be an engineer, and you can't be an engineer if you don't work hard. If I had stayed in Fort Lauderdale, I would've been killed on Sistrunk Boulevard or something. Some of my classmates at Dillard used to laugh at me because I made good grades. I didn't care. I want to make it so I can help my family. Dr.

Tata is tough on us, but that's what we need. If you want to lollygag, you'd better not get in the CARE program. You'd better be motivated."

Although CARE is a great success story, I hope that it does not become a permanent, institutionalized crutch at FSU and at the state's other universities. My hope is that black organizations, civic and otherwise, discover the wisdom of FSU's tough love and start demanding that black students work hard and develop the kind of character and values that successful people worldwide exhibit.

This essential work should not be left to the universities alone. It is a shared responsibility.

The missing man in class

JULY 12, 2009

I do not have solid proof, but I believe that the public school experience of my generation of black males in Jim Crow's South was far superior to that of most young African American males in today's public schools anywhere in the nation.

My generation's experience was better, I am certain, because we had a substantial number of black male teachers as role models. I do not have hard evidence that black men as role models positively affect boys' in-school behavior or their academic achievement, but I have a lot of anecdotal evidence, some of it personal, and testimonials suggesting that black male role models during the formative years often make all the difference.

To this day, I fondly remember all of my black male teachers in every school I attended from Florida to New York. Some were godlike figures. They only had to give you "the eye" or that special nod of the head to make you "get with the program." We saw them as both teachers and learners. My buddies and I wanted to be smart like them; they looked like us; they were our neighbors; I lived within walking distance of all of their homes.

Having black male teachers in the classroom was natural to my generation of black boys. Teaching had not become a feminized domain of mostly white women. (I did not have my first white teacher until I was a freshman in college.) Now, the black male teacher is an endangered species on too many campuses.

The U.S. Bureau of Labor Statistics reports that only 2 percent of the nation's 4.8 million teachers are black men. They make up about 3 percent of teachers in Florida, with only 1 percent at the elementary school level where they are sorely needed. In Pinellas County, according to the district's human resources office, "only 1.7 percent of all instructional personnel are African American males."

I am convinced that the shortage of black male teachers as role models is the source of many societal and school-related problems plaguing young black males. Florida, according to the Schott Foundation for Public Education, has the fifth worst graduation rate for black males in the nation, with Pinellas being among the 10 worst urban districts.

In a recent study, Pedro Noguera, a professor in the Graduate School of Education at Harvard University, reiterates findings that have become common knowledge in many circles: "Black males are more likely than any other group to be suspended and expelled from school. . . . Black males are more likely to be classified as mentally retarded or suffering from a learning disability and placed in special education and are more likely to be absent from advanced placement and honors courses.

"In contrast to most other groups where males commonly perform at higher levels in math and science related courses, the reverse is true for black males. Even class privilege and the material benefits that accompany it fail to inoculate black males from low academic performance."

The challenge is to find ways to permanently repair this crisis and find qualified black males for the classroom. The most prominent and perhaps most successful effort on the national level is Call Me Mister, established by Clemson University to recruit black men to college and to careers in teaching. It offers money for tuition at Clemson and 15 other colleges around the nation. A handful of Florida school districts, community colleges and three universities (Bethune-Cookman University, the University of North Florida and the University of Florida) have signed on.

Although Pinellas schools are not part of Call Me Mister, officials continuously try to find black male teachers, said Sandra R. Hopkins, senior human resources specialist for recruitment and retention.

"Some of our efforts to increase diversity with the district, at the high school level, include our Minority and Florida Future Educators of America Scholarships," she wrote in an email message. "On the collegiate level, we have the Florida State University scholarship for minority teachers. We also have a support-to-staff teacher program, as well.

"Further efforts geared toward the recruitment of African American educators are: forming partnerships with various historically black colleges and universities, community outreach, and placing ads in publications for minority teachers. While recruitment is important, it is also a must to increase retention efforts, as well. We have a mentor program . . . to support all incoming new teachers. As additional support, I personally make contact with and/or follow-up visits with all of our newly hired African American educators to further access their needs."

School officials in most districts nationwide are earnestly trying to recruit and retain black male teachers. Unfortunately, their efforts are falling short for reasons that include low salaries, stereotypes and fear of sexual-related lawsuits.

I do not have any viable answers, but I am convinced that we black people need to start talking among ourselves about the shortage of black male teachers—a crisis that is endangering the future of our boys. I cannot think of a more important issue at this time.

At all-black school, we all thrived

MARCH 28, 2010

Frequent news reports about academic and discipline problems in so many of our public schools make me think about my own school experiences under Jim Crow in Florida, when white and black students were legally separated.

Our black teachers were gods, and our campuses were virtual shrines, where we went to get on the path to "making something out of ourselves." Ours were quintessential, black-only neighborhood schools. Our teachers were black, all graduating from historically black colleges and universities.

The overwhelming majority of us thrived in school. Failure was the exception. It shamed the child. It shamed the family. I began ninth grade with 18 classmates. Four years later, all 19 of us graduated. Seventeen finished college. One who did not attend college established a small construction company, and the other joined the Army and became a career soldier.

Our parents earned their incomes as maids, fruit pickers, grove caretakers, fern cutters, pulpwood harvesters and carpenter's helpers. None earned more than minimum wage, none had attended college and few had graduated from high school.

How and why did so many of us succeed when Jim Crow actively repressed and rejected us? Three factors made the difference: Our parents placed nonnegotiable demands on us. Our parents had close relationships with our teachers and our principal. And our teachers were smart and tough.

Our parents trusted our teachers implicitly and forged a special partnership with them. Our principal was the "professor," an icon in black culture in that era. Our school's pedagogy—the principles and methods and art of instruction—was the guiding force.

I discovered this fact many years later after I had become a college teacher and journalist and after many talks with our principal and several of our teachers.

The school's pedagogy grew out of the principal's mission: "to give Negro girls and boys the best formal education possible." He hired teachers who vowed to carry out that mission.

De facto "separate but equal" school districts meant that we blacks were on our own. For that reason, our principal's goal was to teach us to be "self-reliant" while we were young children, thus empowering us for the rest of our lives.

We were shown the necessity of educating ourselves without expecting substantive help from whites. Almost everything we received from our white overlords in the main office—furniture, lab equipment and books—were hand-me-downs. We never had new textbooks. We played basketball on an outdoor clay court. On winter nights, our fans built courtside fires in oil drums to keep warm. The white school had a modern gym.

No matter. Our teachers believed we should know more than our white counterparts across town. As such, from first grade onward, they taught us valuable knowledge and the correct way to perform certain duties and functions.

During the elementary grades, for example, all of us memorized the multiplication tables. That one achievement made everything else related to math clear and, in some instances, surprisingly easy. We memorized Lincoln's Gettysburg Address, excerpts of the Declaration of Independence, excerpts of Cicero's orations, dozens of poems, including Shakespearean sonnets. I particularly enjoyed memorizing and reciting Blake's "Tyger, tyger, burning bright."

We knew the planets and their unique characteristics. In chemistry, we memorized the Periodic Table of Elements with full names. In biology, we memorized the classification of select animals, their kingdom, phylum, class, order, family, genus and species.

In English, we diagrammed sentences. We learned how to properly enunciate every word we uttered, and, without apology, our teachers would publicly correct us. Our essays were returned with red-ink corrections. In civics, we memorized the names of the U.S. presidents, Florida's governors and the then-48 states and their capitals. We learned the relationships between the branches of government, and we learned how bills become laws.

I am not advocating a return to such things as memorization, sentence diagramming or any other of the old-school methods and activities. I am simply pointing out that these activities taught us mental discipline and were major parts of our school's pedagogy, one that served my generation well. Being able to rattle off the multiplication tables gave us self-confidence, and it made us wholesomely competitive. Imagine how proud we were to know the Periodic Table of Elements with full names.

Many contemporary scholars and educators have disparaged the effectiveness of memorization and other seat-time activities.

Perhaps they are right. I know, however, that those old methods and dedicated teachers helped us become self-reliant at young ages. We fell in love with learning, and we loved going to school. We still are benefiting from the power of order, obedience and respect we learned in our all-black schools.

A defense of scholarly life

AUGUST 28, 2011

As a former university professor, Pope Benedict XVI spoke from experience Aug. 19 when he addressed young university professors in Madrid. He encouraged the professors to resist pressures on the academy to focus on job skills rather than a broader education, which I translate to mean the old ideal of the scholarly life.

Given the utilitarian approach to education most American universities are embarked on, the pope's speech interested me. The United States needs a Benedict who speaks passionately and often about the true role of professors.

"At times one has the idea that the mission of a university professor nowadays is exclusively that of forming competent and efficient professionals capable of satisfying the demand for labor at any given time," the pontiff said, according to a transcript released by Vatican Radio. "One also hears it said that the only thing that matters at the present moment is pure technical ability.

"This sort of utilitarian approach to education is in fact becoming more widespread, even at the university level, promoted especially by sectors outside the university. All the same, you who, like myself, have had an experience of the university, and now are members of the teaching staff, surely are looking for something more lofty and capable of embracing the full measure of what it is to be human. We know that when mere utility and pure pragmatism become the principal criteria, much is lost and the results can be tragic."

In most parts of the United States, professors, especially those at public universities, are fast becoming pawns in political agendas that are discounting their value. Driven by budget crises that give them convenient cover, many elected officials, such as Texas Gov. Rick Perry and Florida Gov. Rick Scott, make no secret of their intentions to "reinvent" public higher education by operating it like a business.

For generations, scholars have cautioned about the tendency in America to see everything, including university education, through the prism of the free market. More than a decade ago, for example, sociologist Robert Bellah argued that freedom in the market is tyranny in other "spheres" such as the professions, politics and education.

He said that a decent society depends on the autonomy of the spheres. When money takes over politics, only a shadow of democracy remains. Similarly, when money takes over higher education, decisions are made based on the bottom line, and professional authority is cast aside.

Departments and programs and faculty are assessed by their productivity, meaning the amount of dollars they bring in and the number of graduates they churn out. Under such conditions, universities no longer are fulfilling their real mission.

American universities should not totally ignore the values and practices of the marketplace. They cannot viably exist if they do. But our universities must not become an industry redesigned to be operated like, say, the U.S. automobile and home loan industries.

Call me out of touch, but I subscribe to the late Cardinal John Henry Newman's idea of the university. The priest, scholar and poet who founded what is now University College Dublin, Newman argued that the university does not exist for the sole purpose of conveying information and expertise.

"A university," he wrote, "educates the intellect to reason well in all matters, to reach out towards truth, and grasp it." He further stated that "the general principles of any study you may learn by books at home; but the detail, the color, the tone, the air, the life which makes it live in us, you must catch all these from those in whom it lives already."

For Newman, as it is with Benedict, the university is a place where students live for scholarship, where labor and leisure go hand in hand, where students sacrifice, where they fashion their lives around their studies and contemplation.

I dare say that at its core, American higher education is being coarsened as our universities increasingly adopt the business model and forsake the scholarly life. I have no doubt that this trend is having a negative effect on our social order. We are losing the sense of what it means to be human.

Black male collegians beat the odds, stereotypes

FEBRUARY 19, 2012

In 2007, then-presidential candidate Barack Obama told supporters at a rally in Harlem that he did not "want to wake up four years from now and discover that we still have more young black men in prison than in college."

Although university researchers and education reporters cautioned that the statistics Obama was using did not paint the whole picture of this phenomenon, he repeated the numbers to standing-room-only crowds.

Obama was unintentionally reinforcing an enduring negative stereotype: Black males as a group are missing in higher education and failing to graduate because of the pathologies in black culture. And make no mistake, cultural and racial stereotypes, whether true or false or incomplete, assume stubborn lives of their own.

The black male stereotype has done just that. Many people, including many African Americans, university presidents, professors, counselors, students, journalists and politicians picture black males as prison inmates before picturing them as college students.

Black males are branded before ever attempting to enroll in a school. Nothing good is in this. I felt the personal sting of this stereotype in 1963, when I first went to college. Because I am dark-skinned and came from a migrant farming family in Florida, I automatically was placed in remedial English—without being tested. I had been labeled as one doomed to fail on sight. I never bought into the stereotype, never for a moment thinking I would fail. After two weeks, my English professor agreed and transferred me to a regular English class.

I was sustained by four caring professors, a handful of over-achieving classmates, a work-study job in our campus library, my obsession to study and support from my mother and grandparents. Although I graduated in four years as summa cum laude and won a fellowship to the University of Chicago, no one ever asked me how I did it. But a lot of people predicted that I would fail.

During my more than 20 years as a college professor, I have taught many black men who beat the odds, who graduate and lead productive lives. How do they overcome the stereotype?

I currently have a black student, Shaquille Malik, in my writing class at St. Petersburg College where I am an adjunct professor. Malik is a 40-year-old ex-convict who is beating the odds. He is one of my best students. He sits up front, participates in discussions, volunteers to read his essays aloud and eagerly accepts constructive criticism.

A father of three, he told me he is determined to graduate with at least a bachelor's degree. I am certain he will succeed and become a role model. I will monitor his progress and do all I can to assist him. I am already telling other students about him, how he is exploding the stereotype.

Having Malik as a student prompted me to read a new report by Shaun R. Harper, associate professor and director of the Center for the Study of Race and Equity in Education at the University of Pennsylvania, focused on 219 black male students who have succeeded. The professor studied students at 42 colleges and universities in 20 states.

Disregarding the old stereotype, Harper wanted to know what distinguishes these achievers. He found a mix of external factors that seemed to give the students a sense that they not only could but must attend college. Among those factors: committed parents who expected a lot from them; at least one teacher in K-12 who wanted them to succeed academically; and money to pay for college. Another significant factor was a transition to college that included high expectations from administrators and faculty and from successful black male juniors and seniors on campus who motivated them.

"The most surprising finding was also the most disappointing finding," Harper said. "Nearly every student we interviewed said it was the first time that someone had sat him down and asked how he had successfully navigated his way to and through higher education, what compelled him to be engaged and what he learned that could help improve achievement and engagement among black male collegians."

Although the report is complex, Harper has a simple and reachable goal. He wants college and university leaders to commit themselves to finding black men on their campuses like those in the report and learn how they achieved. Harper wants black male student success to become institutionalized. He wants to erase the ugly stereotype of failure that hurts black males and society at large.

Charter schools chart a segregated course

JULY 26, 2013

Charter schools are seen by many parents, policymakers and educators as the panacea in public education. Each year, these campuses are increasing in number nationwide.

In a recent survey of research on school choice and charter schools, the *Hechinger Report*, an independent education news affiliate of Teachers College at Columbia University, finds mounting evidence that charters are not a panacea. In fact, they are enabling our return to racial segregation in public education.

Some advocates used to believe that school choice through charters would help diversify public education despite racially segregated housing patterns. But that has not been happening.

"Charter schools and their proponents argue that charters must take any student who wants to attend—and randomly select students through a lottery if too many apply—and, as such, can't control who enrolls," according to the *Hechinger Report*. "Yet some experts are concerned that this trend is an example of the next phase of white flight, following a long history of white families seeking out homogeneous neighborhoods and schools."

At the beginning of the movement, many charters—independent public schools given freedom to be more innovative while being held accountable for raising student achievement—were established in cities, and they served predominantly African American and other minority populations. But this is no longer the major trend.

In most parts of the nation, especially where whites find mandatory busing objectionable, predominantly white charters are being established in suburbia and other communities with high white populations.

No matter how we frame the debate, we are talking about contemporary segregation academies—those private schools that proliferated during the 1950s, 1960s and 1970s as a way for whites to circumvent the desegregation order of the *Brown v. Board of Education* decision. After these academies took hold, many public schools, especially in the South, were left with mostly black students.

Operating with public money, charters are more subtle in determining who attends them. In addition to location and word-of-mouth marketing, many self-select by establishing curricula that appeal to specific groups. Touting their core mission, they do not mention diversity in their recruitment.

Some focus, for example, on classical education, or the "core knowledge model," the ostensible goal being to groom the whole child rather than prepare the child for a specific profession. Research shows that many minorities are interested in a curriculum that trains for jobs, and they shun the core knowledge model. Some charters tout their cultural traditions to attract specific families.

Policymakers and educators disagree on the significance of charters' role in the racial isolation of schools.

"We have a long history of families and communities segregating themselves," Andre Perry, the associate director for educational initiatives at Loyola University's Institute for Quality and Equity in Education in New Orleans, told the *Hechinger Report*. "It's somewhat wrongheaded to say that charter schools are an impetus for segregation. The people are the impetus for segregation."

Myron Orfield, director of the Institute on Metropolitan Opportunity at the University of Minnesota and a charter school critic, says Perry is wrong: "Charters are either very white places or very nonwhite places. (Charters) are an accelerant to the normal segregation of public schools."

Few critics of charters are willing to state that self-selection is an indication of racism. Perry, for example, who laments the self-selection, told the *Hechinger Report*: "Middle- and upper-middle-class families have always tended to—in my opinion mistakenly—connect quality with sameness. It could be an explicit effort to segregate, but it's more likely a result of this notion that diversity is a sign of poor quality."

Evidence shows that most recent immigrants prefer schools in which their languages are spoken and that black families are more likely to place their children in racially segregated charter schools than are white families.

As long as parents seek the best for their children and as long as income, racial and ethnic homogeneity are seen as a sign of quality, diversity will be viewed as an indication of inferiority. Charter schools, therefore, will flourish.

Teachers need a voice in improving schools

SEPTEMBER 4, 2015

"Failure Factories," the *Tampa Bay Times'* superb investigation of five predominantly African American elementary schools in south St. Petersburg, has forced us to face some inconvenient truths about public education in Pinellas County.

Complete with solid numbers and cogent interviews, the series has produced outrage and forced a lot of needed introspection.

In a recent column, St. Petersburg Mayor Rick Kriseman correctly argued that if the district is to fix the problems the investigation uncovered, "sustainable solutions that address the systemic issues must be our focus." Suggesting that all parts of the greater community are interrelated regarding education is appropriate.

While the mayor is right, if all other elements in the systemic process of public education are normal and managed properly, classroom teachers would be recognized for their essential importance. They would be supported and nurtured instead of demonized and used as scapegoats.

How do we get teachers to perform effectively? The surest way is to show teachers they are valued as professionals. This can be done by giving teachers a voice—a meaningful say in decisions that ultimately affect their teaching. And it does not require more money, just action.

In the five neighborhood schools the *Times* investigated, it is apparent that teachers have not been valued to the degree they deserve. Working in a top-down decision-making system, they appear to have little voice in decisions that affect their teaching.

We know because collectively, these schools have the district's highest rate of teacher turnover. Why such high rates? And what are the implications?

Studies show that the revolving door for teachers is a strong indication that schools are ill-serving their students. Richard Ingersoll, who studies teacher retention and turnover at the University of Pennsylvania, told me the main source of frustration for teachers nationwide is not salaries but the lack of classroom autonomy. This frustration is directly tied to why teachers move to other schools or leave the profession.

Student misbehavior and discipline are at the top of problems correlated with teachers' decisions to stay or leave the profession, Ingersoll said on National Public Radio.

"There's an interesting thing in the data, which is that the amount of student behavior and discipline problems varies dramatically between schools," he said. "And poverty is by no means the only or main factor. And some schools do a far better job of dealing with it, coping with it and addressing it than other schools. And those schools that do a better job of coping with it have significantly better teacher retention."

What to do about student misbehavior and discipline?

"Get the teachers on board," Ingersoll said. "You get everyone together and say, 'Look, we have this issue. Do we want to have a rule or not? What would it be? How do we want to address it?' And a decision is collectively made as opposed to being imposed on the faculty. There are all kinds of behavioral issues to address."

Ingersoll said new teachers have the highest turnover rates. Between 40 percent to 50 percent leave the profession within five years. They need a lot of support. A formal movement called "induction," which helps beginners learn the ropes and how to survive, is a form of support that is growing in many districts nationwide.

Induction can mean anything from having a veteran teacher as a mentor to a 20-minute cup of coffee in September with a colleague who comes in the classroom and gives feedback.

"One thing that we've found that's effective," Ingersoll said, "is freeing up time for the beginning teachers so that they can meet with other colleagues. And learn from them. And compare notes. And try to develop some kind of coherence of curriculum."

Another way to give teachers a voice, especially veteran teachers, is to make them part of hiring, but most districts nationwide exclude teachers from the process of hiring their colleagues. Who knows teachers better than other teachers?

A Pinellas School District spokeswoman told me that there is no mandate to directly include teachers in the hiring of teachers. She said that principals are "encouraged" to include teachers. Some do so. Teachers are often members of recruiting teams, but it is rare for teachers in Pinellas to have a voice in who ultimately gets hired.

That makes no sense. We need to give teachers a voice and autonomy as professionals.

There is more to education than standardized, high-stakes tests

APRIL 29, 2016

I recently came upon a small Opt Out movement protest in front of a Miami-Dade elementary school. This was my first encounter with members of the growing movement.

They are parents, teachers, a handful of principals and others who believe that mandatory high-stakes testing is being misused in ways that harm children. Many of them also believe that the proliferation of high-stakes testing is probably part of a plan, fueled by corporate influences and enabled by conservative policies, to alter, if not destroy, public education as we know it.

For these and others reasons, opt-out advocates believe they have the right to reject the tests and keep young children, especially those in traditional minority communities, from taking them.

Felicia Gordon, 27, the mother of a Miami third-grader, said she joined Opt Out after learning what happens to children such as her daughter if they fail the third-grade test.

"They will hold her back, a little third-grader, if she didn't pass one test, even though she's a very good student with high grades and not one discipline problem," Gordon said. "That's crazy. It's unfair."

Gordon has a strong supporter in Ceresta Smith, a teacher at Ferguson Senior High School and an outspoken Opt Out leader. While most of her colleagues in the district fear retaliation from their administrations and remain silent, Smith travels the nation speaking on behalf of Opt Out. Supporters and potential supporters listen to her because she hails from Florida, ground zero for high-stakes testing, which was established by former Florida Gov. Jeb Bush.

"You have a totally test-driven culture," she said. "More and more innocent children are being stamped as failures in their early development."

The high-stakes test industry involves local, state and national politics and economics. Public education institutions are mandated by the federal government to test most students or risk losing funding. So, with millions of dollars riding on testing, states have little patience for school districts that do not comply.

Principals are expected to make sure students sit for the tests, and teachers are expected to prepare their students. Facing threats of being fired, most teachers toe the line and avoid opt-out involvement altogether.

In Florida, not only does it matter that students take the tests, it matters just as much that they make high scores. Schools are given letter grades based on student scores. These letter grades, A through F, can mean the difference between a good or bad reputation; millions of dollars in funding or a few dollars; special programs or no programs; and great teachers or a corps of rookies. A poor letter grade can also mean that teachers can lose pay or even lose their jobs.

Then there is the virtual death penalty: If a failing school does not improve—meaning student scores do not rise sufficiently—the state will take over its operations.

In Florida, evidence shows that to prepare as many students as possible for high-stakes tests, teachers must immerse their students in test prep reviews. The "art of teaching" is thrown to the wind.

One negative consequence of extreme test prepping is that many students do not acquire the deep understanding and knowledge necessary for a smooth college transition. Florida teachers and principals now spend most of their time on three subjects: reading, writing and math. Serious professionals know that we cannot continue to ignore the benefits of subjects such as music, the arts, history and language without dire consequences over time.

A simple message of the Opt Out movement is that children, especially the young, should be treated like the whole persons they are. Our test-driven culture, however, has created the chimera that one high-stakes test can tell us all we need to know about children. These tests also lull us into thinking we know all we need to know about teachers, schools and parents. They do not.

The Opt Out movement, as Ceresta Smith said, might be the only way to slow, perhaps even stop, a testing culture that stamps innocent children as being failures in their early development.

Don't protect college students from distressing ideas

SEPTEMBER 2, 2016

If you are parents who sent your son or daughter to the University of Chicago, you are aware that your child will not find intellectually safe spaces on the Hyde Park campus.

Dean of students John Ellison mailed a letter to all incoming freshmen, the class of 2020, informing them that trigger warnings will not appear on a syllabus. A trigger warning is a statement atop a syllabus alerting students of potentially distressing material.

Richard J. McNally, a professor of psychology at Harvard University, explained that "trigger warnings are designed to help survivors avoid reminders of their trauma, thereby preventing emotional discomfort."

While stating that respect and civility are hallmarks of Chicago's esprit de corps, Ellison is unequivocal: "You will find that we expect members of our community to be engaged in rigorous debate, discussion and even disagreement. At times this may challenge you and even cause discomfort.... Our commitment to academic freedom means that we do not support so-called trigger warnings, we do not cancel invited speakers because their topics might prove controversial and we do not condone the creation of intellectual safe spaces where individuals can retreat from ideas and perspectives at odds with their own."

As a former college professor, a University of Chicago alum and currently an adjunct instructor, I applaud Ellison's declaration. Trigger warnings have no place in academia, places of higher learning where higher-order reasoning should prevail. There should be no silos or echo chambers or sacred cows.

Barring harassment, voicing ideas should be unfettered.

I fondly recall my years as a student at Chicago from 1972 to 1974. Although I was in graduate school, I and fellow graduate students rubbed shoulders with undergraduates in the college. We always were impressed with the intellectual curiosity of these young people. It was second nature for all of us to read everything our professors required and suggested. And, of course, we read on our own, seeking deeper insights.

We truly were creatures of intellectual serendipity. In our classrooms and libraries, on the Main Quad and in Hyde Park taverns and eateries, we freely engaged. Despite our individual histories and discomforts, we lived and examined the zeitgeist of the 1970s—the philosophical ideas, political movements, social currents, racial upheavals, books, poems, plays, films.

I will never forget my introduction to the work of Saul Alinsky, considered to be the founder of modern community organizing. I read his books *Reveille for Radicals* and *Rules for Radicals* with relish. A new world opened for me, a child of migrant farmworkers from Fort Lauderdale. I met neo-Nazis who would march in Skokie, where many Jews lived, some of them Holocaust survivors. I thought these neo-Nazis were goons, but I had to meet them and listen to them to know.

I was in the audiences when Gunter Grass, Amiri Baraka, John Barth, Edward Albee, Saul Bellow, Gwendolyn Brooks and many other luminaries spoke on campus. At Court Theatre, fellow students and I were transported into new worlds of absurdity, protest, anarchy, dystopia and sublimity.

Because we were not protected from the incendiary, the crude, the stupid or the anti-American, we learned to put matters in their proper places. In short, we were shoved into higher reasoning.

When I graduated from Chicago and became a professor, I never thought of warning students that they would face stressful or hurtful ideas in my classes. I led them into the diverse and messy world of competing ideas.

Over time, I was admonished by many black colleagues. They argued that as a black man in America who shares a history of traumatic events with other blacks, I should not assign certain texts, such as *Huckleberry Finn*, and should never invite certain speakers to my classes. I disagreed then, and I disagree now.

President Barack Obama, who taught constitutional law at the University of Chicago, addressed trigger warnings in a commencement speech this year at traditionally black Howard University in the nation's capital.

"Don't try to shut folks out, don't try to shut them down, no matter how much you might disagree with them," Obama said. "There's been a trend around the country of trying to get colleges to disinvite speakers with a different point of view, or disrupt a politician's rally. Don't do that—no matter how ridiculous or offensive you might find the things that come out of their mouths."

This is sage advice from a black man who has endured perpetual racial contempt, who cannot find an intellectually safe space in America even if he wanted to.

Professors beware

DECEMBER 2, 2016

Miami

The alt-right movement, having picked up great momentum and legitimacy during the presidential campaign, is invading academia big time.

One prominent example of the movement's presence is Professor Watchlist, launched Nov. 21. I was introduced to the site by a student in a composition course I'm teaching at Miami Dade College. His class had read "The Case for Short Words," an essay by Richard Lederer, and, as the title suggests, the essay asks writers and speakers to give up their love of big words and "tap into the vitality and vigor of compact expression."

Based on Lederer's essay, I asked students to write a persuasive essay that attempts to convince readers to give up a popular belief. I didn't know what ideas these young people would want readers to give up.

Trouble started when I asked them to openly discuss their ideas. One student wanted readers to stop believing that American citizens don't have the right to burn the United States flag. Another wanted readers to stop believing that "you have to attend church to experience God's grace." Yet another wanted readers to stop "taking it for granted that it's all right to discriminate against gay people." There were more and they were just as provocative.

After class, a male white student stopped me outside the library and said I should be fired for letting "them kind of ideas into the classroom," and he warned that he might report me to Professor Watchlist.

I'd not heard of the site. I went online and learned a bunch. I even found the names of three professors with whom I'm acquainted on the list, all brilliant scholars.

Professor Watchlist is a project of Turning Point USA. The origins of most of the professor profiles on the site can be traced to stories on right-wing blogs and more prominent sources such as Breitbart.com and Fox News.

On its website, Turning Point USA is blunt: "The mission . . . is to expose and document college professors who discriminate against conservative students and advance leftist propaganda in the classroom. . . . TPUSA will continue to fight for free speech and the right for professors to say whatever they wish; however, students, parents, and alumni deserve to know the specific incidents and names of professors that advance a radical agenda in lecture halls."

Classroom veterans are familiar with such anti-intellectual eruptions. We can go back to the 1920s, when the American Legion, one of the most organized groups, went after so-called "un-American professors" with a vengeance.

Today, Professor Watchlist founder Charlie Kirk, a millennial, says the site intends "to identify, educate, train and organize students to promote the principles of fiscal responsibility, free markets and limited government." Its national operations are organized to "identify young conservative activists, build and maintain effective student groups, advertise and rebrand conservative values, engage in face-to-face and peer-to-peer conversations about the pressing issues facing our country."

Kirk went further: "It's no secret that some of America's college professors are totally out of line," writing that students tell him about leftist "professors who attack and target conservatives, promote liberal propaganda and use their position of power to advance liberal agendas in their classroom. Turning Point USA is saying enough is enough. It's time to expose these professors."

The site's list of "out of line" professors is growing and is having a chilling effect. Its most publicly recognizable offender is Robert Reich, Chancellor's Professor of Public Policy at the University of California, Berkeley. Reich is a harsh critic of income inequality. He served in the administrations of Presidents Gerald Ford and Jimmy Carter and was secretary of labor under President Bill Clinton from 1993 to 1997.

Most other professors on the list are ethnic minority and women scholars who document America's institutionalized injustices.

As far back as 1985, the American Association of University Professors, the main organization that protects academic freedom, issued a statement that addressed the harmfulness of movements such as Professor Watchlist: "External monitoring of in-class statements not only presents the prospect that words uttered will be distorted or taken out of context; it is also likely to have a chilling effect and result in self-censorship."

Such monitoring, the statement continued, "can only inhibit the process through which higher learning occurs and knowledge is advanced." Why, I wonder, are conservatives so afraid of higher reasoning and higher learning? Unfortunately, we soon will have an administration in the White House that accepts our increasing anti-intellectualism and attacks against professors viewed as being "totally out of line."

Reasonable people do not want teachers to be armed

MARCH 2, 2018

Public school teachers, arguably America's most convenient scapegoats, are again thrust into the center of a problem not of their making, a problem that they cannot fix.

This time, in the wake of the mass shooting at Marjory Stoneman Douglas High School in Parkland where 17 people were killed, politicians who are lapdogs of the National Rifle Association are proposing to make teachers responsible for the lives of our children.

They want teachers to carry firearms. In addition to being expected to impart knowledge and practical skills, teachers will be expected to be police officers.

Each time I hear an elected official advance this proposal, I think of teachers over the years who have been killed or injured protecting their students from gunmen. Exactly what do we expect of classroom teachers in today's United States? Are we justified in asking them to do more than they do now, even arm themselves to protect our children?

If salaries and other funding are primary measures, very few school districts place high value on teaching as a profession. Teacher salaries are too low. Their hours, which includes work they take home, are extremely long. Training and retraining are constant. Teachers spend a lot of their own money for supplies their districts do not provide. Many spend afterschool hours nurturing their students and volunteering. Most never see opportunities to advance. Yet the profession is widely disrespected by politicians and too many parents.

In Florida, Republican lawmakers want to create a voluntary Florida Sheriff's Marshal Program. Under the program, teachers "may carry concealed, approved firearms on campus. The firearms must be specifically purchased and issued for the sole purpose of the program. Only concealed carry safety holsters and firearms approved by the sheriff may be used under the program."

Some teachers I spoke with said they would resign if teachers on their campuses were armed. Dealing with life-and-death situations in the classroom is unimaginable, they said.

The daily responsibilities of helping students earn high scores on standardized tests, bus and hall duties, communicating with parents by email, meeting parents face to face, counseling troubled students, teaching classes and preparing lessons challenge the stamina of the most experienced teachers.

Adding 100 or more hours of firearms training and performing the role of a first responder to the duties of teachers are a recipe for disaster.

The other night, I watched 16-year-old Alfonso Calderon, a student who survived the Parkland shooting, speak with CNN's Don Lemon about President Donald Trump's proposal to arm teachers. This young man's wisdom, his clear understanding of the essential role of teachers, should shame Trump and other Republicans beholden to the NRA.

"I don't know if Donald Trump has ever been to a public high school, but as far as I'm aware, teachers are meant to be educators," Calderon said. "They're meant to teach young minds how to work in the real world. They are not meant to know how to carry AR-15s. They are not meant to know how to put on Kevlar vests for the other students or themselves.

"This is not what we stand for. We stand for small policy changes and maybe possibly big ones in the future. Because, right now, I am pretty sick of having to talk about teachers being armed. Because that is not even a possibility in my mind. I would never want to see my teachers have to do that and neither do they want to do that."

No reasonable person in today's America believes that our schools will return to being what Republicans disparagingly refer to as "gun-free zones." Reasonable people believe that police officers and other professionals should be permitted to carry weapons. They also believe that school entrances and exits should be improved and that other security measures, such as metal detectors, should be installed.

Reasonable people simply do not want teachers carrying concealed weapons while standing before a roomful of students. They do not want teachers to become armed combatants.

Teachers deserve more respect

JUNE 2, 2019

Former Jennings Middle School teacher Bianca Goolsby recently wrote a guest column for the *Tampa Bay Times* explaining why she left the profession she once loved and invested in.

Although Goolsby describes in painful detail the institutionalized neglect and some of the dangerous working conditions at the Title I school in Seffner, she zeroes in on the core problems at Jennings and many other traditional Florida public schools.

I quote Goolsby at length because she speaks best for herself and because her plea is smart and earnest.

"My school has little to no support from the district administration," she writes. "Many people who make the decisions about my school have never stepped foot on our campus or been with our students for even a day. . . . When a small group of teachers, myself included, joined our voices together the school district pacified our concerns by sending new administrative staff to try to correct the core issues at our school. This happened with fewer than 45 days of the school year remaining. This change has come too late.

"Our Florida Legislature is more concerned with arming teachers and protecting the right to bear arms than protecting students and dealing with the foundational issues that are contributing to why I and so many other gifted teachers are leaving the profession."

Goolsby does more than merely list problems and issues. She offers solutions for repairing what ails our traditional public schools. Teachers, above all, need the full support of the governor, state lawmakers and top education decisionmakers.

Currently, however, GOP Gov. Ron DeSantis, Education Commissioner Richard Corcoran and State Board of Education Chairwoman Marva Johnson are hostile toward traditional public education. Their mission creep favors charter schools and other for-profit academies, even tiny church basement concerns that have no business teaching children.

This situation is disastrous for the long-term health of traditional public schools that educate 90 percent of our students.

Like her colleagues, Goolsby knows that teachers are central to student success. She knows that few experiences are more rewarding than touching the lives of children and making a positive contribution to their futures.

Then, there is the other story, one Goolsby describes so well. While teaching can be rewarding, it also can be one of the most demanding, loneliest and most stressful professions.

It is no mystery as to why each year nationwide, many districts have teacher shortages, why thousands of teachers go on strike, why so many leave the profession altogether.

These problems are directly related to teacher well-being. Recent Brookings research shows that nearly 50 percent of teachers experience high levels of daily stress that affects their health, quality of life and teaching performance.

This crisis—seemingly ignored by Florida officials—costs U.S. schools billions of dollars annually.

Most of us understand the importance of student well-being, but few of us consider the well-being of teachers. When Florida teachers have problems, they are expected to take care of their problems themselves even as officials in Tallahassee threaten "intervention," "takeovers," "accountability," "budget cuts" and other punitive measures and threats.

Education scholars know that distressed teachers are less likely to form positive relationships with students. More often than not, this causes student performance to suffer.

Goolsby and others want the state officials, lawmakers and school districts to realize that teachers thrive intellectually and personally when their plight is treated holistically; when they are seen as professionals performing essential work; when they are included as equal partners in decisions that impact their duties inside and outside the classroom.

"Just to survive teaching at my school, I've had to become someone I don't like," Goolsby writes. "I have become short-tempered, authoritative, controlling and hardened, and it (has) been spilling over into my personal life. I don't like the person I am becoming and it is affecting my mental and physical health."

She quit. Her last day was May 31. Will school officials and lawmakers listen to such cries in the wilderness, or will they continue their active hostility toward traditional public education and teachers such as Goolsby?

These students of color were the most dedicated college students I've ever taught

AUGUST 2, 2019

I recently taught two writing courses at Miami-Dade College Homestead campus as an adjunct professor. Nearly 90 percent of my students were Hispanics, many of them Mexican farmworkers. I'm writing about this experience in light of President Donald Trump's constant attacks on people of color, with Hispanics being one of his favorite targets.

Before Miami-Dade, I'd taught for 20 years at colleges and universities in other Florida cities, Alabama, Illinois and Texas. My 53 Miami-Dade students were the best I ever had even though none had superior SATs, and most didn't write as well as students I'd had at other schools.

But they had something else, something of great value I wish I could explain to Trump and his die-hard supporters. These students were the hardest-working, most respectful and most polite I have encountered. They addressed me as "Professor Maxwell" and "Sir."

After I gained their trust, I learned that many were the first in their families to attend college. Some were Dreamers, those who entered the United States as minors with their undocumented parents. Their hope was to become U.S. citizens.

I spoke with many of them about this. Some wrote essays about it. They said that education is essential to them and their families; that education offers the straightest path to becoming "real" Americans; that respect for and courtesy toward their professors is a must. One student said that college is a family affair. Dreamers want to build successful lives so that, among other endeavors, they can help their parents.

One student wrote that if his parents had remained in Chihuahua after his birth, he would've wound up toiling in sun-drenched tomato fields, wasting away on a factory line, selling drugs for next to nothing or he would be dead. Others described their lives similarly.

After more than two decades in the classroom, I had become jaded, going through the routine of teaching how to write the five-paragraph essay and how to read and write about fiction, drama and poetry.

The Dreamers in my classes renewed my zeal to teach. I spoke with several colleagues who told me that their experiences were similar, that their Hispanic students' commitment to learning inspired them.

As an adjunct, I didn't have an office, so each day for two hours I commandeered a corner table in the library to see students. Every day, many showed up to go over their essays or to simply chat. After the first three weeks, I rarely called the roll. Hardly anyone ever missed class, hardly anyone was ever tardy.

I asked a few colleagues if my experiences were unique. I was assured that they were not, that their students were the same.

On the last day of the semester I taught there, I stayed in the classroom and graded most of the final exams for that class. As I exited the room, more than a dozen students waited in the hallway to thank me for being their professor. Some shook my hand. Some hugged me. I was stunned. This was the first time in my career that students—as a group—had thanked me in such a public way.

A male, who wrote for the campus newspaper, handed me a greeting card and asked me to read it aloud. I did. It simply read: "Gracias." He hugged me and the others hooted and applauded. As I drove to my apartment, my eyes filled with tears. Apparently, I'd made a positive difference in the lives of these young people.

Now, whenever I hear Trump bash Hispanics, I think of my gracious, hard-working Miami-Dade students, especially the Dreamers who are doing everything right to become U.S. citizens.

Environment

Hands off the Preservation 2000 funds

MAY 15, 2002

Mercifully, our GOP-led Legislature has left Tallahassee. Although I realize that name-calling is a terrible logical fallacy, I must say that Florida's state senators and representatives act like a bunch of uncaring hacks.

I followed many of the issues this crowd dealt with. The one I followed most closely was the Preservation 2000 fund.

Yes, I am one of those sandal-clad, tree-hugging, bird-watching, gopher-tortoise-loving weirdos who knows that we are losing this paradise we call Florida. We understand that our tropical peninsula is fragile, that with population growth and unprincipled development, we are in a race against time to save much of what remains of our pristine regions.

Yes, I am one of those natives who has visited (hiking, camping, fishing) all of our major state parks. Twelve years ago, three friends and I even spent seven days kayaking from Flamingo in the Everglades National Park to Everglades City. (Halfway through the ordeal, we questioned our sanity after vampire mosquitoes sucked our blood at will.)

As a nature lover, I was encouraged 10 years ago when the state established Preservation 2000, a $3-billion program that sold bonds to buy environmentally sensitive properties. Thus far, the program has kept developers away from 1-million acres of wild landscapes, including lowly bogs and scrub stands.

As I read the legislation 10 years ago, the fund was to be used exclusively for preserving the environment. A column I wrote at the time persuaded many Florida residents, natives and transplants alike, to invest in the program. I know because some called or wrote letters thanking me for introducing them to a good cause they could support.

Now, some of these bondholders are calling and writing because they are outraged that for two consecutive years, incompetent, cowardly legislators have raided the fund. Last year, lawmakers lifted $75-million from the fund, this year $100-million. One of my neighbors on Coquina Key invested $10,000. Furious, he and his wife came to my house Monday night to tell me they "have been duped."

I agree. All Floridians who thought they were investing strictly in the environment have been duped, and the raids are tying the hands of state-related agencies that buy and protect sensitive lands. The *St. Petersburg Times* reported that the Southwest Florida Water Management District, for example, lost $20-million in land-purchasing money it could have used to protect areas critical to the region's water resources.

How can the Legislature and the governor act so irresponsibly and threaten precious water resources? Supporters of Preservation 2000 see a combination of cynicism, indifference, arrogance, desperation, incompetence.

Frank Jackalone, Florida director of the Sierra Club: "Watching Gov. Jeb Bush and the Legislature manage the state of Florida's finances this year has been like viewing the fumbling antics of the Keystone Kops. After making massive revenue cuts, Bush and legislators have done nothing but scramble to find the path of least resistance to make up for the budget shortfall, whether it be education one day, the state sales tax holiday the next, or, today, the Preservation 2000 land program as the latest target."

Jackalone believes many lawmakers who raided the fund will pay a price at election time: "The Legislature and the governor are arrogantly misreading the pulse of the electorate if they think that cutting land preservation funds won't produce a 'throw the bums out' voter backlash. Have they forgotten that more than 70 percent of the ballots cast in 2000 supported amending Florida's Constitution as the only way to guarantee that the state would raise and spend the dollars needed to acquire those unprotected natural treasures that lay within reach of the state's rapidly advancing bulldozers and construction cranes?"

Other activists, representing Audubon of Florida and the Nature

Conservancy, believe Bush and lawmakers are playing a shell game with Preservation 2000 funds. Legislators say they will use the fund's debt reserve dollars to pay off debt service on the bonds. This move, they claim, would loosen up money for, among other things, education and health care. Activists do not believe Tallahassee, arguing that lawmakers are using sleight of hand to cover for their beloved $262-million corporate tax cut.

Preservation 2000 investors have every reason to believe our lawmakers are a pack of self-serving liars. They promised last year to restore the $75-million they grabbed from the fund. They did not. They promised last year they would not raid the fund this year.

They lied.

South Florida's marine life is limited

JULY 31, 2002

In an effort to save South Florida's marine life, especially the fish we relish at mealtime, scientists are being forced to limit what we can catch and haul from the waters of the Atlantic Ocean and the Gulf of Mexico.

Most Floridians always have believed that fish are an unlimited resource that could never run out. Marine scientists are trying to change that wrongheaded attitude. In what has been hailed the most ambitious study of marine life ever conducted in the United States, scientists recently counted the fish from the Dry Tortugas, through the Keys, to Key Biscayne.

This marine life census is significant to scientists because it is the first count of fish throughout the Florida Keys at one time. The count is critical because wildlife experts have indisputable evidence that South Florida's fish stocks are being depleted by commercial and recreational fishing.

The census, which included the endangered Dry Tortugas, North America's largest living coral reef, also will provide information about how to save and restore this disappearing underwater treasure.

At more than 16-million residents, Florida's population and all the ills that come with it have devastated our once-abundant numbers of grouper, grunt and snapper. In fact, scientists say, we have over-harvested 70 percent of all fish species.

Many fishermen, including some I spoke with in St. Petersburg, do not believe the marine scientists, arguing that they are exaggerating the numbers and discounting the impact of pollution and development.

James Bohnsack, a marine biologist with the National Oceanic and Atmospheric Administration, disagrees, citing our belief that we have dominion over all living things, especially life in the seas: "This is what happens when you have 900,000 fishing boats and people who feel that it is their God-given right to go out and catch fish."

The long-term goal of the census is, of course, to provide information that can help save and replenish marine life in the waters of South Florida. A more immediate goal is to evaluate the impact of existing federal and state conservation measures and to implement new rules. If evidence indicates that no-fish zones work, officials say they will not hesitate to establish more of them. Fishermen, of course, are angry.

Scientists report that in an experiment to determine if untouched fish populations could replenish, federal wildlife officials last year banned fishing in 151 square miles in and around the Dry Tortugas. Five years ago, the Florida Keys National Marine Sanctuary banned fishing in the waters around 23 smaller reefs.

I am happy to report that many other no-take zones are being contemplated as scientists digest the bad news of the Florida Keys census report and that of a study published last year by the British journal *Nature*. The journal states that the global catch has dropped by 360,000 tons since 1988.

A United Nations study indicates that 70 percent of fisheries worldwide are fully used, overfished or depleted. Further, a quarter of the world's 15 major fishing areas are fished at or beyond capacity.

Our fragile coral reefs are essential to the health of Florida's marine life, especially to the fish we enjoy in fine dining. For this reason alone, no-take zones are a necessary tool. Florida's coral reefs extend down the coast for 130 miles. Human activity, including global warming, is destroying them at alarming rates.

The Dry Tortugas, a keystone ecosystem, must be protected at all costs. This reef serves as a home, a source of food and a place of safety for more than 200 species of marine life. It also nurtures larvae and fish eggs that become "catch of the day" in our restaurants and homes up and down the coast.

No-take zones already have proved their value. In protected areas, the number of bigger fish far outnumber those in unprotected areas. Even the Goliath grouper, which was near extinction just 10 years ago, has made a spectacular comeback in the no-take zones.

What other evidence do commercial and recreational fishermen need to see the light, to get onboard the new effort to save one of our most valuable resources? From years of writing about this issue, I know for a fact that overfishing does more than deplete stocks and threaten habitats. It imperils coastal economies that rely on marine life.

Each year, I see more boats returning to shore with fewer fish. Each year, I see more saltwater anglers return home with empty ice chests. When will we learn, and start caring, that fish are a finite resource? Only so many snapper and grouper are left in the Atlantic and the Gulf.

To see real Florida, get on the back roads

JANUARY 24, 2010

After our recent freezing weather, many tourists would question using "paradise" and "Florida" in the same breath. Hundreds of disappointed visitors around the state packed up and went back North. After all, why pay big bucks to freeze in the Sunshine State if you can go home to Ohio and freeze for free?

As a native, I see Florida as paradise despite the occasional freezing weather, egg-frying heat on summer days, hurricanes, tornadoes, lightning storms, swarms of blood-sucking mosquitoes and waves of love bugs that ruin your car's paint.

I have lived in several other states, but I always find my way back to Florida. Few other states possess our spectacular ecology, our social and cultural diversity, our unique entertainment venues and our varied and vital agricultural industries.

Florida is the world's top travel destination, but many visitors stick to the coasts and never see what we natives refer to as "real Florida" or "Old Florida." While our 663 miles of beaches are major attractions, the majority of these beaches are not part of real Florida. Most are near an interstate and major cities and are so commercialized that they have become mere amusement parks.

To see real Florida, you have to leave the interstate and take the blue highways and back roads. You have to ride the trains. You have to explore some of our 11,000 miles of rivers, streams and waterways by small boat or canoe or kayak. We also have hundreds of miles of hiking trails, and I can tell you from experience that the trails in Ocala National Forest are exceptional.

Last week, I visited Fort Pierce and Vero Beach. As always when I make this trip from St. Petersburg, I take State Road 70, which spans five counties across the peninsula. Once you clear the ugly sprawl of the Lakewood Ranch and Panther Ridge developments, the road becomes two lanes, and you begin to see a part of real Florida, passing through Myakka City and Pine Level. Here, many people work on the land.

You see a lot of open space and wood-frame structures dating to 1950, the last year that cows could legally roam freely throughout the state. You have entered a major part of Florida cattle and dairy country. Most people, including many natives, do not know Florida is one of the nation's major cow-calf producers and ranks 12th in the nation in the number of beef cows.

Between Arcadia and Okeechobee, vistas of green open space stretch beneath blue skies as far as you can see, creating the kind of living beauty captured on postcards. Here, I passed three different ranches and saw dozens of real cowboys driving and herding cattle, just like in the movies.

In addition to the food they provide, Florida ranchers along SR 70, like other ranchers statewide, are dedicated stewards of tens of thousands of acres of pastureland and grazed woodland. This land provides much of the state's "green space" for hundreds of animal and plant species, and it is used as an aquifer recharge area.

All along SR 70 from Arcadia to Fort Pierce, there are thousands of acres of citrus groves, all part of the industry that produces 75 percent of U.S. oranges and accounts for about 40 percent of the world's orange juice supply. Our groves, like our grazing lands, provide havens for countless species of wildlife.

In several sprawling groves, I saw crews of pickers climbing ladders to harvest our precious crop. On the road, semi-trailer trucks roared east and west hauling the fruit to packing houses and juice facilities.

Real Florida is a place of natural beauty, where we have not backfilled our swamps, bulldozed our trees, butchered our mangroves, scraped away our shorelines and paved over our grasslands, all for the sake of development.

To see this Florida, you need to head to the interior on the back roads, where land is respected, not so often abused for profit.

Protecting Florida's wild places

One of the benefits of living in Florida is being within easy driving distance of beautiful, wild places. But some of these places may be getting too much attention and love, and human activity has to be carefully controlled.

Big Cypress National Preserve, the 566,000-acre swamp between Fort Lauderdale/Miami and Naples, is one such place. While this treasure is home to many common animals such as turkey and whitetail deer, the endangered red-cockaded woodpecker and the Florida panther find tenuous protection there. The panther is of greatest concern to environmentalists.

The major problem in Big Cypress is the intense use of the off-road vehicle, or ORV, by sportsmen, especially hunters, and other outdoor enthusiasts.

Use of the ORV, always a contentious issue, is the subject of a lawsuit the National Parks Conservation Association, a nonprofit watchdog group, filed recently against the National Park Service. The suit argues that, among other abuses, the National Park Service used faulty science and ignored federal law to approve a management plan that would give swamp buggies use of 130 miles of new trails in a quadrant of the preserve called Addition Lands.

"Off-road vehicles have long been recognized to have significant adverse impacts on natural areas," said John Adornato, NPCA Sun Coast regional director in Hollywood, in a telephone interview.

In 2000, he said, the National Park Service documented that ORVs had created ruts as deep as 2 feet in Big Cypress, affecting surface water flow into Everglades National Park, altering the composition and distribution of plant species and dramatically reducing the hunting and mating opportunities of animals, especially the panther.

"The National Park Service and the Fish and Wildlife Service have the responsibility to ensure not just the protection of the panther, as well as its prey, but also to ensure that the species recovers from its endangered status," Adornato wrote in an email message. "Conflicts between utilizing ORVs and hunting versus the protection of panther habitat and prey are to be addressed by the planning processes of the park service.

"Specifically, the park service must abide by its management policies, as amended in 2006, which specifically state that when conservation and recreation come into conflict, conservation predominates. The decision to eliminate 70,000 acres of wilderness from the Addition Lands of the preserve in favor of 130 miles of ORV trails is in direct contrast to those management policies."

Adornato suggested that the National Park Service may have violated federal law, or at least the spirit of federal law, when the agency relied on an off-road vehicle advisory committee to make recommendations about the management of ORVs in the preserve and is now turning to that committee to help implement the ORV plan.

"Under federal law, when an agency uses an advisory committee to help it make decisions, the committee must have a fair balance of people with competing interests and viewpoints," he said. "The preserve has relied on recommendations by a committee lacking true balance and dominated by ORV users and their supporters."

"Hunters and other swamp buggy and ATV users deserve a place at the table when new trails are being considered. However, this committee has functioned with a majority of such people. . . . The National Parks Conservation Association is asking the court to enjoin this committee from further operations until it has been recomposed in a fair and balanced way."

Adornato said he does not believe that anyone wants to intentionally harm Big Cypress. Most people love the swamp, he said. The NPCA simply wants the National Park Service to use good science and the advice of a panel of residents with competing interests when determining where new ORV use should be allowed.

"Big Cypress National Preserve is a national treasure for all Americans and was created to preserve and protect sensitive lands," he said. "Congress provided that limited hunting could be permitted, with restrictions determined by the park service, and there are already significant trails for hunters and other ORV users in the original preserve."

Parks of tranquil beauty are no place for guns

JANUARY 8, 2012

I spent some of the Christmas holidays in Flamingo, the southernmost point in Everglades National Park. There are not many other ways I would rather spend my time.

Naturalist John Muir captured the wonder and value of the parks more than a century ago: "Everybody needs beauty as well as bread, places to play in and pray in, where nature may heal and give strength to body and soul alike. This natural beauty-hunger is made manifest . . . in our magnificent national parks—nature's sublime wonderlands, the admiration and joy of the world."

The beauty that inspired Muir inspires today's visitors to our national parks as well. But a lethal alien has invaded our parks, and it is destroying our expectations of tranquility.

The lethal alien is the gun.

Before Ronald Reagan's presidency, guns were not permitted in our national parks. Reagan signed a law, the beginning of mission creep, that let gun owners carry unloaded firearms or store them inside while visiting national parks.

George W. Bush overhauled the Reagan ban, allowing people to carry loaded guns in 373 of the nation's 392 sites where the National Park Service has jurisdiction. The Brady Campaign to Prevent Gun Violence and other groups filed a lawsuit, and a federal judge put Bush's measure on hold. Following more litigation in 2009, President Barack Obama signed legislation that restored Bush's rule. Again, licensed gun owners could bring firearms into our national parks and wildlife refuges if weapons are allowed by state law.

I saw an ugly side of the law in Flamingo on Christmas Day when two fishermen stashed handguns in the glove compartments of their pickups before taking their boat into Florida Bay. An hour earlier, coincidentally, I had spoken with a law enforcement ranger about his career. He carried a high-caliber handgun. The weapon seemed out of place strapped to the hip of this helpful and jovial young man wearing that iconic Smokey Bear hat and drab uniform.

I thought of this ranger and the thousands of visitors he must protect as I listened on New Year's Day to reports of the shooting death of Margaret Anderson, a 34-year-old law enforcement ranger in Mount Rainier National Park.

Anderson, who was married with two young daughters, had attempted to stop the car of Benjamin Barnes, who had driven into the park to escape police seeking to arrest him in connection with four shootings in Seattle. Anderson's main goal was to prevent the heavily armed Barnes from harming park visitors and personnel.

Granted, no law would have prevented Barnes from bringing guns into Mount Rainier. But the tragic event shows that firearms, especially in the hands of a dangerous fugitive, are alien to pristine places where families and individuals come for peace and quiet and the enjoyment of spectacular scenery and wildlife.

While we worry about the safety of visitors to our parks, we should be equally concerned about the safety of our law enforcement rangers who may have to risk their lives on a moment's notice. According to the Environment News Service, the park service's 1,000 law enforcement rangers face the highest number of felony assaults and the highest number of homicides of all federal law enforcement officers. Anderson is the latest to be killed. In 2002, a ranger pursuing drug cartel hit men was killed at Arizona's Organ Pipe Cactus National Monument.

The National Rifle Association and its elected sycophants in Congress are wrong. And Obama was wrong to relent and sign the law allowing people to openly carry semiautomatic weapons, shotguns and rifles in our national parks.

"This law is a very bad idea," wrote Bill Wade, chairman of the executive council of the Coalition of National Park Service Retirees. "It is not in the best interests of the visitors to national parks, the resources to be protected in national parks, nor the employees in national parks. . . . Employees, especially law enforcement rangers, will be more at risk. And visitors will not only be more at risk, but will now see national parks as places where they need to be more suspicious and wary of others carrying guns, rather than safe and at peace in the solitude and sanctuary that parks have always provided. It is a sad chapter in the history of America's premier heritage area system."

National parks remain "America's Best Idea." Allowing guns in our parks is one of our dumbest ideas.

Despite veto, Florida habitats still in jeopardy

APRIL 15, 2012

Here in Florida, shortsightedness and greed have always guided and motivated our movers and shakers, our leaders.

These folks have been responsible for paving over our grasslands, butchering our mangroves, backfilling our swamps, gouging our shorelines, damming our rivers and bulldozing our trees.

Shortsightedness and greed have made Florida, one of the nation's most biologically diverse regions, one of its most at-risk ecologically. We are second only to California in the number of animals and plants the federal government has designated as endangered or threatened.

Too many Florida leaders, political, business and otherwise, apparently do not care about the essential link between people and their impact on wild species and their natural habitats. Research shows that negative human impact on the environment includes habitat destruction, pollution and the introduction of non-native and invasive species of flora and fauna.

Most habitat destruction, and subsequent harm to plants and animals, is the result of development that is seen, of course, as crucial to human progress.

But habitat destruction is just as damaging when it is carried out for frivolous purposes. The most prominent example of such frivolousness was in a bill introduced during the recent legislative session in Tallahassee. The zoo bill, HB 1117, dubbed the "Jurassic Park bill" by critics, would have permitted zoos and aquariums to lease state-owned lands to conduct breeding and research on animals such as rhinos, zebras, giraffes and elephants.

Many Florida residents love zoos and take their children and grandchildren to them. But few of these residents would vote to permit exotic animals to be bred and allowed to roam on our public lands. We love our wild places and species and are extremely protective of them, as was demonstrated after the zoo bill was introduced by Rep. Shawn Harrison, a Temple Terrace Republican.

Gov. Rick Scott vetoed the bill following vigorous opposition led by Defenders of Wildlife. Explaining why he rejected the bill, Scott wrote that it "lacks sufficient safeguards" to "ensure the protection of state . . . lands, native species and habitats."

But we should be realistic about the governor and his veto.

In the same letter, he explained that he had little trouble rejecting the bill because he believes state law already allows the governor, Cabinet and the five water management districts to lease state lands for purposes deemed constitutional.

Forget about science and safety. Is it constitutional?

Furthermore, according to the *Tampa Bay Times*, Harrison said Scott told him personally that the state already has the authority to lease state-owned lands to zoos. It just has not happened—which does not mean it will not happen. Why would the governor assure Harrison of this authority?

Apparently feeling triumphant, Harrison said: "I'm happy . . . that we've brought attention to the fact that Florida law already allows this to happen."

Then there is Larry Killmar, the Lowry Park Zoo vice president and president of the Florida Association of Zoos, who shepherded the bill to the governor's desk. During the legislative session, the *Times* reports, Killmar said the association will "certainly plot forward" to find state land suitable for breeding large herds of exotic animals.

While Defenders of Wildlife officials and other environmentalists hope the governor keeps herds of exotic animals off state lands, they are right to be vigilant. They believe, for example, that exotic animals roaming state lands would displace native habitats and species. They also fear that animals could escape and threaten human life, and they are concerned about the spread of non-native seed and feed and the potential spread of disease.

Fortunately, Laurie MacDonald, Florida director for Defenders of Wildlife, has a warning for Killmar and others: "We will be watching very closely any applications for this use."

Although the wrongheaded "Jurassic Park bill" is dead for now, Florida's legendary environmental shortsightedness is alive and kicking.

Natural Florida needs stewards, not profiteers

JUNE 3, 2012

Imagine Gov. Rick Scott as Spanish explorer Juan Ponce de Leon in 1513 landing on the pristine La Florida ("place of flowers") shore in the vicinity of the Caloosahatchee River.

Now, imagine Rick Juan Ponce de Leon Scott discovering the mythical fountain of youth, a source of natural spring water.

Knowing Scott as we do, we do not have to imagine what would happen next: He and his some 200 men would begin capturing the spring water and exporting it for profit. If the water failed to restore youth as marketed, the Scott team would bury the now-worthless fountain and move on to the next treasure hunt, leaving behind the detritus of human progress.

Although fictional, this scenario closely mirrors several assaults on our state's fragile environment by the Scott administration. The latest is a wetlands mitigation scheme involving a pine plantation. On one side are Highlands Ranch, formed in 2008 as a joint venture between a Jacksonville company and the Carlyle Group, a private equity firm. On the other side are science, environmental stewardship and the people of Florida.

Highlands Ranch is trying to pull off a shell game. Florida's wetlands mitigation law is clear: When issued a permit, the applicant has the authority to "impact" wetlands and is required to offset those "impacts" with activities such as wetlands creation, preservation or enhancement. But Highlands Ranch is seeking wetlands mitigation credit for some land that is high and dry.

As *Tampa Bay Times* staff writer Craig Pittman reported, Department of Environmental Protection wetlands expert Connie Bersok was suspended from her job after she followed science and bucked politics in denying the permit.

The Scott administration, with its zeal to give businesses carte blanche in dealing with our natural resources, seems to hold the anachronistic view of wetlands as being peat bogs that breed mosquitoes and other vermin, dirty and dangerous places that should be drained and backfilled for development and agriculture.

The governor and his aides need a primer on the intrinsic value of wetlands. They should log on, for example, to the St. Johns River Water Management website. They would learn that wetlands benefit us by:

—Cleaning, or filtering, pollutants from surface waters.
—Storing water from storms or runoff.
—Preventing flood damage to developed lands.
—Recharging groundwater.
—Serving as nurseries for saltwater and freshwater fish and shell-fish that have commercial, recreational and ecological value.
—Providing natural habitat for a variety of fish, wildlife and plants, including rare, threatened, endangered and endemic (native) species.

Why, then, would anyone—especially the state's highest elected official—tolerate dissembling when the welfare of the state's wetlands is at stake? Scott and his DEP appointees should be the lead stewards of our environment, always protecting our treasures from irresponsibility and greed.

In her bestselling book *The March of Folly*, historian Barbara W. Tuchman discusses a problem that describes the kind of failed leadership in Tallahassee that imperils our environment.

"A phenomenon noticeable throughout history regardless of place or period is the pursuit by governments of policies contrary to their own interests," Tuchman writes. "In this sphere, wisdom, which may be defined as the exercise of judgment acting on experience, common sense and available information, is less operative and more frustrated than it should be. Why do holders of high office so often act contrary to the way reason points and enlightened self-interest suggests? Why does intelligent mental process seem so often not to function?"

The original writers of DEP wetlands regulations appear to have been guided by science and experience and earnestly tried to balance environmental protection with private property rights and economic development—which is certain to continue. They knew that with progress some wetlands would be impacted. For that reason, they devised a permitting system that requires developers to do as little harm as possible to wetlands and to proportionally mitigate damage when it does occur. Mutual trust was a guiding principle.

Our governor and his minions are ignoring the science available to them. And they will not hesitate to come down hard on experts such as Connie Bersok who refuse to bend the rules for powerful friends.

Conservative politics and greed are driving those in power in Tallahassee to pursue environmental policies contrary to the interests of the greatest number of Floridians. It is an example of the march of folly.

Nature meets wrecking ball

JANUARY 6, 2013

In his 1998 book *Some Kind of Paradise: A Chronicle of Man and the Land in Florida*, environmentalist Mark Derr wrote that "in these past one hundred years, man has reshaped and relandscaped the peninsula, leveling forests, draining the marshes. The process continues at such a rapid rate that many residents of more than a decade barely recognize the areas around their homes."

Since Derr wrote those observations, the process of destruction has gone on at breakneck speed.

Two out of three Florida residents come from other states or foreign countries, and they have no memory of our old natural beauty and too often little respect for that beauty. Most have no qualms about electing lawmakers who dismiss the intrinsic value of our environment. As a result, Derr wrote, the "tale of Florida's development often is sordid, marked by the greed of people intent on taking whatever the land offered and leaving nothing in return."

Gov. Rick Scott is an outsider, and he is proving to be no friend of the environment in almost every move he makes.

Most recently, as suggested by an article in the *Tampa Bay Times*, the future of Florida's natural environment was put in jeopardy when Hershel Vinyard, secretary of the Department of Environmental Protection, laid off 58 DEP employees who have what is described as a "history and knowledge" of the state's critical environmental problems.

It is no secret that Vinyard, like the governor, is a probusiness crusader who has little use for environmental regulations.

"The majority of positions they were eliminating are compliance and enforcement positions," Jerry Phillips, a former attorney for the advocacy group Public Employees for Environmental Responsibility, told the *Times*. "They want to essentially turn the agency over to the regulated industries."

Phillips is right, of course. In addition to the layoffs in November, Vinyard brought in several new top administrators who had been high-level consultants or engineers for companies the DEP regulates.

Prior to the layoffs, Scott appointed Juan Portuondo to oversee the South Florida Water Management District, the board ostensibly responsible for protecting South Florida's water supply and wetlands from pollution. Portuondo once operated a trash incinerator in Miami that Greenpeace and other organizations showed was "a major source of mercury emissions" that were responsible "for much of the contamination in the Everglades." He also was linked to air and water pollution in Miami-Dade, and the company was heavily fined for violations.

No matter. Scott deemed Portuondo the best person for the board.

In another travesty, DEP suspended wetlands expert Connie Bersok from her job after she bucked politics and denied a permit to Highlands Ranch, formed in 2008 as a joint venture between a Jacksonville company and the Carlyle Group, a powerful private equity firm. Highlands wanted to turn a pine plantation, which was mostly high and dry, into a business that makes up for wetlands that are destroyed by new roads and development.

If Bersok had granted the permit, the company potentially could have collected millions of dollars in wetlands "credits" that could be sold to the government and developers.

The Scott administration's assaults on the environment keep piling up. Common sense, if not a little pragmatism, should show rational lawmakers and other officials that threatening our fragile environment also threatens our economy.

They do not seem to know that our natural environment creates our tourism, our most lucrative industry, attracting nearly 90 million visitors annually who put $67 billion into the state's economy. In fact, Florida is the top travel destination in the world.

People come here to experience our parks, beaches, wetlands, woodlands and amusement venues. They come to swim, scuba dive, fish, bird watch, kayak, boat and hike.

More business leaders and state lawmakers need to realize that viable tourism is directly connected not only to our pleasant weather but also to the health of our waters, beaches, greenery and clean air.

We need leaders who respect this interconnection. They need to be stewards of the environment, not profiteers who destroy and leave nothing in return.

Politics mustn't bog down progress in Everglades

JANUARY 20, 2013

You cannot overestimate the value of Everglades National Park. Unlike other parks that were created for their scenery, Everglades was established to preserve the 1,542,526-acre ecosystem as a wildlife habitat, with surface water as its most important resource and lifeline.

Decades before the park was established in 1947, those trying to protect this unique habitat had to cope with natural forces and fight human degradation and politics. That fight continues, led today by the Everglades Coalition, an alliance of 57 local, state and national conservation and environmental organizations.

More than 300 activists, politicians, and federal and state agency officials attended the coalition's 28th annual conference this month in Coral

Gables. The three-day meeting reaffirmed the coalition's mission to re-store what is known as the Greater Everglades Ecosystem, the vast area from the Kissimmee Chain of Lakes into Lake Okeechobee, through Everglades National Park out to Florida Bay and the Keys.

Everglades habitat restoration projects, the largest in the world, have been faring well during the last four years, with several dedications and groundbreakings. On Jan. 11, for example, a ribbon cutting was held at a facility in south Miami-Dade that will pump needed freshwater into Everglades National Park and into a troubled part of Florida Bay.

More good news is that a ribbon cutting will take place next month at a 1-mile bridge along Tamiami Trail. This popular road has blocked water flow for generations.

Progress has been possible because the Obama administration rein-vigorated the Everglades' restoration with $1.5 billion. One clear result of this infusion of money is that polluted water is being cleaned up. This newly clean water directly benefits South Florida homes and businesses.

But coalition members fear that congressional partisanship may stall progress.

"We can't let politics stand in the way of Everglades restoration," said Dawn Shirreffs, co-chair of Everglades Restoration and the Everglades program manager for the National Parks Conservation Association. "There are key issues that Congress is going to have to address in 2013. If we don't, we could really hurt restoration. We need bipartisan effort so that we can break ground on other projects.

"Right now, every project that is authorized is under construction. We understand that money is tight. But at the same time, conditions continue to decline. If we pull back on funding, we increase the cost of restoration. You'd have more delay, construction costs will increase, and you wouldn't be able to take advantage of some of the great progress we've had during the last couple of years."

Many important projects are authorized through spending bills called Water Resources Development Acts. These bills used to be voted on ev-ery two years. Not anymore. A divided Congress has not voted on a bill since 2007, slowing restoration momentum and threatening entire projects.

And there are vital economic reasons why Congress needs to pass the 2013 water bill.

In a study for the nonprofit National Parks Conservation Associa-tion, Mather Economics, a business consultant specializing in applied economics, found that Everglades restoration projects provide many jobs and numerous economic benefits to Florida and the nation. For every dollar invested in Everglades restoration, four are returned to the economy. If Congress approves future water bills, Mather estimates that more than 400,000 jobs will be created by Everglades restoration over time.

According to the National Park Service, Everglades National Park created more than 2,000 jobs in 2010 and generated more than $140 million in tourist spending.

If Congress fails to pass this year's water bill, Everglades wetlands will continue to be degraded by commercial, residential and agricultural development. Vital water will continue to be drained and channeled, the entire landscape will continue to be altered, and thousands of jobs will be lost.

If nothing else, the politicians in Washington need to remember that Everglades projects provide clean drinking water for more than 7 million Floridians. This fact alone is reason to set politics aside.

To save and protect precious Everglades

APRIL 12, 2013

Imagine the emphasis the state would place on Everglades restoration if our lawmakers and citizenry understood it as Marjory Stoneman Douglas did— as a giver and protector of life, the vital ecosystem that stretches from north of the Kissimmee Chain of Lakes to the waterways of Florida Bay and the coral reefs of the keys to the south.

New York Times

As a South Florida native who spent many years fishing, hiking and canoeing in the Everglades, I have watched this natural treasure come under assault from decades of pollution, overdevelopment, agricultural abuses and other human acts of greed that are exempt from rigorous government oversight.

I'm convinced that precious few of our elected officials have ever understood the value of the Everglades beyond its being a dumping ground and money pit. The best Floridians have been able to hope for is that their elected leaders at least acknowledge the role the vital ecosystem plays in providing clean drinking water for the most populous part of the state.

In a recent column for the *South Florida Sun-Sentinel* in Fort Lauderdale, for example, Gov. Rick Scott wrote, "As Florida's economy continues to grow, it is essential that we work to protect and restore our Everglades."

But I wish the governor and all state legislators appreciated the Everglades as a living, natural place that has inherent value beyond our limited imaginations.

"There are no other Everglades in the world," as Marjory Stoneman Douglas wrote in her 1947 book, *The Everglades: River of Grass*. "They are, they have always been, one of the unique regions of the earth, remote, never wholly known. Nothing anywhere else is like them. . . . They are unique in their simplicity, the diversity, the related harmony of the forms of life they enclose."

There's hope, at least, that some legislators want to encourage this broader and more sophisticated appreciation. Last year, Sen. David Simmons, a Republican, and former Rep. Steve Perman, a Democrat, sponsored legislation making April 7, which is Douglas' birthday, the annual Everglades Day in Florida. It is largely a symbolic gesture, but one that acknowledges that Everglades stewardship must become a shared effort that reaches across party lines.

"The Everglades is a vital ecosystem and an important aspect of South Florida's tourism, agricultural, real estate, and recreational economies," Simmons said. "Dedicating April 7th as Everglades Day provides an opportunity for all of us to recognize the Everglades for its local, as well as global, significance."

The challenge is to not stop at symbolism. Last week, 45 advocates, including volunteers, retirees, students and Everglades Coalition groups from nine counties statewide, traveled by bus to Tallahassee "to educate" lawmakers on the vital and ongoing restoration efforts and remind them of the important economic issues at play.

During the last four years, as a result of financial and legislative support from the Obama administration, restoration projects in the Everglades, the largest of their kind in the world, have been going forward.

"We need strong leadership and support from our state officials to build on this momentum and fund restoration and water quality projects," said Dawn Shirreffs, Everglades Coalition co-chair. "Everglades restoration is a sound investment for Florida that could amount to up to $46.5 billion in gains to Florida's economy."

Shirreffs and other advocates aren't naive. They know they are in a tough battle. I was with them as they walked the hallways of the Capitol, as legislative leaders were fine-tuning a bill that would circumvent the "Polluter Pays" protection in the Florida Constitution. The measure would undercut the state's commitment to the Everglades by shifting the costs for cleanup from polluters, particularly the sugar industry, to taxpayers, meaning the project will have to compete against other state needs.

From what I saw and heard, Everglades advocates have a lot of hard work ahead because too many legislators are in bed with polluters. They chose to ignore the detriment they're causing to the state's economy by not ensuring a long-term clean water supply and to future generations who may never get to see the Everglades in all its wonderful splendor.

Everglades Day and events surrounding it must become more than symbolic. Somehow, self-interested lawmakers must be convinced that a healthy River of Grass is more important than currying favor with special interests.

Stopping the slithering invaders

MAY 31, 2013

We Floridians love international visitors. Showing them a good time is a major way that we sustain our economy. But there are some visitors we can do without. In fact, we want them out of here. They are a menace, and they have overstayed their welcome in paradise.

I'm referring to invasive animals, those exotic and dangerous species. People around the globe still remember the photo several years ago of the 13-foot Burmese python and the 6-foot alligator that fought to their deaths in the Everglades. A few weeks ago another photo showed a Florida International University student with an 18-foot, 8-inch python he caught and killed in the Everglades. This was the biggest python killed thus far in South Florida, reminding us that we have been invaded.

Scientists estimate that there are thousands of pythons in the Everglades, some longer than 18 feet. We probably will never get rid of them because they live in inaccessible areas and reproduce annually, the females sitting on up to 100 eggs until they hatch.

The reptiles are a danger, not only to public safety but to natural resources. Full-grown Burmese pythons, 200 pounds of muscle, can overpower their owners and are a threat to residents if they wind up on the loose. Several have been captured or killed in South Florida neighborhoods.

But they also threaten biodiversity because they eat native species, including endangered ones. "It's only a matter of time until we find a Florida panther in a snake belly," said Jenny Conner Nelms, Florida director of government relations for the Nature Conservancy. "Pythons also have the potential to make some common species 'rare' in the future. Baby birds, adult wading birds, bobcats, kitty cats—pythons eat them all."

Until recently, Florida lawmakers seemed to have put the livelihoods of animal dealers ahead of the greater good of the state. Rules and oversight were lax. On top of that, many snake owners simply released their pets in the Everglades once they became too large to manage.

To their credit, state lawmakers began working with the pet industry, scientists and environmental organizations and crafted legislation that brought some sanity to reptile trade and management policies. The state identified nine reptiles that no longer can be sold for personal possession, and there are stricter rules for caging and transporting reptiles to reduce chances of escape. The new law also gives the Florida Fish and Wildlife Conservation Commission authority to control sales into the state, including mail order and Internet transactions. The commission also has the authority to fine lawbreakers.

Nelms said these regulations are a good beginning, but we still need what she refers to as a "pre-import screening tool" at the state and federal levels. In other words, wildlife officials need the authority to screen and keep out dangerous species such as the python.

Currently, the 111-year-old Lacey Act is the federal law for invasive species. Nelms wrote recently in the *Palm Beach Post* that most experts consider the Lacey Act to be ineffective in addition to being costly.

"The United States receives hundreds of millions of live wild animals each year," she wrote. "At least 2,500 species of non-native wildlife were imported in the past decade."

Research indicates that more than 300 of those species are known to be potential invaders or present disease risk. However, the Lacey Act process to review typically occurs after the harmful species has been brought into the country.

"The Burmese python invasion is a prime example of how federal reforms to screen species for risk before importation could have saved the nation's natural resources, and hundreds of millions of dollars in control costs," Nelms wrote.

There is a potential solution in the offing. A bill in Washington, HR 996, the Invasive Fish and Wildlife Prevention Act, would give the U.S. Fish and Wildlife Service more authority to screen exotics such as the python. That makes sense not only because prevention is the most effective tool, but also the least expensive one. But so far, the plan is failing to win enough Republican support in the House. House members who remain unconvinced should re-read last month's tale of FIU student Jason Leon killing the record-sized Burmese python and ask themselves why they won't take action.

Fouling Florida environment? Simply insane

OCTOBER 15, 2013

Albert Einstein said that insanity is "doing the same thing over and over again and expecting different results."

In Florida, environmentalists have their unique definition of insanity: knowingly destroying our environment—one of our major economic resources—while blocking efforts to slow or stop the destruction.

This brand of insanity plays out daily and has for decades, from the moment business owners, their political supporters and lobbyists learned that the abuse of our precious wild places can bring huge profits.

Here on the southeast coast, the Indian River Lagoon, the St. Lucie River and its estuary are being polluted like never before—perhaps irreversibly—by an algae slime that proliferates from excess manure, sewage and fertilizer released by municipalities and, of course, from Lake Okeechobee.

Research clearly shows that most of the nutrients flowing into Lake Okeechobee come from tributaries in the northern Everglades. This is Big Sugar country, the Everglades Agricultural Area, where most of the nation's sugarcane is grown. Adjacent regions also are affected by discharges from the lake.

Elected officials and others have known for more than 30 years about our nutrient-rich water problems, but they consistently have put business interests ahead of eliminating the sources of the pollution. The discharge of dirty water from Lake Okeechobee is not new. It has been going on since the U.S. Army Corps of Engineers constructed the dike around the lake decades ago and created a reservoir system that enabled the sugar industry to operate without major interruptions or effective regulation.

That is a clear sign of the insanity.

This year, because of unusually high rainfall into the lake, the Army Corps discharged unprecedented volumes of polluted water into the tributaries, further enriching algal blooms and releasing muck that smothers vital sea grass beds. Many scientists believe the toxic blooms, which have been increasing over the years, may have caused the deaths of untold numbers of fish, hundreds of pelicans, dozens of dolphins and more than 100 manatees.

Although this damage is taking a heavy toll on businesses that depend on a healthy environment for their incomes, too many owners continue to contribute money to the same cast of characters in Tallahassee who refuse to pass legislation to curb the pollution.

For many years, environmental groups have identified several key areas that elected officials and other leaders need to address to fix our most serious water pollution problems. In August, a coalition of environmentalists sent a statement to lawmakers outlining measures to stop the toxic algae scum in the Indian River Lagoon and other waters.

Here is part of the statement: "Septic tanks need to be cleaned out and connected to treatment plants, failing sewer lines that pour sewage into the estuary need to be replaced, sewage treatment plants must be upgraded, fertilizer ordinances must be adopted statewide, and, most importantly, agricultural pollution—the primary source of the filthy water flowing into Lake Okeechobee—needs to be regulated."

Over the years, our governors and legislators, both Democrats and Republicans, have done little to fix these problems. They have let the polluting industries and their lobbyists write the regulations. It does not take rocket science to spot the loopholes. The fox is being allowed to guard the henhouse.

How insane is that?

Last week, the Indian River County Commission, the St. Lucie County Commission, the Martin County Commission and the cities of Fort Pierce and St. Lucie Village signed a resolution asking Gov. Rick

Scott to declare a state of emergency regarding the Indian River Lagoon. The resolution implored the governor to issue an executive order to protect the waters of these areas. Scott has the constitutional authority to issue the order and to hold violators accountable.

We should be encouraged by the action of these local governments. However, because the governor and the Legislature value business over the environment, we should expect the environmental insanity to continue unabated.

Living in the river of grass

NOVEMBER 22, 2013

Everglades National Park

"When I was a boy in Scotland I was fond of everything that was wild, and all my life I've been growing fonder and fonder of wild places and wild creatures," conservationist John Muir wrote in his essay "A Boyhood in Scotland."

If you change Muir's Scotland to Florida, you get a good description of my childhood and how my love grows each day for what remains of the Sunshine State's wild places, particularly Everglades National Park.

Muir was born in a tiny town on the North Sea, where the wilderness reached for miles in all directions. I was born in Fort Lauderdale, a mid-sized city on the Atlantic Ocean. The Atlantic, too, is a wilderness. It was not accessible to a child. I could only stare at it from shore, swim near shore and fish from shore.

To the west of Fort Lauderdale, however, wild regions of Greater Everglades sprawled west toward Naples, north toward Orlando and south to Florida Bay. I began my forays into the Everglades when I was 6 or 7 years old, when I went with an uncle to fish in "secret spots" he and a buddy discovered along U.S. Route 27.

My uncle constantly had to yell, "Boy, you got a bite," to let me know my bobber had been submerged a long time.

I would be daydreaming, mesmerized by swaying sawgrass, strands of bald cypress and the spectacle of snowy egret, white ibis and other waders on the hunt. Cypress domes and hardwood hammocks in the distance intrigued me. I imagined that they concealed deep pools where alligators and other ferocious animals hid from human eyes.

As I matured, becoming a self-assured adventurer, I trekked deeper into what naturalist Ted Levin calls our "liquid land." When I was 14, I discovered Everglades National Park itself. Since then, I have returned countless times, slogging the sloughs, camping, kayaking, fishing, bird-watching, staying in the now-gone cabins and relaxing for extended periods on a houseboat.

During my first slog through a periphyton marsh, I learned that this so-called swamp is not a wasteland of putrid, stagnant water. I saw that the shallow, slow-moving water is clear, revealing a world of fish, other creatures and plants.

When I taught at Florida Keys Community College and Broward Community College, I brought hundreds of students to the park for writing assignments and for the sheer enjoyment of this treasure.

And today, I am living a dream.

As a journalist who often writes about nature, I am an artist-in-residence in Everglades National Park. I have been here since Oct. 30. My residency ends Dec. 8, after which I have a year to publish an in-depth commentary on the progress of the Comprehensive Everglades Restoration Plan. I am spending my time exploring, researching, interviewing sources, keeping a journal and enjoying my good fortune.

Living in the park has taught me something that Muir, Aldo Leopold, Henry David Thoreau and other nature writers were keenly aware of: Those of us who love natural places, especially our national parks, have a special way of being in them. By being, these writers meant our state of consciously existing in wild environments. Some nature writers even describe wilderness as "sacred" places.

Being in the Everglades is unique to each person. But all of our ways of being have one thing in common: We are individually transported beyond our normal selves as we sense the essence and uniqueness of the River of Grass.

Everglades National Park, a World Heritage Site, is special. Unlike other national parks, it was not established for spectacular vistas and awe-inspiring scenery. Its purpose is to protect our wildlife and waters. When we enter the park, we do not expect to see geysers, glaciers or bottomless canyons. We expect to see alligators, wading birds, raptors and plants that do not exist anywhere else on Earth. And we wistfully hope to see an endangered Florida panther.

We come here to see wild things.

That expectation alone gives us a special way of being in the park: I am reminded that I am an animal, the human animal, a term used by conservationist Ian McCallum in his book *Ecological Intelligence: Rediscovering Ourselves in Nature.* Indeed, I realize that I am naturally linked to other living creatures here and that I am the only animal in the park possessing the power to destroy everything here. Instead of giving me a sense of dominion, this awareness humbles me, making me grateful to be in this one-of-a-kind wilderness.

Having the good fortune to be an AIRIE artist-in-residence has taught me that I am part of the great chain of being of life in Everglades National Park.

Florida's vital challenge: to save the Everglades

NOVEMBER 1, 2014

Everglades National Park

The health of Florida's environment never should have become a partisan issue, but we keep electing officials who make it partisan. As a result, we see the continued degradation of our water and land and serious threats to many plants and animals.

Many ecologists and other experts argue that as the health of the natural world diminishes, the quality of human life diminishes in equal measure.

In Florida, nothing epitomizes our need for vigilance and challenges our commitment to environmental stewardship more than the health of the Greater Everglades, the state's most vital wetland ecosystem.

The Greater Everglades is not just the iconic national park near Homestead. It is the region that stretches from north of the Kissimmee Chain of Lakes south into Florida Bay. Historically, this ecosystem encompassed 18,000 square miles. Today, because of agricultural and urban development, just half of it remains. Scientists call this leftover the "remnant Everglades."

Proposals to help restore and protect this treasure and many other sensitive places are divisive. Even in South Florida, where some 7 million residents of Palm Beach, Broward and Miami-Dade counties depend on the Everglades for potable water, politicians who oppose water-related projects still get elected.

In addition to being a source of drinking water, the Everglades brings in more than $146 million in tourist and recreation spending and creates thousands of jobs annually.

To their credit, some lawmakers are working with environmentalists to make the Everglades healthy again. The major effort, the $10.5 billion Comprehensive Everglades Restoration Plan, began in 2000 and was to be completed in 30-plus years. That will not happen.

For a century, disastrous projects tried to control the Everglades by building levees and digging canals. Led by the U.S. Army Corps of Engineers, the replumbing south of Lake Okeechobee was to prevent flooding in residential areas and to drain the so-called swamp for agriculture, especially sugar. These actions began the slow death of the Everglades by altering the depth, timing and distribution of water flow in the ecosystem.

Engineers apparently did not know or care that the Everglades' flora and fauna evolved and thrived on low levels of nutrients. With human encroachment, levels of nitrogen and phosphorous rose, severely damaging the ecosystem.

Scientists involved in CERP agree that high levels of phosphorous, mainly from sugar production runoff, is one of the major obstacles to restoring the Everglades. And they agree that although the sugar industry has reduced levels of phosphorous discharge in recent years, it must do much more.

But demanding more of Big Sugar can kill dreams of incumbency in Tallahassee. Only a few politicians will take the gamble. Worse, it is such a corrosive issue that few scientists will say publicly that the sugar industry is the proverbial elephant—the big polluter—in the room.

As far back as 1996, nearly 70 percent of Florida voters approved the "Polluter Pays" constitutional amendment that calls for Big Sugar to pay its fair share of the then-estimated $2 billion to clean up water in the Everglades. Evidence strongly showed that the industry produced 62 percent of the pollution. But with powerful friends in the Legislature and in select government agencies, Big Sugar has yet to pay its fair share for cleanup, saddling taxpayers with most of the tab.

A viable way to restore the Everglades emerged in 2008, when then-Gov. Charlie Crist announced that Florida intended to buy up to 187,000 acres of land from the state's largest cane grower, U.S. Sugar Corp., for $1.75 billion. Although the deal had drawbacks, it would have given the land back to the people and let scientists implement programs that would effectively reduce levels of phosphorous flowing south.

But the recession and politics killed the deal, and the state settled for a much smaller parcel of land, too small to aid in significant cleanup.

Today, the reality of restoring the Everglades remains as it was: The state needs to buy out U.S. Sugar Corp. Not surprisingly, the company is threatening to develop the land for housing, perhaps looking for more money than in 2008. If the state does not buy the land, a handful of noncontroversial CERP projects will remain on the fringes, doing little to clean the dirty water.

Florida's gubernatorial election is Tuesday. There is not a proposed amendment on the ballot that specifically earmarks funds for restoring the Everglades. But there is Amendment 1, calling for land and water preservation statewide, allocating one-third of an existing tax that is already used to fund water and land protection. More state-owned land and clean water in other regions will benefit the dying Everglades.

Furthermore, Amendment 1 tests politicians' long-term vision for the natural world. Republican Gov. Rick Scott opposes the amendment, and his first-term record on the environment lacks vision. Democrat Charlie Crist supports the amendment. He has a positive environmental record and promises to restore programs and funds Scott has gutted or eliminated.

More than ever, paradise needs a pro-environment governor, a steward, who has the courage to renew the buyout of U.S. Sugar Corp, putting us back on course to restore the Everglades and in a position to safeguard precious land and water statewide.

Don't be fooled by environmental bills in Washington, Tallahassee

FEBRUARY 28, 2015

Game on!

How else do we describe the portent of President Barack Obama's veto of a GOP-sponsored bill that would have forced authorization of the 875-mile Keystone XL pipeline? By rejecting the bill, Obama not only enraged Republicans; he deepened the wrath of the oil industry and other businesses with financial interests in the venture.

The veto is being called a "milestone" in Obama's presidency. Not only will it bring more partisan gridlock in Washington, its ideological impact will be felt nationwide, especially in Florida, where environmental problems such as water pollution, sea level rise and wildlife habitat loss are worsening.

While the environment did not play major roles in midterm Senate races, triumphant Republicans are gearing up for a broad and sustained assault on environmental policies they deem harmful to the bottom lines of businesses.

Senate Majority Leader Mitch McConnell said his top priority is "to try to do whatever I can to get the EPA reined in."

A Washington-based writer dubbed the remainder of Obama's presidency as the congressional Republicans' "regulation-hunting season." It is an apt description.

To begin the well-planned assault, the GOP-dominated House Transportation and Infrastructure and Senate Environment and Public Works committees convened a joint hearing to attack the Clean Water Act. Members of the committees grilled Environmental Protection Agency administrator Gina McCarthy on the agency's proposal to expand the authority of the Clean Water Act.

According to the *National Journal*, a nonpartisan magazine that reports on politics and policy trends, the GOP has staked out 10 environmental rules to kill: the Clean Power Plan; Endangered Species Act; Ground-Level Ozone Standards; Methane Regulations on Oil and Gas Production; Renewable-Fuel Standard; Rules for Fracking on Public Lands; Waters of the United States; Coal Ash Disposal; Stream Buffer Zone Rule; and the Social Cost of Carbon.

Although these rules clearly protect the environment and public well-being, Republicans see them as job-killers and constraints on free enterprise itself.

States with Republican governors and Republican-controlled legislatures are eagerly adopting Washington's anti-environment and anti-Obama agenda. In Florida, voters tend to approve measures that protect the environment, especially the Greater Everglades. But the governor and Republican legislators routinely find ways to circumvent the will of the people to please various industries, many of them heavy polluters.

Agriculture Commissioner Adam Putnam, for example, is pushing a bill (HB 7003) that will alter how the state manages water. Putnam's apparent goal is to loosen rules and lower enforcement. Under the bill sponsored by Republican Rep. Matt Caldwell, standards for water quality will be rolled back while the state works more aggressively to harvest new water resources.

Now the governor, with enforcement powers, heads the Department of Environmental Protection and the water management districts. This bill puts more oversight authority into the hands of Putnam, a man who hails from a wealthy agricultural family and who is a good friend of Big Sugar, the state's worst agricultural polluter.

The new arrangement puts Putnam in the lead of cleanup efforts for the 3.5 million acres of land north of Lake Okeechobee. Although the Department of Agriculture has only eight staffers to manage those 3.5 million acres, Putnam has assured lawmakers that these eight souls can perform inspection miracles.

The most harmful provision of the bill is that the relatively effective permitting process now used by the South Florida Water Management District to reduce discharge into Lake Okeechobee would be scrapped and replaced by an industry standard of so-called "best practices."

In other words, agribusiness, developers and other polluters—who profit from cutting corners—would be trusted to do the right thing, to earnestly reduce toxic discharges into Lake Okeechobee.

During seasons of excessive rain, the lake's dirty water is moved south and to each coast by the U.S. Army Corps of Engineers and SFWMD. The phosphorous-laden water that goes south ends up in the endangered Everglades, where, ironically, the world's largest restoration effort struggles to make a serious dent in eliminating hazardous conditions.

In a statement following the House Appropriations Committee's approval of the water bill on Feb. 19, Putnam served up boilerplate rhetoric to hide the duplicity: "I thank (House leaders) for supporting a water bill policy that will secure the supply and quality of Florida's water for generations to come. Florida's water is one of our most precious resources, and the management of water quality and conservation has been and always will be a partnership."

Do not be fooled. The legislation is mostly a diversion that will please developers and farmers. Like many other GOP efforts in Florida, Washington and elsewhere, the bill is part of a campaign to roll back environmental protections.

Florida needs new amendment to protect environment

MAY 2, 2015

Enough is enough.

In its familiar dissembling way, the Republican-led Florida Legislature is contravening the official will of the people.

Last November, a supermajority of voters approved Amendment 1. It was supposed to strengthen Florida Forever, substantially protect natural habitats and enable the purchase of vital land statewide. Most notably, Amendment 1 money would position the state to purchase 46,000 acres owned by U.S. Sugar Corp. that would be used to help restore the Everglades. The option to buy the land expires in October.

Republican conservatives and cowed Democrats in Tallahassee have no intention of using a fair share of the millions of dollars from the amendment's documentary stamp tax proceeds to buy land. They intend to spend a lot of it on wastewater projects and to clean up agriculture's pollution.

The Legislature's dismissal of Amendment 1 is yet another example of the voters' powerlessness and the need for drastic action. Citizens who understand the value of the natural environment must take back the state from the sycophants in Tallahassee who put wrongheaded ideology, campaign contributions and incumbency ahead of the state's greater good.

We must use our only viable weapon: another constitutional amendment.

I acknowledge that the Legislature has effectively ignored previous environment-related amendments, one of the most far-reaching being the 1996 "Polluter Pays" amendment. With nearly 70 percent voter approval, the amendment called for Big Sugar to pay its fair share of the then-estimated $2 billion to clean up water in the Everglades.

But with bought-and-paid-for members of the House and Senate, armies of lobbyists and lawyers and shills in the water management agencies, Big Sugar has yet to pay its fair share for cleanup. Taxpayers continue to be cheated.

So, what would we gain from yet another amendment?

I am not a lawyer, but I wager that an amendment with incontrovertible language that gives Floridians a constitutional right to clean air, safe drinking water and a healthy environment would be a game-changer. This is not a new concept. In her 1962 book *Silent Spring*, Rachel Carson argued that Americans have an inalienable right to a healthy environment. After all, a healthy environment is an apex human right.

Now consider the concept of the constitutional right to a healthy environment more broadly. In his book *The Environmental Rights Revolution: A Global Study of Constitutions, Human Rights, and the Environment*, David R. Boyd, an internationally acclaimed environmental lawyer, writes that as of 2012, 177 of 193 United Nations member nations recognized the right to a healthy environment in their constitutions. The United States was not one of them. With all of our purported wisdom and sense of justice, we are in the company of China, Afghanistan and North Korea.

Boyd shows that in nations that have adopted environmental amendments, the outcomes have been remarkable, including stronger environmental laws, better enforcement of those laws, landmark court decisions, the cleanup of pollution hot spots and the provision of safe drinking water.

But merely stating in a constitution that a healthy environment is a human right is not enough. Countries with the most effective environmental rights in their constitutions crafted precise language describing shared responsibilities between the public and the government and gave courts the power of judicial review.

This movement is described by Erin Daly, a professor of environmental and constitutional law and the associate dean of faculty research at Widener University Law School.

"In many instances," she writes, "environmental rights are recognized not as substantive entitlements (which would allow litigants to sue if the government polluted their rivers or clear-cut their forests), but as procedural rights. Examples of procedural rights include imposing on governments the obligation to consult with communities before they take actions that will affect their environment or giving individuals the right to participate in governmental processes that will affect their environment. While procedural rights do not guarantee a particular outcome, they may be more effective in preventing environmental degradation."

The time has come for Florida voters to fight for a constitutional amendment that outlines clear procedural rights to a healthy environment. One result should be the option of eminent domain. Floridians should have the right, for example, to take Big Sugar land at a fair price to restore the Everglades.

Big Sugar's polluting practices must end. The industry should be forced to pay up with cash or land or both.

Dismissing the environment

NOVEMBER 3, 2017

In 1973, Congress had the foresight to pass the Endangered Species Act. To amplify the need to protect the nation's plants and animals, a House committee wrote a report on the importance of the new law.

The report stated: "Man's presence on the Earth is relatively recent, and his effective domination over the world's life support systems has taken place within a few short generations. Our ability to destroy, or almost destroy, all intelligent life on the planet became apparent in this generation. A certain humility, and a sense of urgency, seem indicated. . . . From the most narrow possible point of view, it is in the best interests of mankind to minimize the losses of genetic variations."

The authors probably never thought that untold numbers of legislators one day would think little or nothing of destroying, or almost destroying, plant and animal life.

That day has arrived. All states in the union, even those with the most vulnerable wildlife, land, water and air, have elected officials who actively support and write bad environmental policies. And, of course, the nation's capital is dominated by anti-science and anti-environment lawmakers. The president leads the pack.

Americans who worry about this trend should monitor the ecological destruction in Alaska and Florida. Although thousands of miles apart, Alaska, bordered by the North Pacific Ocean, and Florida, bordered by the Atlantic, are prime laboratories for bad environmental policies and practices.

Lawmakers responsible for the Endangered Species Act, or ESA, clearly understood that protecting the environment protects people. Unfortunately, the 115th Congress has politicized the ESA and many other science-based laws and agencies that protect wildlife on federal lands. Opponents of environmental regulations are using either budget maneuvers or changes to the intent of original authorizations to open up public lands for use by private business.

The Arctic National Wildlife Refuge, the nation's largest refuge, has been politicized and is at risk of being opened to oil and gas exploration and drilling. Weakening or destroying the Endangered Species Act will enable paving the way for exploration and drilling in the refuge. Although preservationists question the economic benefits of these actions and predict ecological degradation, Congress is determined to move forward.

Such shortsightedness is dangerous, said Laurie Macdonald, a Florida-based consultant for Defenders of Wildlife.

"Along with being the ancestral and sustaining home of the Gwich'in people, the Arctic NWR is a unique and truly wild ecosystem depended upon by polar bears, the porcupine caribou herd, musk ox, Arctic fox and nearly 200 species of birds," she said.

"Migrations take place to six continents and 50 U.S. states. Florida provides important winter habitat or resting and feeding points along the flyway for many species of Arctic birds. Besides the migration connections between the Arctic and Florida, we share in being two of the most vulnerable areas of the world to climate change."

Destructive policies for the Arctic NWR closely mirror those being concocted in Florida. During the last week of April, for example, Florida lawmakers approved a proposal to distribute $300 million to eight Panhandle counties to compensate for damages from the 2010 Deepwater Horizon oil spill in the Gulf.

Several days later, these same people, including Gov. Rick Scott, mostly stayed quiet when President Donald Trump issued an executive order that could open up more waters of Florida's coast to drilling for oil and natural gas. Sen. Bill Nelson, a Democrat, outright opposes Trump's order, but Republican Sen. Marco Rubio has not leveled with Florida residents as he tries to satisfy his supporters in the oil industry.

Many Floridians do not know that the state already allows oil drilling, producing about 2 million barrels a year, a thimbleful in satisfying the nation's use of oil. In reality, there is no need for more drilling in the Sunshine State. The risks are too great.

Still, a major real estate company in southwest Broward County has applied for the rights to drill an exploratory well on its 20,000 acres that is part of the Greater Everglades ecosystem, which includes Big Cypress National Preserve. Elected officials in the cities that will be impacted oppose the project, but many officials in Tallahassee, including Scott, are poised to give the go-ahead.

Apparently, these lawmakers are not seriously thinking about the health of the Everglades and other vital areas that do not need more man-made intrusion. And, for sure, Scott could use his friendship with Trump to stop the project.

The trouble is that Scott, a climate-change-denying Republican, probably will be followed by another anti-science Republican. Until Floridians begin to care about the health of our precious environment and make their wishes known at the ballot box, the destruction will continue unabated.

Homeowners protest Big Sugar's burning of cane fields

JUNE 2, 2018

Belle Glade

This town's motto is "Her Soil Is Her Fortune." The soil, called "muck," is the moist, dark earth where sugarcane thrives. Also called "black gold," the soil does indeed provide a financial fortune for the growers who have powerful influence on lawmakers and other important leaders.

The bittersweet irony is Big Sugar uses a process called "pre-harvest burning" to make its fortune. From October to April or May, the companies ignite huge fires in their fields to burn off so-called "trash," the outer leaves of the cane stalks, before harvesting.

The fires send billows of smoke and stench into the air. Ash rains down over four counties.

Impoverished residents of the western Everglades Agricultural Area, mostly low-income African Americans and foreign temporary laborers, call the falling ash "black snow."

A small group of activists began meeting to find ways to encourage sugar growers to switch to "green harvesting," the use of machines and human labor rather than fire.

Hardly anyone listened to them or took them seriously.

Steve Messam, 35, one of the activists and an associate pastor at Glades Covenant Community Church in South Bay, was born in Belle Glade. He grew up taking his heavy breathing and allergy flare-ups for granted. Many neighbors and schoolmates had the same symptoms.

When he went to college in Michigan, his respiratory ailments disappeared. But when he returned for Christmas each year, his ailments also returned. Today, his wife and 4-year-old son have similar problems. His son uses a breathing machine during the burn season.

Messam said that in addition to causing medical problems, the emissions negatively impact residents' quality of life. Homeowners are especially plagued by inconveniences and unnecessary expenses.

"There's nothing like opening your door and being greeted by ash rushing into your home and over your body or going outside and seeing your car covered with it," he said. "I have to pressure clean my doors and porch at least once a year."

His home air conditioner filters should last three months or more, but he changes them monthly during the burn season.

"Pre-harvest burning is like having a bad next door neighbor who takes all his trash from his yard and throws it across the fence into your yard," he said. "We're paying to clean up someone else's trash."

Former South Bay Mayor Shanique Scott said she sees relatives and friends suffering from asthma, migraines and sinus and respiratory problems that worsen during burn season.

"When I walk out my front door, I see the black snow and smell the pollution," she said. "I'm appalled to see clouds of billowing smoke, not knowing if a neighbor's home is on fire or if it's just another day of sugarcane burning. I have difficulty breathing during the burning season."

Teachers such as Mariya Feldman share Scott's experiences and outrage. Feldman, who has a master's degree in environmental science, taught for two years in Pahokee, which is surrounded by cane fields and has a sugar refinery nearby.

She said most of her students showed symptoms of asthma during burn season.

"I had two students who would wear garbage bags over their heads to get to the school bus because of the burnings," she said. "I have spoken to parents who are angry that their children aren't getting help from the exposure to the smoke. I spoke off-the-record to scientists and even with officials who told me these burnings are archaic. Ash falls in the school parking lot. Some days, it was unbearable for me to go from my car to the school because the smell from the burning would give me cramps in my lungs."

Feldman visited the U.S. Department of Agriculture in Palm Beach County on two consecutive days for answers, but no one was available to speak with her. She emailed sugarcane officials, but no one granted her an interview. She complained to the fire department. An official promised to "look into it." She called the Sheriff's Office and was dismissed as being "naïve" for accusing Big Sugar of harming the environment, she said.

Local community activists, seeking attention for their cause, became hopeful after learning about a press conference in which the possible link between sugarcane burning and human health was a topic. Shortly afterward, the grassroots Stop the Burn campaign was initiated.

Sugar growers have accused the Sierra Club and the Stop the Burn campaign of trying to end agriculture south of Lake Okeechobee. They point out that they receive burn permits from the Florida Forest Service, and that air quality is good in counties such as Glades, Hendry and Palm Beach.

"Neither the Sierra Club nor local activists involved in the campaign want to destroy the sugar industry," said Patrick Ferguson of the Sierra Club. "A shift to green harvesting would benefit the industry in the long-term rather than put them out of business. Investing in the infrastructure to utilize the trash, instead of wasting it, would create more local jobs and provide new sources of revenue for sugar growers. Green harvesting is a win-win-win."

Florida's land of black snow

JULY 1, 2018

When I was told Florida gubernatorial candidate Chris King would visit Belle Glade to meet local activists who are trying to persuade sugarcane farmers to change their pre-harvesting method, I wondered why he would invite the ire of the powerful industry.

After all, Belle Glade, south of Lake Okeechobee, is one of Florida's poorest towns. Agricultural and conservative, it has a population of roughly 19,000. Only about 10 percent is white, and median household income is $26,859.

Running a serious campaign for governor requires millions of dollars. King, a 39-year-old Harvard-educated Democrat and business owner, will not find much money in Belle Glade and in two other nearby towns, South Bay and Pahokee, together nicknamed The Muck.

"I traveled to Belle Glade," King said, "because I wanted to better understand the communities that live there, the challenges they face from sugarcane burning and why few leaders in our state have tried to understand this issue and figure out if there's a better way forward. For seven to eight months a year, and six to seven days a week, this community is on fire. I came away astonished, incredibly concerned and angry."

He is referring to pre-harvest burning, Big Sugar's method of igniting huge fires in their fields to burn off so-called "trash," the outer leaves of the cane stalks, before harvesting. Activists want growers to switch to "green harvesting," using machines and human labor instead of fire.

"Before my visit, I was aware that this was one of Florida's areas of greatest poverty and shameful treatment, but I don't think that prepared me for what I saw there," King said. "I've done charitable work in countries experiencing dire poverty across the world, but I never expected to view similar conditions in Palm Beach County. It unnerved me that in a county with tremendous wealth and resources, that prosperity has not been shared with the people who are helping to generate it."

Most news outlets that cover the area focus on environmental problems such as water levels in Lake Okeechobee and algae bloom in once-pristine waterways flowing east and west.

King said he wanted to know more after hearing about human health problems that are rarely addressed objectively.

"I learned that sugarcane burning has had real public health consequences for the families that live around the lake," King said. "Residents shared with me generations of concerns about respiratory illness, asthma and associated health problems from the air quality. I also learned they live in the one community in Florida where it snows seven months of the year thanks to the ash from sugarcane burning."

From October to April or May, pre-harvest burning sends up billows of toxic smoke and stench that come down over four counties. Local residents call the falling ash from the process "black snow."

Since King will not grab many voters in The Muck, I asked him to explain what he hoped to gain from the visit.

He said few politicians acknowledge the "extraordinary poverty" in the area, and even fewer have the courage to take on Big Sugar, the industry that has created some of the very conditions residents face. "What's happening in Belle Glade is at the intersection of race, poverty and environmental neglect and justice, and our state has turned a blind eye to the public health and economic impacts of sugarcane burning," he said. "Since my visit, I've asked myself why, and it's because one industry, sugar, has a vise grip on Florida politics."

If elected, he said he would make "substantial efforts" to get the Florida Department of Environmental Protection to conduct research and publish the findings showing the public health effects of sugarcane burning on communities around Lake Okeechobee.

To gain the trust of likely voters unfamiliar with his commitment to fairness and to put detractors on notice, King pledged during his first campaign speech to never take "a dime" from the sugar industry. "After $60 million in political donations from the sugar industry to politicians on the left and right, the next governor of Florida must be an honest broker and lead the argument against Big Sugar's environmental abuses and their corrosive effect on our democracy," he said.

Based on statements on his website, King believes the governor should be a competent financial steward while serving the greater good. "I have always believed that it's a false choice that we either do well or do good," he said. "I believe we can grow an economy at the same time we better care for all of Florida's families.

"The issue in Belle Glade and other communities around the lake is that the sugar industry has told us that if we begin using green technologies and innovation on pre-harvest burning, which are proven to be better for people, we will hurt the economy. I reject that premise and false choice."

Let's save the paradise that is Florida

FEBRUARY 1, 2019

Apparently, the new governor wants to restore some of the old pristine Florida he enjoyed as a child growing up in Pinellas County. Whatever his motivations, Floridians should support his early environmental initiatives.

Many old Florida natives like me used to believe we were living in paradise, a special place "full of flowers," as Juan Ponce de Leon had observed. Our peninsula was mostly pristine and undeveloped, more sand dune than pavement, more earthy green than kitschy pastels, more shoreline than seawall.

We old-timers were awed by our wilderness. We instinctively understood that healthy bodies of water, including our springs and wetlands, were our essence and major drivers of our economy.

In his 1998 book, *Some Kind of Paradise: A Chronicle of Man and the Land in Florida*, Mark Derr wrote: "In these past one hundred years, man has reshaped and relandscaped the peninsula, leveling forests, draining marshes. The process continues at such a rapid rate that many residents of more than a decade barely recognize the areas around their homes. . . . The tale of Florida's development is often sordid, marked by the greed of people intent on taking whatever the land offered and leaving nothing in return."

Today, paradise is spoiled. And we voters have ourselves to blame. We are left with, among many other problems, choking algal blooms, dying fish populations, red tide and human health concerns.

Election after election, with rare exception, we choose lawmakers who place little, if any, value on the long-range health of the environment. These officials, Republicans and Democrats alike, are more beholden to the interests of businesses than they are to the interests of ordinary voters. For decades, our water management districts—charged with protecting out waterways—have allowed business lobbyists, especially those who work for agriculture, to write regulations that circumvent the public good.

Last month, during the 34th annual Everglades Coalition Conference in Duck Key, former Gov. Bob Graham, an environmentalist, did something unique for a politician. He acknowledged that he had failed to do enough to prevent the catastrophes the South Florida Water Management District has allowed to occur year after year because of its policies. While acknowledging his failures, Graham also gave current and future lawmakers a path forward.

I quote him at length: "The current federal law that regulates federal action . . . was written in 1948. That's a long time ago, and it was written primarily—almost exclusively—for the goal of flood control. . . . We now have a much broader palette of issues and the federal statute that authorizes the Army Corps to be engaged with managing those issues needs to reflect that broader palette.

"So the first federal assignment (for attendees) is to initiate the process of rewriting the 1948 flood control act on which all the actions of the Corps of Engineers are now predicated.

"I'm going to be self-critical. I was in the Senate for 18 years. I failed you. I should have done this while I was there. I didn't. Now it's your responsibility."

The hopeful news is that Gov. Ron DeSantis seems to be where Graham never was. One of DeSantis' first moves was to appoint replacements for SFWMD, which oversees Everglades restoration and Lake Okeechobee efforts.

DeSantis also issued an executive order that creates a chief science officer. This office will prepare the state for rising seas and seek solutions to algae outbreaks. These moves are remarkable in light of former Gov. Rick Scott's anti-science actions.

In addition to offering progressive views on the environment, DeSantis is doing what his GOP colleagues historically would not do: find substantial amounts of money for the environment. At two different stops in the state last week, he unveiled a $625 million plan to be spent on water resources.

"I don't want this to take forever," he said in Broward County. "I think there's a sense of urgency."

Even more, he vows to spend $2.5 billion on water resources over the next four years.

"What we're doing in the budget is historic," he said. "It will have a very big impact on the quality of life for Floridians."

Apparently, the new governor wants to restore some of the old pristine Florida he enjoyed as a child growing up in Pinellas County. Whatever his motivations, Floridians should support his early environmental initiatives.

Favorites

Transforming ideas of drug rehabilitation

MAY 21, 2000

Operation PAR Inc., a Pinellas Park-based nonprofit drug treatment agency, is providing hope for many who are victims of drug abuse. Such facilities provide treatment as well as life skills to help the abuser to stay off the drugs and become a successful parent and employee. Programs like these are transforming how Florida's leaders are treating drug abuse.

Sundae, a Florida native, is divorced and has a 4-year-old son. She wants a successful future for the boy, and she dreams of owning a restaurant.

She could just as easily have been a statistic in America's politically charged war on drugs, except that she found a place in Largo that taught her how to turn her life around. She came to grips with her "insanity," as she calls her drug habit, through the help of PAR Village, a residential drug treatment and parenting center.

Sundae's story, and that of PAR, offer some simple human lessons in our societal struggle with demon drugs. They also speak to a remarkable political embrace in a county that long has prided itself on conservative principles of law and order.

From birth, Sundae's home life was dysfunctional. Her parents fought constantly, drank excessively and used drugs. They had diagnosed mental health problems, and they divorced when Sundae (whose last name is being withheld to protect her identity) was 4. During the next 10 years, she went back and forth between the two households. Despite the volatile circumstances, she made excellent grades and was a star athlete.

But when she was 14, her mother committed suicide and everything fell apart. Her grades dropped, and she started drinking booze and smoking marijuana. At 16, she graduated to cocaine and began selling it to schoolmates and whoever else would buy. She got into fights and was arrested for assault and battery and put on house arrest. She went through three high schools and ultimately dropped out.

"I became very self-centered, hateful and very angry," she says.

She got married at 19, entering what she now calls an "abusive relationship that included drug use." After becoming pregnant, she stopped smoking cigarettes, drinking and using and selling drugs. Three months after her son was born, however, the father was convicted and sent to prison. Shortly afterward, her father was sent to federal prison for 20 years.

She returned to drugs.

"To get cocaine, I started spending every dollar I made working and then wrote bad checks and started on a crime spree," she says. "I was insane and ended up in jail 10 times."

Her arrests included grand theft, forgery and possession of drug paraphernalia. She turned to prostitution, robbery. She says she was raped, and her life was constantly in danger. She neglected her son, who was raised by her family.

Then, a police cruiser tried to pull her over one day and she sped away. The police gave chase. She lost control of the car, hit a tree, and, in the process, her boyfriend lost an eye and the mobility in his right leg. She was treated at the hospital and taken directly to jail.

Instead of giving Sundae long jail time, an empathetic judge sentenced her to PAR Village. Perhaps best of all, Sundae's son was permitted to live with her at the 50-bed center for women during her eight-month treatment. Today, because of Operation PAR Inc., a Pinellas Park-based nonprofit drug treatment agency, Sundae and her child are living in their own apartment. She is drug free and is working.

"PAR has provided me with the opportunity to raise my child," she says. "I have a clean slate and have hope for my future. I now have stability in my life. PAR gave me structure and taught me responsibility."

Sundae's plight shows that drug abuse, especially among young people, is not so easily resolved by some of the more fashionable political prescriptions of the day, by elected officials who want to lock 'em up and throw away the key. Thanks to an inspiring community drug treatment program, some of those same politicians are now able to see Sundae in all of her complex humanity, as a vulnerable young woman who gave in to the worst temptation, who did not have the inner strength to create a firewall of self-definition that would protect her.

Today, agencies such as PAR are leading the way in rescuing the Sundaes of this state and nation. At PAR, part of the real story is that it was founded by Republicans, a political party that has had a national history of supporting draconian solutions to drug problems. When Florida's current governor, Jeb Bush, ran against Lawton Chiles the first time in 1994, he was hardly a guy who would have spent time with the likes of Sundae.

Now, however, Bush can be seen at PAR singing the agency's praises. When he recently unveiled his $60-million drug control plan, he did so at the Shirley D. Coletti Academy for Behavioral Change, a PAR residential treatment center for juvenile offenders. His outreach has attracted bipartisan support, as Republicans and Democrats have rallied behind his efforts to combat youthful drug abuse.

In other words, some of the old divisive politics of the war on drugs have given way to an acceptance of the complex, personal face of drug addiction. And old rivals have come together to fund programs such as PAR Village.

Since 1992, when it was established with a five-year grant from the Center for Substance Abuse Treatment, PAR Village has rescued nearly 500 women such as Sundae. When these women improve, their children's chances of living healthy, happy lives are doubled. The agency also has served 853 children either born prior to or during their mother's stay there. Each child born at the facility was drug free at birth, according to official reports.

The profile of typical women entering the center is numbing:

77 percent used cocaine; 5 percent, marijuana; 12 percent, alcohol.
90.2 percent have criminal records.
87 percent were referred by the criminal justice or social system.
60 percent were involved in prostitution.
95 percent were unemployed.
60 percent were pregnant at the time of admission.

The average education level was ninth grade.

36.1 percent had custody of their children, and the average had three children.

Given these statistics, PAR's task of steering its female clients toward a new way of life is daunting. Professionals, such as Rebecca Wade, PAR's nurse educator, know that many addicts have mental-health problems. As part of their preparation to rejoin society, mothers receive parenting training, techniques in discipline and recognition of stages of child development, vocational assessment and employment counseling and advice on sexual trauma. They also attend classes on depression and self-defeating relationships. And academic courses are a centerpiece of the daily routine, which includes: wake up at 5:30 a.m.; roll call at 6:45; dorm clean-up after roll call; breakfast at 8; taking the children to the on-site day care or putting them on their buses to public school; and dorm check at 10:30 p.m.

Training mothers alone, however, is not enough. The children, who in the past would more than likely have been taken from the mothers, also must learn to overcome the effects of their parents' addiction. Most of them have been severely neglected. Therefore, they receive, among other things, speech therapy, medical attention and motor-skills therapy and after-school care designed for those with perinatal drug exposure, which occurs near the time of birth.

PAR Village works because of its systemic, common-sense, practical method. Wade, a registered nurse who conducts group therapy sessions, says that PAR's staff members know their clients want the same things that everyone else wants.

"They want to get a job, have a family and be safe," she says. "They want to be happy. PAR gives them that opportunity. They gain back their self-respect. When you give people back their lives, they become taxpayers and citizens. That's why we help clients with education and help them get jobs. The lack of an education and jobs are what hold addicts back. It's a vicious cycle. It's hopelessness."

Cheryl, 34, is a mother of two boys, and is one of those clients who wants help. She has been at PAR Village for 11 months, after 20 years of abusing drugs and alcohol.

"I finally couldn't do it anymore," Cheryl says. "I wanted to stop the insanity of my addiction. I gave up everything I had for my addiction—my home, my children and any values I had ever been taught."

Cheryl found out about PAR from the state Department of Children and Families, and she was surprised to find out her children could live with her during treatment. Her 4-year-old attends PAR's day care, and her 8-year-old attends a public school. Scheduled to leave PAR in November, she is realistic about her condition and her chances of succeeding on her own. She is ready to go home but knows that she has not totally kicked her addiction.

"I am not cured," she said. "PAR has taught me how to live with my addiction. I have a great support system now, something I didn't have before. I am a better mom now. I spend a lot of time with my children. My 8-year-old knows what's going on. I've explained it to him. He grew up with my addiction. I think I have a bright future now."

Cheryl's new perspective explains the acronym PAR—Parental Awareness and Responsibility. And the seed for PAR was planted in 1969, when Pinellas-Pasco State Attorney James T. Russell, then-Pinellas Sheriff Don Genung, County Commissioner Charles Rainey and others organized a volunteer group to slow youthful drug abuse in the area. One evening, Russell received a telephone call from a neighbor and friend, Shirley Coletti, who told him that her teenage daughter was using drugs.

Coletti wanted help—and information. When the homemaker found nothing, she formed a group of volunteers and went to work. The result today is a private agency with an annual budget of $25-million, a staff of more than 600 and integrated addiction and mental health services at various sites in Hernando, Pinellas, Pasco and Manatee counties. Last year, PAR treated nearly 12,000 clients.

Even after 30 years as PAR's president, Coletti still speaks of her mission with passion, and her determination to keep families and their children away from substance abuse is stronger than ever.

"When we talk about drug rehabilitation, we are really talking about habilitation," she says. "We're talking about teaching people new skills so they can learn to live quality, drug-free lives. This also includes leisure skills. Just ask an addict what they do during their leisure time, and their answer will be 'get high' or 'go to the bar.' Most drug abusers, regardless of their age, have never experienced healthy hobbies or recreational activities."

Like other veterans of the nation's therapeutic community, Coletti is tough, and she is realistic about the profound allure of drugs and their far-reaching impact. "Recovering from drugs and alcohol use requires a lifelong commitment from the drug user, their family and their community," she says. "On average, one or two episodes of treatment cannot arrest an individual's addiction, particularly severe chronic use."

The main key to solving drug abuse, Coletti says, is making entire families aware and responsible. Too many children, such as 18-year-old Josh, grow up seeing one or both of their parents using drugs. Although his mother has been drug-free for 11 years, Josh remembers the old days and how her addiction influenced him to start smoking marijuana.

"When I was 14, I was smoking a lot of pot," he says. "I came to treatment just to keep from going to prison. But now that I've been here, I see that my life has changed a whole lot. When I get out of here in June, I want to go to college or a vocational school. I know I can do it because I have faith in myself now. I'm also very close to my mother, grandmother and brother. I believe I can make it now."

Susan Latvala, chairman of PAR's board of directors and a member of the Pinellas School Board, knows that PAR can help teenagers such as Josh turn their lives around. Like Coletti and many others with the agency, she is a veteran of the drug wars and carries personal scars. She sought Coletti's help several years after her teenage son became addicted to drugs.

"My commitment to PAR developed through my son's treatment and the fact that our whole family was educated on the facts of drug addiction, treatment, relapse and long-term recovery," she says. "Drug addiction cannot be cured by inoculation. It requires long-term behavioral change as well as a strong family and community-support system.

"I am convinced that we can dramatically improve the quality of life in our community, state and country if we prevent children from ever using drugs and provide long-term treatment to those families already affected. There is no pain like the pain of seeing your own child suffering and headed for failure. There is no joy like seeing that child whole again."

To his credit, Gov. Bush, unlike many of his counterparts in other states, is listening and acting. He has rejected the harsh, punitive approach to youthful drug abuse popular just a few years ago. Florida's therapeutic community welcomes his goal of reducing substance abuse in Florida by half in five years through prevention, treatment and increased law enforcement. His plan will add approximately 10,000 beds to treatment centers statewide and two drug-enforcement units in South Florida and one in Central Florida.

While many other residential treatment programs around the country are reporting negligible success with their clients, PAR's statistics remain impressive. Studies show that individuals who remain in residence for more than 90 days reduce their use of drugs and criminal activity and are more likely to return to school and find a job. The overwhelming majority of those who complete their treatment stop using drugs altogether—especially when family, friends and others support them.

PAR's success is directly attributable to the hard work of Coletti and her staff and perhaps, unwittingly, to the bipartisanship that has begun to transform how Florida elected officials and civic leaders view treating youthful drug abuse. In other words, when a child is in trouble with a substance, both Democrats and Republicans are helping. It is this shared willingness to look at the faces of individuals, such as those of Sundae, Cheryl and Josh, that offers perhaps the greatest hope of all.

A favorite spot of quiet inspiration

JUNE 7, 2000

The affliction lacks a proper name, but a lot of us have it and most of us are not looking for a cure. It is a passion for libraries.

Paul Dickson, author

Even as the Internet moves more and more information into cyberspace and away from human touch, the public library system, including libraries on college campuses that are open to the public, remains one of the nation's most important institutions. And, by the way, the first library in America was founded in 1638 at Harvard University.

The first library I fell in love with was in Crescent City. My grandmother was a maid, and one of her sites was the Crescent City Women's Club. In addition to being a meeting place and dining room, the facility served as the public library, housing about 2,000 books.

When my grandmother took me to help clean the building one Saturday morning when I was 15, I fell in love with the smell of old leather and parchment. From that morning on, I came with her often, spending more time reading than cleaning. The woman in charge let me check out books. I was the only black person who used the library in those days.

Wherever I lived after leaving Crescent City, I found a library. At Wiley College in Texas, I had the campus Carnegie Library. In the Marine Corps, I found a local public library. In Chicago, I had the University of

Chicago's Regenstein Library and the Newberry. In Gainesville, I had the University of Florida libraries.

Here in St. Petersburg, the Nelson Poynter Memorial Library on the University of South Florida's Bayboro campus is my favorite hangout. Over the years, I have written dozens of columns on the third floor. In fact, I am writing this column at my favorite carrel. Sometimes I use my laptop. Other times I write in longhand.

For me, this is an ideal place to write because I am surrounded by books. It is quiet even when many students are around. And the scenery to the east is spectacular. When I feel burned out or otherwise distracted, I come here for respite and inspiration. I have a view of Bayboro Harbor and Tampa Bay beyond the Coast Guard facility. Sailboats come and go in the water below, and ships plow the far horizon. Mullet and other fish leap into the air.

On a clear day, I can see the outline of Ruskin and its environs. To the south, the grassy promenade between the library and the Dali Museum serves as a playground for children and tourists. Often, I spot lovers strolling hand-in-hand or lying entangled on the grass. A group of African American boys used to swim in the harbor before the seawall was erected. It is a serene place. A variety of small- to medium-sized terns are in abundance. I love to watch these sleek, slender-billed hunters. They fly in a buoyant or hovering fashion and dive headfirst for tiny fish. Often, baby terns, no bigger than golf balls, take their first flights from the library's roof. Staff members routinely rescue those that fail to become airborne. Occasionally, a brown pelican will swoop down toward a fishing boat in search of a freebie.

Tall palms, their fronds gently swaying, stand like sentinels outside the window, and huge white clouds linger against a blue sky.

My greatest challenges are remaining focused and not becoming too distracted by the beauty and quietude of the place. Until now, I have told only a few other people about this spot. I have shown it to even fewer people.

Interestingly, Kathy Arsenault, the library's interim director, tells me that I have several soul mates who use this spot to write. And who are they? Ministers who need peace and quiet to write their sermons. Perhaps I have found the right place after all.

Sad goodbye to 28th Street Drive-In

JUNE 21, 2000

If you are a Pinellas County resident nostalgic for drive-in theaters, you had better unfold that rumble seat, rinse out that favorite thermos and truck out to 4990 28th St. N. On June 30, the county's one remaining ozoner—the 28th Street Drive-In—will not see another moonlit, starry night. Gone, too, will be those steamy car windows. Remember them? The 50-year-old theater is shutting down forever.

The land it is on has been sold to the school board. Citing stricter zoning laws, high land prices and a shortage of large tracts of land, Harold Spears, president of the company that owns the theater, told the *St. Petersburg Times* that "it is practically impossible to build a new drive-in theater today."

I, like thousands of other Floridians, fondly remember the drive-in theater. In fact, my family, many of my childhood acquaintances and I had a love affair with the drive-in. I grew up in the 1950s and early 1960s as a migrant farmworker. Each year, I followed my family and others from South Florida to Virginia, Delaware, New Jersey, upstate New York, Michigan and back to Florida. We harvested melons, potatoes, tomatoes, beans, apples and cherries. We rarely stayed in one place longer than two months.

We worked hard, often six days a week, from first light to last. But at the week's end, everyone—old men and women, teenagers on hormones and young children—knew that a great reward awaited us down the road or in a neighboring town: the drive-in theater.

Indeed, no matter where we traveled, a drive-in was within driving distance. As black migrant farmworkers, we were always strangers. Few local blacks wanted us in their part of town and, of course, no whites wanted anything to do with us. We always lived in migrant camps or in designated sites out of town.

Rarely were we welcomed in indoor theaters. But drive-ins were different. Each Saturday or Sunday night, no matter where we were—Hastings, Fla., Raleigh, N.C., Exmore, Va., Dover, Del., Long Island, N.Y.—we found a Sunset or a Starlite or a Sky-Vue or some other named drive-in.

And we were a sight to behold: dozens of migrants in a caravan of old pickups and beat-up Buicks, Chevys, Fords and Pontiacs pulling up to the entrance of a theater. The owners loved our hard-earned bucks, and we loved the amenities of the outdoor theater.

The movies, always awful, were a wondrous respite from the daily toil in the fields, orchards and groves. The cherry Cokes, the hot dogs and burgers, the candy bars, the popcorn and other treats made us feel as if we were part of the human race after all.

"Drive-in night," as we called it, was the one time that we dressed up and put on perfume or cologne. The concession stand gave us our one real opportunity to mingle with the local residents. At the stand, the locals seemed to forgive us for being "dirty outsiders" as we forgave them, at least temporarily, for having snubbed us during the rest of the week.

In a strange way, the drive-in experience gave us dignity. All week, as we sweated in the hot sun, ate our meals in the fields, rested under trees or beneath truck beds or wagons, we laughed and talked about the latest stupid zombie or biker movie we had seen.

The drive-in, always reasonably priced, fortified us like nothing else could.

Each weekday was one day closer to drive-in night. Even now, I believe that knowing we were going to the drive-in at week's end made farmwork bearable, at least for the children. The movies also gave our parents some greatly needed time away from their energetic offspring. More than a few future fieldhands were conceived on drive-in night.

So, if you remember drive-ins fondly and want to re-create that old under-the-sky feeling, time is running out in Pinellas County and the rest of the country. Short of physically going to a drive-in, the best ticket these days may be the vicarious experience found on drive-in websites and in books.

Me—I prefer books. The best on the market on this subject are written by husband-and-wife team Don and Susan Sanders. Published in 1997, their first such book, *The American Drive-In Movie Theatre*, is a colorful work that covers nearly every aspect of the industry. Some of the photographs, such as those of lovers making out on the front seat of their car or those juicy hotdogs dripping with mustard, make you go back in time. Their second book, *Drive-In Movie Memories*, is a wonderful collection of the personal experiences of writers nationwide. A version of my experiences above is published in *Memories*.

I say goodbye to the 28th Street Drive-In with a lump in my throat. This old under-the-stars emporium, like others nationwide, was a valuable piece of Americana that will not be forgotten.

Florida Crackers, a vanishing breed

JUNE 28, 2000

Last weekend, while checking on wooded property I own in Levy County, I visited a friend I had not seen in two years. He, his wife, three adult children and four grandchildren live in the same three-bedroom, dog-trot house that has been in the family since the 1920s.

They are, in the tradition of Florida's last governor, Lawton Chiles, Florida Crackers. And they are a vanishing breed. I always enjoy visiting my friend and former neighbor because his lifestyle is fascinating. No, it is inscrutable. Although I spent many of my childhood years near Crackers, I understand very little about them, except their fierce independence.

In many parts of the state today, they are virtually invisible—staying to themselves, moving on the outskirts of society.

Author Marjorie Kinnan Rawlings had a well-known love-hate relationship with her Cracker neighbors. Many become characters in her fiction.

"Here, in the uncivilized Cracker interior of Florida, you insult a man in half-friendly fashion by calling him a damned Georgia Cracker," she writes in her short story "Cracker Chidlings." "Nine times out of ten you have hit the mark. Georgia Crackerdom, joined by a thin stream of Carolinians and a still thinner one of Virginians, has flowed lazily into the lakes and rivers, and created Florida Crackerdom.

"Georgia Cracker and Florida Cracker have a common ancestor in the vanished driver of oxen, who cracked yards of rawhide whip over his beasts and so came by his name. One hates the other as mothers and daughters sometimes hate. I saw the hate flicker into words at the doings in Anthony."

Indeed, in Mascotte and Groveland, where my family lived across the pond from several Cracker families, I witnessed intra-Cracker fury between Georgia and Florida strains. These clans—men, women and children—never used guns or knives. They beat the hell out of one another with fists, kicks, teeth and clubs. The sheriff, the infamous Willis McCall at the time, and a deputy would drive out to the homes but would sit in the truck or cruiser and observe.

Somehow, the combatants always stopped short of drawing too much blood or breaking enough bones to hobble someone. All the while, screams and profanities would leap across the pond, and seven or eight hungry- and mangy-looking dogs would start a parallel fight.

Then, the strangest thing would happen: Each Saturday morning, these enemies would gather in one yard and travel to town together. Here is how Florida historian James M. Denham describes this phenomenon:

"It was a sort of gala occasion. . . . Each family formed a little procession of its own, all in single file, with the head of the household leading off, with his long rifle on his shoulder. . . . Then came the cart—the family carriage—driven by a half-clad urchin mounted on the back of the horse or mule with his knees drawn up and his feet resting on the shafts. In the cart rode those of the family too young or too feeble to walk; and these shared the limited space of the clapboard buggy with the whiskey jug and two or three dry hides brought along to barter. The mother, always at the head, (was) followed by the daughters in the order of age."

My friend is the quintessential Cracker. He is, as Rawlings describes them, lawless. "They are living an entirely natural, and very hard life, disturbing no one. . . . Yet almost everything they do is illegal. And everything they do is necessary to sustain life."

Indeed, my friend, for example, hunts out of season and fishes beyond the limit. Although he has a driver's license, he does not believe in licenses of any kind. The earth is his to pluck—without government interference. His grandchildren carry this same attitude to public school each morning.

None of the children holds a traditional job. They, including the women, do odd jobs for friends and neighbors and somehow live off the land. In fact, he cleared the land for my house, built the barn and stable for my horse, helped me fence my pasture and often mowed my yard. At the same time, though, he regularly stole my apples, pears and peaches and raided my vegetable garden when I was out of town. I have no proof, but I am certain that he took my chicken eggs, too.

In 1975, Florida historian Clark I. Cross summed up Cracker life: "There is an Old Florida, call it Cracker Florida if you will, where a distinctive way of life and attitudes persist, where houses and barns seem little changed but this Florida exists only in pockets and seems harder to find every passing year."

Today, Old Florida—Cracker Florida—is vanishing faster than ever.

Honored diplomat felt racism at home

JULY 19, 2000

As the most important Mideast peace talks in a generation wind down at Camp David, I am reminded of the years 1948 and 1949, when United Nations diplomat Ralph J. Bunche—an African American—was the chief mediator between Arabs and Jews on the island of Rhodes for 81 days non-stop.

He negotiated a truce in the Arab-Israeli war and was influential in the first partition of Palestine that gave half of the nation to the Arabs and half to the Jews, that placed Jerusalem virtually under UN control. He urged the Arab states to recognize the new state of Israel and helped to legitimize the Jewish state in the world community.

For his singular efforts, Bunche, U.N. Under Secretary General for Special Political Affairs, was awarded the Nobel Peace Prize in 1950, becoming the first African American so honored. Although he is best known for his work in the Middle East, he brought his mediating skills to many other international hot spots, including Congo, Cyprus and Kashmir.

Few people today know anything about this extraordinary man, whose image was placed on the 20-cent stamp in 1982.

Born in Detroit in 1903, his parents died before he was 14. Orphaned, his sister and he went to live with their maternal grandmother in Los Angeles. He immediately proved himself a brilliant student and graduated valedictorian of his 1922 class at Jefferson High School. He attended the University of California at Los Angeles on scholarship. There, he excelled in football and basketball.

After graduating from UCLA with a bachelor's degree and Phi Beta Kappa honors, he went to Harvard and earned a master's degree and doctorate in government and international relations. He went on to do advanced study in anthropology at Northwestern University, the University of Cape Town and the London School of Economics. Then, he joined the faculty of Howard University in the nation's capital, where he organized and chaired the Political Science Department.

Old sports injuries kept him out of military service during World War II, but he joined the War Department as an analyst of African and Far Eastern affairs. His rise through the ranks of the Strategic Services was meteoric. At war's end in 1944, he was one of the officials who helped to establish the international agency that would be the United Nations. Bunche's negotiating prowess became apparent immediately, and Secretary General Trygve Lie hired him as a top assistant.

He served with distinction in various capacities until his death on Dec. 9, 1971. With the exception of Andrew Young, Donald McHenry, Ron Brown and Bunche, few blacks have figured prominently in U.S. foreign policy. The irony, which most of his contemporaries tried to bury, was that while Bunche was blazing new trails in international diplomacy, he was the victim of racism in his own country. He could not, for example, rent or buy in Washington's racially segregated neighborhoods or dine in downtown restaurants. And he suffered countless racist snubs and remarks from legislators.

Early in his career—even as he served on the board of the NAACP and marched with the Rev. Martin Luther King Jr. in the Selma to Montgomery march—Bunche did not discuss the bigotry he faced each day. Later, after recognizing the similarities between colonialism in Africa and racism at home, he argued that "segregation and democracy are incompatible."

The year following his triumph in Rhodes, he was asked to become assistant secretary of state. He rejected the post, saying, "Frankly, there's too much Jim Crow in Washington for me. I wouldn't take my kids back there." Even though his name was constantly in the news as Secretary General Dag Hammarskjold's point man, his son was refused membership in the West Side Tennis Club at Forest Hills. Bunche went on the attack, received an apology and was offered club membership. He rejected the offer, believing it was because of his personal prestige and not on the ideal of racial justice.

"No Negro American can be free from the disabilities of race in this country until the lowliest Negro in Mississippi is no longer disadvantaged because of his race," he said.

When he died at age 67, his accomplishments in foreign affairs were not fully appreciated by a nation that measured him by the color of his skin.

Lake Wales

AUGUST 31, 2000

The flowers are beautiful, yes, but they aren't the only attraction. There's another glorious garden resident: the butterfly.

Less than two hours from the Tampa Bay area lies Bok Tower Gardens, one of Florida's best-kept secrets.

I discovered the gardens as a child in the late 1950s. My father and I were driving from Groveland to Belle Glade when I saw the famous Singing Tower rise above the distant tree line and punctuate the sky. My father, a labor contractor, took little interest in nature for nature's sake, so I had to beg him to detour and drive to the gardens.

Once there, however, even he was moved by the beauty of the place: the interplay of every shade of green imaginable, the commingling of shadow and light. When the carillon sounded, everyone, including my old man, stopped and looked up. I knew then that I was home.

The vibrant colors of the plants bordering the paths held my attention. Never had I seen so many different colors in one place. But my real love affair with the gardens became permanent when I discovered the butterflies.

Here was a year-round, teeming color show that was mine for the price of a few dollars and an appreciation for one of nature's most alluring creatures. After that first day, I have returned there many times, often just to observe butterflies.

I recently befriended several avid butterfly watchers, who have shown me that specific knowledge enhances the experience tenfold. Florida butterfly lovers should know that Byrum and Linda Cooper of the Lake Region Audubon Society in Winter Haven have developed a provisional checklist of Bok's 56 species of butterflies.

For each, the common and scientific names are given, and the months it is in the gardens and the degree of its abundance are listed. Here, for example, is how an entry reads: "Species: Pipevine Swallowtail / Battus philenor / Month: 1-12 / Abundance: common to uncommon." The two other abundance designations are "abundant" and "rare."

Abundant means that you are likely to see more than 20 of that species per visit to the right habitat; common, you are likely to see four to 20 per visit; uncommon, zero to three per visit; rare, unlikely to see any per visit, but they do appear from time to time.

Everyone with whom I have spoken finds the checklist useful. Free copies are in the gardens' gift shop. On my most recent visit, I bought a copy of *Florida's Fabulous Butterflies*, a colorful book by University of Florida entomologist Thomas Emmel and *National Wildlife* and BBC wildlife photographer Brian Kenney. Although the gift shop stocks other butterfly books, I like this one best because of its lush pictures, detailed information and easy-to-read prose. Most of the insects in the book can be found in the gardens.

One recent Sunday, I used the book to identify a Florida viceroy, or *Limenitis archippus*. The viceroy, found statewide, is one of my favorites because it is a trickster. While in South Florida, it adopts a rich brown to mimic the queen butterfly. When in the northern counties, it becomes red-orange to mimic the monarch. Emmel writes that the viceroy favors moist terrain and swamps along lakes and streams where willow trees thrive.

Near the reflection pool and tower, I spotted the stout, hairy body of a male tropical checkered skipper, its black checks arranged in bands on a white background. True to form, it was flying a few inches above the ground hunting for a female. A few yards away, a female, with darker coloring, fed on reddish flowers. The male detected her and flittered toward her. As if teasing, she caught a breeze and floated into a tall orangish lantana.

With my book, checklist and binoculars, I wandered throughout the gardens for two hours. I saw a cloudless sulphur, cassius blue, white peacock, Carolina satyr, several dorantes longtail and an ocola skipper. I wrote on my checklist each habitat, type of plant that attracted the insects, brightness of the sun and time of day.

I have learned that in many cases, consistency pays off when looking for a butterfly showing. For example, I head straight for multicolored impatiens, native milkweed, lantana, blazing star, butterfly bush and thistle going to seed. Nine times out of 10, I will find colors darting in and out of flowers.

The beauty of journalism

APRIL 15, 2001

Believe it or not, journalism can be a dangerous profession. In 1999, 34 journalists were killed around the world just for doing their job, reporting and writing. Eighty-seven others were imprisoned. A *Tampa Tribune* reporter, whom I knew, was killed in Peru several years ago as he investigated drug trafficking in the mountains there.

Two years ago, I had the dubious honor of spending a day in a Gaza City jail for photographing a Palestinian Authority building.

All that said, journalism can be fun, and it is always interesting, especially for those of us who regularly get out of the office. For us, finding a place to write and a way to transmit our copy are the greatest challenges. Quite often, the process is down-right crazy.

As a boy in Florida during the height of the civil rights movement, I used to marvel at the journalists who came down South. To me, they were as brave as Marines, and I wanted to be like them.

In St. Augustine, the scene of some of the nation's most violent racial confrontations, reporters and commentators faced down armed Klansmen, some in St. Johns County sheriff's uniforms, snarling German shepherds, powerful water hoses, billy clubs and civilian mobs who wanted to kill "nigger lovers." These were white men, many fresh out of college, trying to do their job, trying to report on bigotry and injustice. To this day, I love their memory.

Some of the bravest reporters I have known wrote for the tiny *Daily Commercial* in Leesburg. They had the dangerous task of covering the deeds and misdeeds of the late Willis McCall, the infamous sheriff of Lake County. McCall, the representative of decency and law and order, thought nothing of eliminating black men: He shot one prisoner to death, shot and wounded another, and, a few years later, kicked another prisoner to death in a cell. That act finally brought the governor down on McCall's head.

Those who wrote about McCall, such as Emmit Peter and Mike Archer, did so knowing that the big, pot-bellied sheriff might take revenge.

He often did. In 1954, for example, according to news accounts, Mabel Norris Reese, editor of *Topic*, Mount Dora's weekly newspaper, wrote some scathing stuff about McCall. The angry lawman poisoned Reese's dog, painted "KKK" across the windows of her office and placed a burning cross in her yard.

The tough editor persevered, however.

Even today, reporters risk physical harm in many parts of the country. Mob hits remain a real possibility. During the Florida Senate race last November, a Republican candidate approached me in a grocery store parking lot and threatened to rearrange my face and kick my "black" hind quarters. Fortunately for me, or the candidate, a St. Petersburg Police Department employee witnessed the encounter and saved the day.

A *St. Petersburg Times* reporter was accosted on election night of the city's recent mayoral contest.

Finding a suitable place to write always makes journalism interesting. I have seen reporters sit on the ground in battlefields typing away or writing in longhand. I have seen them duck bullets and mortar fire while taking notes. The legendary Ernie Pyle was killed while writing in combat. Ernest Hemingway writes of near misses in combat.

I was not a reporter in the Marine Corps, so I never experienced writing under fire. But I have written whole columns on airplanes, in airports, in telephone booths, in the front and back seats of cars, in the bed of a pickup. While writing about floods in Arkansas several years ago, I had to climb up a tree to write. It was the only dry spot around.

I will never forget when I covered Hurricane Elena. I wrote from the roof of my Chevy pickup. From that perch, I could see the Gulf of Mexico pound the old buildings, including one of my favorite seafood restaurants on Cedar Key.

Over the years, I have written many columns in bathrooms. I write in bathrooms when I am traveling with someone else and I must work late at night or into the morning hours. I do this so as not to keep my companions awake.

As for transmitting copy, difficulties crop up like weeds, especially in the electronic age. When I was in Israel in 1996, I had no trouble sending my copy by modem from the Laromme Hotel. Two years later, however, I had a bad telephone line everywhere I stayed and wound up downloading to a disk, printing and faxing. Last year, in Poland and Romania, I was forced to telephone the office and dictate everything.

That East European experience reminded me of the good ol' days, when frantic reporters would phone in their stories to rewrite editors, those living legends who could make a hack sound like a genius. I should know. The first daily newspaper I wrote for had a rewrite man who made lousy prose sing. He set my linguistic monstrosities to music, often.

My biggest fear these days while on the road is this: Staring at deadline, I may wind up having to write with pen, pencil and paper. My laptop (the company's laptop) has ruined my ability to write by hand. My thoughts do not come well when I am not in front of a computer. A blank computer screen does not scare me. A blank sheet of paper does. Sure, I have written complete columns in notebooks. I wrote a piece about New York's Cardinal Egan in a bar on Amsterdam Avenue. But I struggled.

Despite the dangers, the unconventional offices (trees, parking lots, toilets) and transmission headaches, I do not want to do anything else for a living. Sometimes journalism is true high anxiety. That is the beauty of it all.

The source of my interest in the Middle East

APRIL 7, 2002

Because I often write about the Middle East, especially about the Israeli-Palestinian conflict, many readers have asked me to explain why I—an African American who is neither Jew nor Muslim—cares about this subject so deeply. It is a fair question, and I feel compelled to answer.

I visited Israel for the first time when I was 13 years old. The occasion, along with everything that occurred before and after that trip, inspired my interest in the region and shaped my politics toward it today.

My paternal grandparents, like the overwhelming majority of African Americans of their generation, were devout Christians with a love for the Holy Land. Everyone I knew as a child dreamed of traveling to the Middle East, especially to what we called "The Land of Israel" and Egypt.

For my grandfather, Israel was more than a dream. This little old man, a presiding elder in a Pentecostal denomination, announced to his congregation of 35 members that he was going to Israel and would be delighted if others would accompany him.

That service turned into a marathon planning session. Women went home and cooked dishes and brought them to the church, men barbecued and other members fetched cold drinks. We had what is called "dinner on the ground."

Before the day ended, 20 adult members had signed up to travel with Grandfather. They would depart one year later.

For us, the Holy Land, which included all the nations in the region, was destiny. It was where Jesus Christ was born and was crucified. It was where Moses led the Israelites from bondage, where the Red Sea was parted, where the walls of Jericho tumbled, where Saul marched toward Damascus, where Adam and Eve dwelled in the Garden of Eden, where Mount Sinai was shrouded in clouds, where Solomon handed down wise decisions, where Jesus performed miracles.

The Holy Land was a mythic and mystical place where everything—including rising from the dead—was possible.

Members went to work raising money and getting passports. They cooked, washed cars, held raffles, begged and reached into their pockets. Within six months, they had enough money to send the entire congregation to Israel for seven days. In the end, 26 adults and eight children went. I was one of the children.

This was the trip of my life.

When we arrived, Israel was not two decades old. Zionism was not a dirty word and kibbutzim was the way of life for many. Our group was a wonder to behold for most Israelis who had never seen black people in the flesh. But we were treated respectfully and had full access to all of the Christian holy sites.

Steeped in the region's history and folklore, my grandfather hired the right guide. We stayed in a kibbutz near the River Jordan. Imagine how I felt, a mere child, actually dipping my toes in this famous body of water, where Jesus had been.

We saw the Dead Sea, and we sailed across the Sea of Galilee, also called Lake Tiberias. As a child, I was there, in the place where Jesus and his disciples had been, where rough waters had tested the faith of devout believers.

Our group walked where Jesus had walked. I noticed that my childhood companions, who normally would have been unruly, were awed by the historicity and geography.

We were in a holy place.

In Bethlehem at the Church of the Nativity, the site of Jesus' birth, some members broke down and cried uncontrollably, Grandfather among them. In Nazareth, where Jesus spent his childhood and adult life, we walked the narrow streets trying to imagine the daily activities of Jesus the carpenter.

Our visit to Jerusalem, the final leg of our tour, changed the lives of many in our group. During our three days there, we relived the agony of Christ's final days on earth. We visited the Mount of Olives and the sites where Christ was put to death and rose from the dead.

Even before we left Israel, I knew I would return often. My grandfather dreamed of returning, but he died without seeing the Holy Land again.

For my part, I have returned many times, most recently nearly two years ago. During my early trips, I was what could be called an unequivocal Friend of Israel, which meant that I sided with Israeli Jews in all of their relations with the Palestinians.

Today, I am not an unequivocal Friend of Israel.

I am a friend of Israel, and I am a friend of the Palestinians. I want peace for the region, for all of its people. I believe, however, that Israel—with the upper hand, with vast military weaponry, with the power to shut down borders, with the power to detain thousands of people at one time, with the power to restrict travel and determine where people live, with the power to destroy entire cities—must learn to use its power to bring dignity to the lives of the Palestinians.

My travels to the region and my reading have taught me that the Israelis can change the politics of this enduring conflict whenever they want to.

I had planned to return to Israel this summer. Obviously, I must put this plan on hold. Each day, I look at a coffee mug I bought in a Haifa gift shop on my second trip to Israel in the 1960s. It reads: "Pray for Peace in the Holy Land."

Indeed, my hope for peace keeps me returning to the region, and this desire to return keeps my interest refreshed.

A friendship that endured in racist time

MAY 19, 2002

I am one of those African American men who can sincerely say that he has had a true white friend. I will call him Paul (not his real name) because many of his relatives are still alive and my column is published in newspapers some relatives may likely read.

Ours was a friendship born of its time and place, the racially turbulent 1960s in the American South. Ours was a friendship defined by race, racism and the fractured dynamics emanating from old hatreds we were cast into.

I met Paul during the summer of 1964, when I was a 19-year-old sophomore at an all-black Texas college. I had traveled to Birmingham, Ala., with students from my campus to establish a system for registering blacks to vote. Paul, also a sophomore, was a reporter for the University of Alabama student newspaper. He spent three days shadowing my group for a story.

What struck me first were his long red hair, Howdy Doody features and thick Southern accent. I hardly understood him the first time he interviewed me. But I noticed something else about him, a significant trait I have seen in other whites in subsequent years and circumstances: He approached our all-black group with an earnest desire to understand. He did not have a bias to satisfy. He wanted to know what compelled a group of privileged black students to risk limb and life in George Wallace's and Bull Connor's Alabama.

When we left Birmingham a week later, Paul promised to visit my campus, Wiley College in Marshall, Texas. His sincerity and non-judgmental manner convinced me that I would see him again. Two weeks later, Paul came to Wiley. I introduced him to my handful of friends and my favorite professors. I was still on the football team, and Paul watched us play a losing game against Jackson State University.

During the rest of the year, we saw each other often. I would visit his campus, and he would visit mine. A year later, I quit college and joined the Marine Corps and went off to war. Paul went on to graduate, and he took a reporting job with a small newspaper in southeastern Alabama.

There, his life changed forever, and the bond between us became stronger although we were thousands of miles apart. As a reporter, he focused on the civil rights movement and the violence surrounding it. He covered the marches of Dr. Martin Luther King and the Southern Christian Leadership Conference, and he wrote several articles that exposed Klan activity. For his efforts, he was brutally beaten three times, the last beating putting him in the hospital for three weeks.

When I was discharged from the Marine Corps, I returned to Florida and graduated from Bethune-Cookman College in Daytona Beach. Paul already had taken a reporting job in South Florida. Many years later, after teaching at several colleges in Illinois and Wisconsin, I again returned to Florida, and Paul and I wound up writing for the same paper.

We covered street gang-related stories together. On one occasion, Paul probably saved my life by wrestling a handgun from a skinhead hell-bent on "taking out a nigger," as the skinhead had said pointing the weapon at my chest.

Paul and I fished together, sailed his sloop in the Atlantic and the Gulf of Mexico, bar-hopped, camped, hiked and traveled the state in search of interesting stories. I introduced him to two black women. He fell for both. He lived with one for three years and asked her to marry him. She refused and left him because the "racism mess," as she called their encounters with other people in public, was too high a price to pay. Her biggest regret was that Paul's relatives, all in Alabama, refused to meet her.

His relatives also barred me from their homes and refused all of my invitations to have dinner in restaurants. In time, they disowned Paul, calling him "the nigger loving branch of the family."

I often asked Paul to explain how he turned out so differently. He did not have an instructive answer, only a personal revelation: "I simply don't hate black people. I have no reason to hate. I just don't feel it."

He was good for me. His example made me re-evaluate my views about race and white people as a group and as individuals. My segregated, racist upbringing in the South had marked me with a simmering hatred of whites. I trusted few of them and always expected the worst when I encountered them.

Through his actions—not through a complex philosophy of words— Paul enlightened me. Sure, I recognized—and still do—racism and racist whites when I see them. But Paul taught me to accept individuals one at a time, each on his or her merits.

I have white male friends today because Paul—born into a family of incorrigible racists—taught me how to trust.

Paul died two weeks ago of complications related to diabetes. He was 56. I telephoned his brother in Alabama and said I wanted to attend the funeral. His response, which I wrote in my journal, was clear: "Stay away from us. We don't want your kind around here."

Even in death, racism is a powerful force. But it cannot diminish the bonds of true friendship.

Words of advice for a young, black male

OCTOBER 16, 2002

San Angelo, Texas

A few days ago while I was shopping for groceries, a young African American teenager and his father approached.

"My son says you're Bill Maxwell, the writer," the man said, his tone suggesting doubt.

When I nodded affirmatively, the boy shouted, "I told you!"

The father, an airman 1st Class stationed at Goodfellow Air Force Base in San Angelo, shook my hand and said he had wanted to meet me.

He had read my columns about black children and liked them. His son, a ninth-grader, is performing poorly in school and has "fallen in with the wrong crowd."

He wanted to know if I had advice for his child. The boy rolled his eyes and leaned back, signaling he did not want to listen to the bromides of a gray-haired stranger. The father also rolled his eyes, signaling to the youngster that his negative attitude was showing.

To make a long story short, the father invited me to eat lunch with him and his son at a Mexican restaurant. He wanted me to talk to the boy, who stayed in trouble in and out of school.

"You're a writer and a professor," the father said. "Maybe he'll listen to you."

The boy rolled his eyes as I began what has become my sermon to all black children, especially males, struggling with self-identity, peer pressure and parental expectations. I am summarizing what I said because some of it may be useful to other young people:

In all public settings, black males need to realize that they are being watched constantly, that they are rarely invisible, that they are judged by how they play out a host of negative stereotypes. The questions become: How do you want to be perceived? Do you want to be accepted in this environment? How do you want to be treated? And, of course, do you have any control over what happens to you?

Many black males see themselves as victims of a world filled with arbitrary adult rules. Indeed, society is rule-bound. At the risk of oversimplification, I believe that each person either chooses to obey or disobey the rules. Life is much easier and more enjoyable when we obey time-tested rules.

"Obeying rules gives you power over your life," I said. "If you want to be accepted and treated well, you must act appropriately in any given circumstance."

The boy said he wanted to fit in with his black friends. I sensed his confusion and earnestness. Who does not want to fit in with one's peers? Children must learn, however, when to draw the line, when to recognize that certain ideas, behaviors and acts are negative and yield negative, self-destructive results. Black males, especially, should avoid the negative. The very notion that being smart equals acting white, for example, is a sure path to failure and rejection in a culture that relies more and more on accountability and performance.

African American boys should learn how to say no—not merely in word but in action. From my work with young people through the foundation I am associated with and through teaching, I have learned that standing up and refusing to follow the negative wishes of the crowd often becomes a source of inner strength that builds self-confidence.

If the group wants to skip class or play a video game rather than complete homework, refuse and tell your pals why you refuse. I have seen children in our foundation turn their lives around for the good by standing up for themselves, by holding firm to the positive.

Racism is a major problem for black children, especially males. It has caused many youngsters to hate themselves and to hate others. The self-hating child believes that he is inferior to others, especially to whites. Here is a piece of wisdom my grandfather, the preacher, taught me: "You're inferior only when you let people make you inferior."

Look inside yourself and find the good whenever others paint you negatively. You are never devoid of goodness. Recognize that goodness, and let it guide your thoughts and actions.

When I was his age, I told the teen, I wanted to be a writer. My friends, along with some grown people, told me that migrant farmworkers were too dumb to write. I knew they were wrong. Why? Because I secretly wrote every night no matter where we were in the country. I was told that migrants did not attend college. Although we could barely feed ourselves sometimes, I knew I would attend college.

"I looked for the good and the positive inside myself," I said. "I'm not inferior. I'm as good as anyone else."

I have no way of knowing how much of my sermon got through to this youngster. But I do know this: He was leaning forward, and he was not rolling his eyes when I finished.

Don't be afraid of democracy

MARCH 23, 2003

One of my favorite thinkers, environmentalist Edward Abbey, observed: "I love America because it is a confused, chaotic mess—and I hope we can keep it this way for at least another thousand years. The permissive society is the free society. Who gave us permission to live this way? Nobody did. We did. And that's the way it should be—only more so. The best cure for the ills of democracy is more democracy."

Since the Sept. 11 attacks, American democracy—that confused, chaotic mess—has been put to the test like never before, and the very meaning of citizenship is being redefined.

In fact, what we have in the United States today is a war between two or more views of democracy and the definition of what we mean when we call ourselves a "free society."

Civil liberties are not what they used to be. Many of the freedoms that we, at least I, took for granted before the World Trade Center and Pentagon attacks are being obliterated by a Republican administration that is blinded by its messianic zeal.

Go out today and speak of privacy, the bedrock of our culture. Chances are, you will become an object of derision. Privacy is whatever the president and the attorney general say it is.

And, for sure, as the president presses the Bush war in Iraq, you had better be careful where you attempt to practice your right of free speech. You could wind up doing it in the wrong place—in your town square, on your college campus, near a military base—where so-called patriots have decided that opposing government policy is un-American.

Few things make me happier than seeing thousands of the nation's college students protesting the Bush war. These young people, like students of the Vietnam era, are right to voice their opinions and are courageous to do so. In an ironic way, I am glad that right-wing war supporters are coming after these supporters of peace.

These young people will grow stronger in their convictions, and their respect for the confused, chaotic mess of democracy will grow deeper.

During a peace rally at Florida State University in Tallahassee the other day, a war supporter wore a T-shirt emblazoned with these words on the back: "Kill 'em all and let God sort 'em out." These words were on the front: "I support the war on Iraq."

One of my former students, now a graduate assistant at FSU, who attended the rally and who saw the T-shirt, sent me an email, saying: "This guy & his crew were there to intimidate us. They want war & they want us to shut up. Well, we won't shut up. One of them spray-painted 'f— terrorists' on one of our placards. Mr. Maxwell, this stuff makes me know we have to fight even harder to keep the right to speak out.

"Patriotism doesn't have to be stupid. I'm a patriot & I am hurting for what is happening to our country. We're attacking a nation that did not declare war against us. Why? Because we can get away with it. I think that's wrong. I will never support that kind of policy. I'm being attacked in my own country because I oppose bad policy. I fear that things will never be the same. Conservatives want us to be quiet; they want us to go along with the program, right or wrong. Democracy isn't about either/or. It's about the right to be true to your individual conscience. Too many people have become afraid of democracy. Peace."

Absolutely. Democracy is about being true to your individual conscience. It is a confused, chaotic mess. It is permissive. As Abbey wrote: "The best cure for the ills of democracy is more democracy."

By the way, the student above, a history major, sent me the Abbey quote. I love learning about American freedom from one of my former charges—a young woman who is not afraid of democracy.

Our celestial high

At 6:21 a.m. Thursday, I watched the landing of the space shuttle *Atlantis* on television.

The giant craft suddenly appeared through the darkness of Cape Canaveral and touched down, smoke shooting up from the landing gear. The parachute opened, and *Atlantis* coasted to a smooth stop, ending a successful 12-day construction mission to the international space station. I did not turn off the TV and leave for work until I saw the six astronauts emerge from the craft and step onto the runway.

Many people believe that space exploration is a waste of time, money and scientific know-how. I disagree. A dreamer, I have been a supporter of space exploration since I was kid, and if I could start life over, I would try to become an astronaut.

Over the years, I have been fortunate to have witnessed 21 liftoffs in person. I was at Cape Canaveral with members of my 11th grade class on Feb. 20, 1962, when John Glenn blasted off in *Friendship 7* to orbit the Earth. We watched from a great spot reserved for public schools. After that day, I was hooked on spaceships and our space program in general.

My personal feelings notwithstanding, space flight has held a special place in American life since the program's inception. It is embedded in our collective self-perception. Either by design or by coincidence, most of our important flights occur at the right time, always pulling the nation closer together during times of real or perceived crises.

Consider Glenn's triumph on *Friendship 7*. The voyage of that tiny *Mercury* capsule restored the nation's pride after the seemingly invincible

Russians had orbited Earth twice already. Other successful U.S. launches followed *Friendship 7* during the 1960s—when our spirits needed lifting.

Here is how Walter Cronkite, then the CBS News anchor and the nation's unofficial cheerleader for the space program, described the significance of NASA's successes: "The space program was a major factor in maintaining some balance of what our country was all about. That period was the most traumatic decade this country had seen since the Civil War. The Kennedy and King assassinations, the civil rights struggle, the Vietnam War, Watergate. The country was splitting apart. The great thing about the space program in those days was (that) it kept us dreaming about the future, which had a very salutary effect in maintaining national sanity."

Speaking to the *New York Times* many years later, Glenn apprehended the importance of his historic flight: "It was almost like we had turned a corner in our national psyche, almost as though we were at a low point and were starting back."

And then came the dark times of space travel, when our national psyche was plunged into mourning following the tragedies of *Challenger* in 1986 and *Columbia* in 2003.

As a columnist for the *New York Times* Regional Newspapers, I witnessed the *Challenger* explosion. For several years, many Americans, including me, could not bear to view pictures of the explosion. Some of us, including me, still turn away from the fiery images. Many TV stations still refuse to air footage of that national horror.

These explosions temporarily disillusioned us as a nation and made us question our sense of scientific superiority. Some questioned the value of space exploration per se. Others felt responsible for our dead space pioneers. We had failed them. We had become hurried and too cavalier about safety, even though human life was at stake.

I was at Kennedy Space Center in 1998, when Glenn soared into space the second time, on the space shuttle *Discovery*. And I was there several weeks later when the first module of the international space station was launched.

Thousands of journalists from around the world crowded the media viewing area. I made a point of reading press badges: Argentina, Australia, Brazil, Canada, China, England, France, Germany, India, Israel, Japan, Mexico, New Zealand, Norway, Russia, South Africa, South Korea, Spain, Sweden and others.

Although the space station is a collaboration among 15 nations, that first launch was an American moment. And last Thursday, when *Atlantis* returned to American soil, the event symbolized our technological strength and, most importantly, our essential role as a peacemaker in the world.

Atlantis' achievement is good for our national psyche during these dangerous and uncertain times.

Where I began to look inside

OCTOBER 22, 2006

The other day, I had a blast from the past.

A loyal reader, a woman who was one of my mother's playmates in Mascotte, Fla., telephoned from her Lake County home to welcome me back to the *St. Petersburg Times*. Our talk drifted into memories of the one-room schoolhouse in the then-all-black village of Stuckey. Blacks attended the school from first through 12th grade until passage of the 1964 Civil Rights Act.

That building, she said, was the single-most important place to her during childhood. I surprised her when I said that my grandfather's barn, not the little white clapboard schoolhouse, is the structure I hold most dear. I spent only one full year and three summers in Stuckey, but that was enough time for me to fall in love with "Ben Maxwell Barn," as it was called.

It was a typical poor man's barn. Years before I was born, my grandfather, a farmer, and his sons hammered together thick, hand-sawed pine and oak boards for the exterior and interior walls, and they used second-hand tin for the hipped roof. The tin was red, but the walls were left unpainted. The floor was dirt, and the two transport wagons, a cart and a sled were parked beneath the hips.

When I first saw the building, about age 7, it was weathered and gnarled like an old man. But I thought it was beautiful. I enjoyed it most when heavy rains tattooed the tin roof.

It was only about 50 feet from the main house's back doorsteps. Inside, the hayloft was on east wall, the corn bins on the north wall. A wide dogtrot divided the stalls for the mules, Pete and Patsy Mack, from the main work area where the women canned and where machinery, implements and simple plunder were stored.

The smokehouse, which my cousins and I often raided for slices of ham and turkey, was attached to the south wall. The chickens and turkeys were kept in a coop away from the barn. The ducks roamed at will. A lean-to space was attached to the west wall for the unaccountably mean bluetick that kept to itself when it was not hunting with the pack.

We would dump corn into the mules' wooden troughs and watch and listen as the tired and hungry beasts ate. If you have never heard mules grind corn between their teeth—their eyes closed in pleasure and their tails swishing—you have not heard magic. I loved the experience so much that I fed Pete and Patsy Mack each day, before they went into the fields and after they returned. I even enjoyed mucking their stalls.

The building, about 1,000 square feet, had a special odor, the commingling of grain, old hay, manure and urine, animal and human sweat, dogs and so on. I never tired of it.

For me, a typical day in the barn was a day at the zoo. In addition to the mules and pet dogs and cats as inhabitants, the barn was the permanent home to mice, owls, bats, snakes, wasps, dirt daubers, spiders, frogs and toads and my grandfather's pet raccoon. I had a ringside seat to a show of the survival of the fittest: I saw a litter of kittens born, a snake swallow a mouse and an owl perched on a rafter tearing apart a baby rabbit.

A few bad things—of the human kind—also occurred at the barn during the early 1950s, following the famous Groveland rape trial in 1949, when four black men were accused of raping a white woman. The barn became a gathering place for scared black men. Later, and ironically, it also became a temporary rest area for white Florida Guardsmen sent by Gov. LeRoy Collins to protect my uncles and other black men from being lynched by a white mob, all inspired by Lake County Sheriff Willis McCall.

More than anything else, the barn was special to me because it was my own private universe. It was where I was free from adult supervision, where I made the rules, where I tinkered with contraptions, where I played with animals, where I daydreamed and where I learned to love being alone.

"Ben Maxwell's Barn" was torn down in 1962. I have never found another place like it—a place where I can be myself.

'Swanee River' out of flow as state song

APRIL 6, 2008

We call Florida the Sunshine State. We should call it the Benighted State, mainly because our lawmakers, mostly Republicans, are a bunch of ideologues whose constituents follow them blindly. And our Democrats can't even hold a legitimate primary to send delegates to their national convention. We're funny folks.

And so here we are again making ourselves the laughingstock of the nation. This time, we're debating whether to keep the contemptible old state song, Stephen Foster's "Swanee River (Old Folks at Home)," or adopt a new one that's 21st century, inclusive and inspirational.

GOP lawmakers Jim King, Stephen Oelrich, Ed Homan and Charles Dean are heading up a gang of fellow Bubbas to block the adoption of "Where the Sawgrass Meets the Sky," by South Florida elementary school teacher Jan Hinton. Her song truly is about Florida.

"This is history," Oelrich told the *St. Petersburg Times* of "Swanee River." "I'm not in favor of changing the song. Nor are my constituents."

History? What history? "Swanee River" didn't become the state song until 1935, when bigoted legislators, longing for plantations and pliant slaves, adopted it by resolution.

In my high school in Crescent City, we didn't sing "Old Folks at Home," with its strange, insulting dialect: "de Swanee Ribber"; "Dere's wha de old folks stay"; "All de world am sad and dreary"; "Ebry where I roam"; "playing wid my brudder"; "my kind old mudder"; "Oh! Darkeys"; "One dat I love"; and "I hear de banjo tumming."

I do recall that our music teacher, Mr. Florence, tried a few times to coax us into singing it. Each time, however, we boys laughed until we cried. Laughing himself, Mr. Florence finally gave up on us.

Our homeroom teacher, Constance Howard, dismissed the song as "sickening blackface minstrelsy." Years later, I learned that she was right. Foster, a white man, wrote "Old Folks at Home" in 1851 for a minstrel show. Most historians say he never set foot on Florida soil.

At Middleton High School, whenever someone wanted an instant laugh, he'd bellow a few lines from "Swanee River." Satirizing Foster, I penned a very bad song about the "de ole St. Johns Ribber," which flows into "big" Lake George near Crescent City. Instead of the travails of a "darkey," I used those of a "white Cracker" pining for "mah fishing camp on dar St. John's Ribber." Most of the lyrics, which I've pretty much forgotten, were foul. We never sang them when adults were around.

I learned many years ago that rural, white Floridians are pitiful when they wax nostalgic. They lose all sense of reality, forgetting that Florida is a long, funny-shaped peninsula of contradiction and paradox. Here's an apt description I found in the book *Florida: A Guide to the Southernmost State*: "Florida has its own North and South, but its northern area is strictly Southern, and its southern area definitely Northern."

Rural Florida, mostly in the north, loves "Old Folks at Home." Urban Florida, mostly to the south and on the coasts, wants to get rid of it.

For the record, I've yet to meet a single African American, rural or urban, who favors keeping "Swanee River." Anyway, since lawmakers apologized for slavery, why not just get rid of the "darkey" ditty?

"Where the Sawgrass Meets the Sky" is a respectful song that embraces the character of the Sunshine State. Here's a sampling of its lyrics: "Florida, land of flowers, land of light"; "Florida, where our dreams can all take flight"; "mockingbirds cry and 'gators lie out in the sun."

We should adopt this song.

On travel, terror and living to tell the tale

AUGUST 2, 2009

La Paz, Bolivia

Even before I had adjusted to the altitude of the world's highest capital, my hosts and friends, members of a generations-old Bolivian family, hauled me off to a parade. Nearly 1 million people from every South American country and tourists from elsewhere flooded the streets and sidewalks of the central city.

When we left the parade, freeing ourselves from the throng, we had to cross several streets along the parade route and pick our way through lines of other spectators. My La Paz-savvy friends slipped through easily, but two indigenous women shoulder-bumped me as I tried to squeeze between them. That is when I realized that I was a stranger in a remote, Third World land whose customs and etiquette I did not understand.

For the first time, I was afraid for my safety. Because of my many years of covering big outdoor events, I am wary of festive multitudes. I had been present in the late 1970s when a woman was trampled to death after a soccer match in Johannesburg, South Africa. I imagined myself getting trampled to death here in La Paz if trouble broke out.

Catching up to my friends, I pretended that nothing was wrong. In reality, nothing was wrong. I was practicing what I had been preaching to aspiring writers throughout my careers as a journalist and a teacher: Travel every chance you get. Go to places that make you feel uncomfortable. Meet peoples from all parts of the world and seek out unfamiliar and challenging experiences.

During my three weeks in several parts of Bolivia, I often was uncomfortable, and I was constantly introduced to the unfamiliar and the challenging, even the truly frightening.

I do not speak Spanish beyond perfunctory greetings. When one of my friends was not with me, I was virtually lost. I did not know when I was being ripped off for simple purchases; I could not order in restaurants with confidence; and I could not read the newspapers, a real downer for a print news junky. After two days of linguistic disorientation, I tossed my U.S. pride and asked my hosts to translate for me.

Besides my dark skin, my tall frame, gray hair and beard made me stand out like a llama in a fancy dog show. I am much taller than most Bolivians, especially the indigenous people, causing curious eyes to follow me everywhere. Vanity is alive and well in Bolivia. My friends told me that the moment most Bolivians, male and female, see a gray lock, they rush to the store for dye and use it for life. Indeed, I did not see gray hair anywhere I went. And hardly any men have noticeable facial hair.

When my friends and I went out, I used their toilet beforehand, trying to avoid using a public toilet. The first time I used one, I plunked down a peso, and the man pointed to sheets of pink paper on a beat-up counter. I realized that the pink sheets, about eight, were my allotment of toilet paper. When I opened the toilet door, the stench was overwhelming. I held my breath and entered. I must acknowledge that some of the public toilets were clean, but the stench of the first one never left my mind.

The abrupt changes in Bolivia's climate, environment and altitude from one region to another were pure culture shock. In La Paz, the average temperature was 38 to 50 degrees Fahrenheit. We had snow two days in July. Down in the lower elevations of the subtropics—merely three hours from La Paz—we had temperatures as high as 80 during the day.

Almost everything about Bolivia is chaotic, and nothing is more emblematic of the chaos than vehicle traffic. In La Paz, only upscale sections of the city have traffic lights and stop signs that are observed. Elsewhere, drivers' expertise and nerves determine who survives. Lane markings and center lines do not exist, and vehicles, their horns blasting, jockey for space. Imagine thousands of bumper cars in a finite, mountainous space trying to avoid collisions. That is La Paz.

On the open roads, the fastest and biggest vehicles rule the sharp curves and steep inclines. For good luck, many truck, bus and taxi drivers pour a drop of liquor on the ground each time they hit the road. The liquor is for Pachamama, Mother Earth or god of nature. One of our Copacabana bus drivers performed the sign of the cross each time he got behind the wheel. Many passengers also prayed.

I had the harrowing experience of traveling on some of the world's most dangerous roads. When we took the unpaved Yungas Road, which goes to the tropics, I thought I was going to die. Only a few spots in the road are wide enough for an oncoming large vehicle and car to pass each other. When a place is too narrow, the vehicle going up has the right-of-way, and the one going down must pull into a designated safe zone or back up.

I spent many terror-filled moments looking down into dizzying gorges as our minivan backed up. Sometimes, we were as high as 3,000 feet, with a roaring river below, maneuvering hairpin turns or backing up for a tour bus to go by. Memorials to those who have plunged to their deaths are built along the road.

Each time I travel to a faraway place where I am uncomfortable, where things are unfamiliar, I return with a greater appreciation for the United States and a deeper understanding of another part of the world. All of the inconveniences and the fear are worth every minute.

In crises, rule of law steadies us

JANUARY 23, 2011

Because Americans fundamentally are a people more alike than different, the recent massacre of the innocent in Tucson shocked most of us. It will leave us with a defining memory of the senseless loss.

We will carry on with our lives despite the combustive politics raging around us, the very politics that may have somehow pushed the very disturbed shooter to act. Unlike people in many other nations where similar tragedies occur, we do not fall apart even though our sense of well-being and our unique American ethos have been breached by one of our own, this time by an apparent madman.

It is not in our nature to commit widespread, organized acts of revenge. We are prepared to let justice take its course.

Since my undergraduate days of reading the likes of Alexis de Tocqueville, Frederic Jackson Turner, William Whyte, Margaret Mead, Carl Becker and Gordon Allport, who wrote about the mythic "American character," I have tried to understand the forces that give the United States the ability to maintain basic calm following homegrown, politically motivated atrocities.

In the same way, I have tried to understand our ability to maintain the peace when we have a change of top leadership. How could Barack Obama replace George W. Bush so seamlessly? As Americans, most of us take the transfer of power for granted. I do not. It is emblematic of what makes us who we are even with our many ethnicities and religious faiths. It manifests the taproot of our national character.

During a weekly commentary in January 2009, leading up to Obama's inauguration, CBS Evening News chief Washington correspondent and *Face the Nation* host Bob Schieffer said: "As it has been from the beginning, the old president will go and the new president will arrive for no other reason than that it is the expressed will of the American people which is at once our greatest strength and the core principle on which America came to be."

I am convinced that the "core principle," which also accounts for our resilience in the face of domestic atrocity, is our unblinking commitment to the concept and the practice of the rule of law. For the rule of law to prevail, argues Ronald Cass, dean emeritus, Boston University School of Law, there must be the elements of consistency, predictability, rules from valid authority and transparency of the law.

These elements are underpinned by the U.S. Constitution.

"The nature of the judicial system is critical to the rule of law," Cass writes. "Impartial judges, governed by clear legal rules, committed to enforcing the rules as written, independent of political influence are essential if law is to be a reliable guide to individuals and a constraint on those in power."

The rule of law works because while the judicial system circumscribes activity, the U.S. Constitution and the Bill of Rights and state constitutions and their bill of rights limit the power of government over the individual.

"The one right, above all others, that makes the rule of law work is the 'freedom of speech,'" according to Rule of Law in the United States, an online publication—ruleoflawus.info. "The ability to speak one's mind, to challenge the political orthodoxies of the times, and to criticize the policies of the government without fear of recrimination by the state are the things that are the essential distinction between life in a free country and a dictatorship."

I volunteer for World Partnerships Inc., an affiliate of the U.S. State Department that brings hundreds of foreign visitors from around the world to our area each year. These visitors include politicians, educators, diplomats, law enforcement officials, journalists and scientists. Some of our guests tell us they are astounded by the freedoms Americans enjoy. Whenever I am asked to discuss the sources of our freedoms, I always have the same answer: our commitment to the rule of law and our willingness to reach consensus, often a messy process, for the greater good.

I told one Middle East visitor that freedom of speech in America does not include the freedom to gun down or otherwise physically attack our fellow citizens because we disagree with them.

As we condemn the horror of Tucson, the sane among us, which is the majority, will grow from it just as we grew from the 1995 Oklahoma City bombing. We have a system that provides for a fair trial for the alleged shooter. We will remember, and we will gain an even deeper appreciation for the rule of law.

Get it straight: I'm no conservative

APRIL 10, 2011

All of my writing life, I have remained silent about being labeled a conservative. Friends have regularly encouraged me to set the record straight, but I refused until now for two reasons. First, I thought it would be self-serving. Second, I learned decades ago that disabusing critics of erroneous beliefs, illogic and convenient lies is next to impossible.

But here goes. I am not a conservative, and I am deeply offended to be seen as one.

Here is a definition of a conservative: a person who is averse to change and holds to traditional values and attitudes, typically in politics, religion and social practices. I have never been afraid of change, particularly change that promotes the common good for the greatest number of Americans.

I came of age as a college student at the apex of the civil rights movement during the 1960s. As a member of the Southern Christian Leadership Conference, I marched from Selma to Montgomery; registered voters in Alabama, Georgia and Mississippi; and organized maids, hotel workers and garbage collectors in Florida. Like many other activists of my generation, I went to jail several times for acts of civil disobedience. Was that conservative?

These are some of the organizations I support: National Public Radio, American Civil Liberties Union, Humanist Association of Florida, Unitarian Universalist Association, Amnesty International, Southern Poverty Law Center, NAACP, Coalition of Immokalee Workers, United Farm Workers, Defenders of Wildlife, Nature Conservancy, Environment America, National Parks Conservation Association, and Role Models Foundation Inc.—rolemodelstoday.org.

In addition to newspapers, these are among the magazines and journals I read: *Mother Jones, The Nation, Slate, American Scholar, Daedalus, Chronicle of Higher Education, Inside Higher Ed, Education Week* and *The Journal of Blacks in Higher Education.*

Here are a few of my core beliefs. You decide if they are conservative. Gay Americans have the same rights as heterosexuals, including the rights to marry and to adopt children. Women have the right to have an abortion. Marijuana should be decriminalized. All Americans should have health insurance, and the federal government should find a way to make it happen. American taxpayers owe the wealthy nation of Israel nothing.

I am a staunch supporter of labor unions. During the 1970s and 1980s, I was the steward of my teachers unions at Kennedy-King College in Chicago and Broward Community College in Fort Lauderdale. I spent many years in fields and groves advocating for the rights of farmworkers. As a journalist, I continue to focus on the injustices these laborers endure. I grew up in a migrant family, and I am intimately familiar with the callousness of management. I will never forget the atrocities I witnessed as a child.

I reject the banning and censoring of any works of art—books, plays, films, music, paintings or sculptures. The works of Robert Mapplethorpe and Andres Serrano are as legitimate as those of Georgia O'Keeffe and

John Singer Sargent. *Naked Lunch* and *Tropic of Cancer* need not take a literary backseat to *The Call of the Wild* and *The Good Earth*.

So what is the source of this nonsense that I am a conservative? My race. When it comes to race in the United States, we practice a cruel double standard in matters related to so-called values, the area in which we are judged most quickly to be either liberal or conservative.

When my white liberal friends believe that education is essential to success and insist on their children doing well in school, they are called good, normal parents. When I, a black man, believe and do the same, I am dismissed as a conservative freak.

My white friends seek to rear their children in crime-free neighborhoods. I want black kids to grow up the same way. For wanting what is normal, I am condemned as a conservative and an enemy of black people.

Liberal whites I know read to their children and grandchildren and take them to museums and other venues of culture. Blacks should do the same for their children. For this belief, I am condemned as conservative.

My white acquaintances enjoy the benefits of nice homes and clean streets. I want the same for blacks. I want blacks to stop destroying their own neighborhoods and slaughtering one another. I want them to become zero-tolerant of crime, a normal sentiment.

Why do whites escape negative judgment for desiring normalcy while I am excoriated as being a conservative? The answer lies in America's double standard—practiced by both blacks and whites—when race and values converge.

Don't take voting for granted

NOVEMBER 4, 2012

Voting is a right best exercised by people who have taken time to learn about the issues.

Tony Snow, White House spokesman for George W. Bush

On Tuesday, Americans will vote for the president of the United States, members of the U.S. Congress, state and local officials, referendums and constitutional amendments that will determine the quality of our lives for years to come.

Voting is a duty of citizenship none of us should take for granted.

One of the most enduring observations I have read on the importance of voting is that of Daniel Webster, who served in Congress for 29 years before the Civil War: "Impress upon children the truth that the exercise of the elective franchise is a social duty of as solemn a nature as man can be called to perform; that a man may not innocently trifle with his vote; that every elector is a trustee as well for others as himself and that every measure he supports has an important bearing on the interests of others as well as on his own."

As one who came of age when regions of the United States had laws that prevented many citizens from voting, I am confounded to see so many Americans today who choose not to vote.

Ironically, my most memorable experience with voting came in 1994, in a foreign country. As good fortune would have it, I was vacationing in post-apartheid South Africa when Nelson Mandela was elected president. Not only was Mandela the first black to become the Republic of South Africa's leader, the event marked the nation's first fully representative democratic election.

After generations of violence and racial repression, the voting process was surprisingly peaceful. In Cape Town, I was surrounded by jubilant black voters from townships and distant villages who had not dreamed of living to see a black president for whom they had voted. I still see the circle of Zulu women in colorful dress dancing near a fountain.

Looking at the throng of newly freed people—especially the very old who had suffered a lifetime of degradation and disenfranchisement—I was ashamed to acknowledge that I had come to take voting for granted back home in the United States.

Now, I vividly recall that euphoric day in South Africa as we Americans prepare to vote on Tuesday.

Our issues are many, and the candidates are well-financed, clever and determined. Some of our problems are so potentially catastrophic that they will require leaders who can work together, who are committed to serving the public interest above all else.

The ineffective, gridlocked Congress has caused more problems than it has solved.

James Garfield, our 20th president, wrote that "the people are responsible for the character of their Congress. If that body be ignorant, reckless, and corrupt, it is because the people tolerate ignorance, recklessness, and corruption."

We should not trifle with our votes. We have a duty to earnestly educate ourselves before we mark our ballots, letting reality and truth guide us.

Do we know the real issues, or are we merely reacting to our biases? Have we personally researched the issues, or are we relying on the opinions of, say, our favorite talking heads or columnists or drinking and golfing buddies or professors or pastors?

Do we know where the candidates stand on the issues? Do their positions support the public good, or do they hew to the party line? Do the candidates blindly follow the tenets of an ideology or religious dogmas?

These are questions we can answer with logic and reason if we have done our homework.

Voters should look to the future before casting their ballots, honestly assessing where the country is now and how it got there, and then envisioning where they want the country to be in four years and beyond.

Based on our informed opinion, who can best solve our problems in ways that benefit the greatest number of citizens?

Merely complaining about the issues and the candidates is useless. Eligible voters who choose not to vote have no legitimate place in political discourse. I read somewhere that "bad officials are elected by good citizens who do not vote."

Read it and, yes, weep

FEBRUARY 10, 2013

Bookstores, like libraries, are the physical manifestation of the wide world's longest, most thrilling conversation.

Richard Russo, novelist

The world I love and enjoy most is shrinking.

Corporate or independent or public or whatever, I don't care. Show me a bookstore and I'll find a dozen reasons to love it and spend a few or a lot of dollars. My world is shrinking because each year, bookstores are shutting down without being replaced.

A little more than a year after Borders shuttered its 411 remaining stores, Barnes & Noble Booksellers, long the nation's largest chain, has announced it plans to close at least 20 stores a year for the next decade.

The *Wall Street Journal* reports that since 2003, Barnes & Noble closed an average of 15 stores a year but opened about 30 a year, many on college campuses. Last year, though, it shut down 14 stores and opened no new ones.

Will the company, which opened its first store in New York City in 1917, eventually go dark like Borders?

My love affair with bookstores began when I was in third grade. Actually, it wasn't a proper bookstore but a secondhand shop with a lot of junk. My parents, who were migrant workers, went shopping for kitchen utensils in a little town in Cumberland County, N.J., where we were harvesting tomatoes. While they searched for pots and pans, I discovered a bookcase with dozens of books.

I found tattered copies of Edgar Rice Burroughs' novels *Tarzan of the Apes*, *The Return of Tarzan* and *Tarzan and the Leopard Men*. Some boy had loved these books nearly to death. Each book cost a whopping 10 cents, but the owner, apparently seeing how I clutched these treasures, sold all three to us for 15 cents. These books provided the escape and adventure a migrant boy needed. They made life in the labor camp tolerable.

The rest of that summer and during all the other summers we were on the road, I bought books at secondhand shops and real bookstores.

As a college student, I learned that bookstores were essential to my intellectual, spiritual and physical well-being. In Marshall, Texas, where I first attended college, I found a tiny Christian store that stocked Jean-Paul Sartre and Albert Camus alongside treatises on Jesus, the Gospels and symbols in Revelation.

Over the years, I have fallen in love with bookstores in all parts of the United States and in several foreign cities. I make these stores destinations.

Before moving to St. Petersburg in 1994, if I had to travel to the Tampa Bay area or farther south, I would set aside a few hours to visit Haslam's Book Store in St. Petersburg. It is the quintessential locally owned, independent store. The owners and employees know me, and we always have stimulating discussions. They know what's on their shelves, which is important to me.

Down the street from Haslam's is another independent gem, Book-Lover's Cafe. I have bought many great books in this little store, some out of print. And the roasted coffee is always delicious.

All book lovers have a favorite store. Mine was the eclectic Borders in Fort Lauderdale, my hometown. It had one of the best, if not the best location of any bookstore in the country. It was on Sunrise Boulevard on the Intracoastal Waterway that flows into the Atlantic Ocean. I would make my purchase, get something to drink and find a spot beneath an umbrella on the water. I would read and watch yachts head toward the ocean. Sometimes I would take a water taxi to downtown and back.

That store is gone. It closed more than a year ago. Whenever I go to Fort Lauderdale, I drive past the building out of habit. I feel miserable each time. An old friend is dead and cannot be replaced.

And now Barnes & Noble plans to shrink. Given the rising popularity of e-readers, inexpensive tablets and Amazon's massive online marketplace, how much longer will the brick-and-mortar stores survive? It is a question I hate to think about.

You can just call me 'Sir'

MARCH 3, 2013

A transformative moment for many black males of my generation came as we watched *In the Heat of the Night* for the first time, the 1967 film starring Sidney Poitier as police investigator Virgil Tibbs. The moment is when Rod Steiger, the racist sheriff, says to Poitier: "Virgil. That's a pretty funny name for a colored boy from Philadelphia. What do they call you up there?"

"They call me Mister Tibbs!" Poitier says.

His delivery is so powerful that blacks, especially males, in that recently integrated theater applauded and screamed for joy. The sheriff has been put in his place by a black man.

We walked into the street feeling a bit taller. Poitier taught many of us that we should care about how we are addressed and greeted by white males, especially by those to whom we hand over our hard-earned money for services rendered. He taught us that we are defined by the names we are called.

Label me a hypersensitive old man for caring about how I am addressed and greeted by white male employees in customer service after all these years. How I am greeted or addressed, in fact, determines if I stay to be served or immediately walk out of a place. I never return to some businesses.

Few things anger me more than to sit at a table in a restaurant only to have a white male waiter ask, "Can I get you something, boss?" or, "How's it going, boss man?" or, "What's up, buddy?" or, "You need a menu, bud?" or, "What can I do for you, chief?"

My reaction depends on whether I'm alone or with others. If alone, I walk out without a word or stay and lecture the offender before ordering. If I'm with someone else, I bear the insult. I leave a small tip or no tip if it's Dutch treat.

What prevents a white male from simply asking: "Good evening, sir, what can I do for you?" What compels him to use "boss" or "boss man" or "buddy" or "bud" or "chief"? I often stand aside to observe how the white clerk who just called me "boss man" treats white male customers. In almost every instance, the whites are called "sir."

Following is a brief lexicon of the terms black men of my generation find insulting.

BOSS: This is a disingenuous form of address. It pretends to be deferential when, in fact, it is masking disrespect. It is a term in the workplace, where underlings take orders from the person with the top job. It does not belong in relationship between the paying customer and the service employee.

BUDDY: When a white man, a total stranger, addresses a black man with this term, it is condescending and demeaning. A black acquaintance told me that "Buddy was the name of a mangy old hound dog" he recalled from childhood. He said that when called "buddy," he feels as if he's not being taken seriously, like he's an object in a game.

CHIEF: It may sound benign, but it's a vicious address. Urbandiction ary.com defines it as a condescending term, equivalent to "buddy, pal, boss, ace, slick, and champ." Its use reminds me of our shameful history with American Indian chiefs. We disrespected them, took away their power and killed many. Why would a person in customer service address a black male, a complete stranger, with this term?

Not a single white female has ever addressed me any other way than "sir." I've never heard a white female use "boss" or "buddy" or "chief" with a black male.

So what's up with white males?

Although I'm not a social scientist, I am convinced that racism, conscious or unconscious, drives many white males in customer service to use these demeaning addresses and greetings. They cannot bring themselves to use terms of respect for black men, particularly graybeards like me.

Employers whose bottom lines depend on quality customer service should adequately train their white male employees to treat blacks with respect. That training should begin with the simple lesson of always using the gold standard of addresses and greetings: "sir."

Leading the world in volunteerism

MARCH 10, 2013

Sequester is now reality, meaning that $85 billion in automatic across-the-board cuts to most discretionary federal spending programs has begun. Many of these programs already depend on a corps of volunteers to operate effectively, and some managers are predicting that as funds disappear, volunteerism will become more essential.

Over the years, I have volunteered for many organizations, including Meals on Wheels, Habitat for Humanity, literacy programs and nature parks.

For the last seven years, I have volunteered for World Partnership Inc., an affiliate of the U.S. State Department that brings foreign visitors to the United States. I have hosted guests in my home, dined out with them, conducted seminars and attended Tampa Bay Rays games with them.

I know of no other organization that does as much to teach foreigners about volunteering. Ironically, our visitors constantly remind us that the United States is unique in the world when it comes to volunteerism. They're right. According to the Corporation for National and Community Service, approximately 63.4 million Americans, or 26.3 percent of the adult population, gave 8.1 billion hours of service worth $173 billion in 2010, the last year for complete numbers.

I never will forget the night at a Rays game when a Ukrainian guest, a security officer, asked me through an interpreter about my work with World Partnerships Inc. When the interpreter said I was a "volunteer," the guest asked if being a "volunteer pays well." The guest was incredulous when the interpreter said I didn't get paid. I realized that I had taken volunteering for granted.

The overwhelming majority of our visitors come here knowing nothing about the role of volunteerism in civic life. Once they experience it, they clearly see that their countries need this kind of philanthropy.

President Barack Obama showed that he understands the diplomatic power of volunteerism when he authorized the State Department to create a special international leadership exchange program, Volunteerism: United We Serve, in 2011. It brings leaders from foreign countries to the United States to participate in volunteer efforts.

Gary Springer, president of World Partnerships Inc., worldpartnerships.org, said the new program was designed as a "hands-on examination of the impact of volunteerism both on volunteers and the communities they serve. It shows young foreign leaders how volunteers of all backgrounds and ages, especially young people, are inspired to participate in community service."

He said our visitors know that when a major disaster occurs in their countries, the United States is first on the scene for rescue, recovery and rebuilding.

"But the depth and breadth of volunteerism they encounter during their visits astounds them," he said. "In Tampa Bay, our international visitors seek the 'volunteer experience' during their three-week official programs in the United States. To paraphrase many of them, Americans are so kind, and we volunteer to help so many causes. Americans just seem to do this naturally."

Springer said he tells visitors that Americans have the "habit" of volunteerism instilled in them at an early age through their families, neighborhoods, churches and schools.

"One visitor, who asked us why so many people attended a dinner for her group, remarked that 'in my country, we would have to pay people to attend such an event.'"

While in the Tampa Bay area, Springer said, visitors work with hundreds of local residents, community organizers and student interns on beach clean-up projects, in soup kitchens and in community food gardens.

"Volunteering is an infectious experience for them," he said. "Many visitors return to their communities and organize volunteers for all manner of projects previously unthinkable without the spirit of volunteerism."

Nationwide, Springer said, an estimated 88,000-plus volunteers, known as "citizen diplomats," organize professional meetings, cultural activities, social events and home hospitality for approximately 5,000 visitors annually.

Springer is not an alarmist. He worries, though, that as a State Department affiliate, World Partnerships Inc., like others nationwide, will be affected by sequester when the current fiscal year ends and after some State Department staff members are furloughed.

"There is nothing like breaking bread with our international visitors to give them insight into who we are, and how we live, work, learn and play," he said. "With sequester, all hands, including volunteers, will be needed on deck."

Memories of the hippie van

AUGUST 27, 2013

When I read that the last Volkswagen campervan would roll off the assembly line on Dec. 31, I was transported back in time.

The company in Brazil that is the world's last manufacturer of this automotive icon will stop production. It says it can't make money and meet the country's new safety mandates of antilock braking systems and air bags beginning in 2014.

I fell in love with the Volkswagen campervan during the summer of 1964, at the end of my freshman year of college. I was driving with a schoolmate in his old Plymouth sedan from Texas to Atlanta. Outside Vicksburg, Miss., the car broke down and we started walking in search of a service station. We didn't dare hold out our thumbs as hitchhikers because—as two young black males in the Deep South—we were afraid to attract attention.

Trudging along the fence, away from the road, we were surprised to hear tinny beeping behind us and to see a psychedelic-painted VW campervan, a mobile mural, stop on the easement a few yards from us.

We were ready to run when two tie-dye-clad young white men hopped out. The driver waved and asked if that was our car about 5 miles back. His smile and that strange fragrance emanating from him—which we learned was patchouli oil—put us at ease. He offered to drive us the 15 miles to Vicksburg to find a mechanic.

As we approached the van, the side door slid open, and we were greeted by three young white women wearing flowing, ankle-length skirts. They made room for us on the L-shaped seat even though we were sweaty. Incense filled the air. One woman opened the icebox, grabbed two cold beers and handed them to us. Nothing had ever been more refreshing.

As we drove to Vicksburg, our rescuers sang Bob Dylan's "The Times They Are A-Changin'" and "Blowin' in the Wind," and we joined in, all of us laughing. They drove us to a service station and stayed with us. A truck towed our car to the station, and we learned that the clutch needed replacing, which we couldn't pay for on the spot. Our rescuers drove us to Atlanta and dropped us off.

We never saw or heard from them again. That was my introduction to the campervan, nicknamed the "bus," the "hippie van" and many other endearing terms.

In 1974, when I taught at Northern Illinois University, I bought a campervan, a 1972 mustard-colored gem with the spare mounted in front. I was inspired to buy it because of my memories of those five hippies who aided my schoolmate and me during one of the most racially violent periods in the South.

That bus, its psychedelic paint and incense, has stayed in my imagination as a symbol of adventure, freedom, friendship, peace and love.

First sold in 1950, the bus was integral to America's counterculture during the 1960s and 1970s, becoming the top-selling auto import in the nation. It was the vehicle of choice during 1967's Summer of Love, when as many as 100,000 people descended on the Haight-Ashbury neighborhood of San Francisco. It was ubiquitous at Woodstock in 1969, and legions of Deadheads piled into their buses to follow the Grateful Dead to concerts nationwide.

From 1974 to 1978, I drove my van from coast to coast to camp and fish. I got rid of it after I bought a travel trailer, replacing it with an eight-cylinder Chevy pickup. The van's engine wasn't powerful enough to constantly pull the trailer in the mountains. I still hear angry motorists screaming profanities and raising their middle finger as they flew by.

Two hours after I placed an ad to sell the van on a campus bulletin board, a colleague came to my office and handed me a check for the price I was asking. He said he'd coveted the van for the two years he'd seen it on campus.

To this day, I regret selling my bus. I've owned several vehicles since then but without becoming attached to any. I don't think there will ever be another auto with the spiritual pull and adventurous allure of the hippie van.

Courageous, black and white

JULY 8, 2014

I came of age during the summer of 1964, when I was an 18-year-old sophomore at a historically black college in east Texas. It was a special 10 weeks, 50 years ago, known today as Freedom Summer. It is a fitting name because of the hope we sensed around us, hope that inspired more than 800 student volunteers from around the nation to put their bodies in harm's way in some of the most violent, racist places in the American South, a region apart from the rest of the nation.

I came of age, and the nation itself came of age, or, at the very least, learned that a new day had dawned for human rights in the so-called "Land of the Free." As a child of the South, that summer gave me my first white friends and acquaintances. Until then, I had seen all whites as the enemy. I had never had a whole conversation with a white person, my interactions with them having been primarily four simple utterances: "yes, sir," "no, sir," "yes, ma'am" and "no, ma'am." White people were not in my intimate life, not in a positive way.

All that changed when I joined the Southern Christian Leadership Conference and the federally endorsed Voter Education Project as an organizer. I was dispatched to Alabama and Mississippi where I met idealistic white students determined to subdue Jim Crow. They believed they could help improve the lives of African Americans. Most of these students were with the Student Nonviolent Coordinating Committee, led by Stokely Carmichael, and most hailed from colleges and universities in the Northeast.

When I arrived in Mississippi during the first week of July, white New Yorkers Michael Schwerner, 24, and Andrew Goodman, 20, had been shot to death on a roadside along with their companion James Chaney, a 21-year-old black Mississippi native. Their bodies had been found in an earthen dam near the small town of Philadelphia.

Eight white students and I were assigned to register voters in Nashoba County. The church where we were to work had been burned to the ground weeks earlier. Public accommodations were closed to us, so we stayed in the homes of blacks and whites who risked everything to shelter and feed us. We changed locations each night trying to avoid the Ku Klux Klan. We were shocked that Schwerner and Goodman were killed, naively believing that Mississippi racists would not kill whites. How wrong we were. Other whites would be killed during the movement.

Unable to establish a suitable location for our work, we were dispersed to other parts of the state. I joined a group, mostly whites, in Greenwood to register voters and assist in a Freedom School. I was awed by the courage and selflessness of my white companions who apparently were unafraid to trek into remote areas. They did not have to be there, and I respected them. Because I was familiar with the klan's violence from my experiences in Central and Northeast Florida, I was wary of venturing into the unknown. However, to save face, I always went along.

The white students had been trained to endure abuse the same way we black students had been trained. They, too, had been taught, for example, what to do if someone spat in their faces or yelled abusive names. They knew what to do if arrested or beaten by a civilian mob or by policemen, many of whom were deputized klansmen. Knowing how to react to insult and violence saved our lives, prevented many injuries and often kept us out of jail.

The landmark Civil Rights Act was passed that summer, paving the way for future legislation and societal changes that made all the sacrifices worthwhile. Although irreparable conflict developed between some of the prominent black and white leaders of the movement, many student volunteers forged lifelong friendships. Doubtless, the civil rights movement would have taken a different course if courageous whites had not joined the front line of the battle. Many paid dearly, losing their personal wealth and social standing—some dying for the cause.

Fort Jefferson's maritime legacy

OCTOBER 30, 2015

Dry Tortugas National Park

We visit our Western national parks such as Yellowstone and Grand Canyon for their flora and fauna, awe-inspiring vistas and other natural wonders.

Although Florida's Dry Tortugas National Park, a string of seven coral reef islands, is beautiful, that beauty belies a one-of-a-kind past. Dry Tortugas is a treasure because its strategic location, 70 miles west of Key

West, gave it vital roles in the nation's maritime, cultural and political history.

From the beginning, in 1513 when Spanish explorer Juan Ponce de Leon saw the islands, the region was one of contention. Ships from different countries competed with the Spanish for dominance in the deep waters and in the narrow passageways among the islands.

In 1819, the Spanish sold Florida to the United States, which included the Dry Tortugas. Immediately, a plan was hatched to build a fortress on Garden Key, the largest of the islands. Over time, after piracy became widespread, the U.S. Army began construction of Fort Jefferson, a formidable gunnery post that would control ship movement.

Although construction continued for 30 years, the fort was never completed. The big guns never fired a shot at an enemy, and no enemy ever fired on the fort. It became a military prison, and at the peak of the Civil War, it had a population of some 2,000, a wild mix of military personnel, civilian workers, Union Army deserters and black slaves.

Fort Jefferson was an expensive experiment in folly, a behemoth appropriately dubbed "America's Devil Island." An armada of skilled workers, including stone masons, specialty carpenters and blacksmiths, labored on the project. Not surprisingly, slaves were the largest group of workers, enduring years of degradation sanctioned by the U.S. government and Florida.

Key West, which did not have slaves, had a large population of white Northerners who brought their black servants south with them. Once in Key West, many of these Northerners leased their servants to Fort Jefferson for $20 a month—quite a sum. Once in the Tortugas, these black servants were reduced to the status of slaves.

Fort Jefferson was also a staging site for slave ships destined for other places. Few slaves attempted to escape because of the miles of dangerous reefs, unpredictable storms and unknown destinations.

The best-known escape attempt began shortly after midnight on July 10, 1847, when seven slaves fled in a small boat belonging to the lighthouse keeper.

In a hastily repaired boat, a crew of eight men pursued the slaves who somehow survived a violent storm. They were captured days later on Key Vaca, 120 miles east of Fort Jefferson.

Such stories have remained an alluring force in art, literature and popular culture worldwide. One of the earliest references to the Dry Tortugas appears in *Treasure Island*, Robert Louis Stevenson's 1881 serialized novel. Billy Bones, the drunken pirate, would hypnotize his audiences. "His stories were what frightened people most of all," the narrator says of Billy Bones. "Dreadful stories they were—about hanging, and walking the plank, and storms at sea, and the Dry Tortugas, and wild deeds."

Although maritime exploits and piracy provide many plot lines and themes, nothing attracts authors to Fort Jefferson like its history as a federal prison for some of the nation's most notorious bad guys. The prison's most infamous inmates were four of the conspirators in the assassination of President Abraham Lincoln. One was Samuel A. Mudd, the doctor who set the fractured leg of John Wilkes Booth, Lincoln's assassin.

Novelists such as Sarah Vowell, who wrote *Assassination Vacation*, visited Fort Jefferson to experience the place of Mudd's confinement until he was pardoned by President Andrew Johnson in 1869. One of Mudd's best-known criticisms of the prison, as Vowell notes, was that Fort Jefferson was a place of "bad diet, bad water, and every inconvenience."

Not to be outdone, Brad Meltzer focused his novel *The President's Shadow* on Lincoln's assassination. The third installment in the Culper Ring series, the novel cleverly combines history and fiction as the president's death is linked to scoundrels in Fort Jefferson. The narrative, held together by Meltzer's research, is a thrilling trek back in time.

While the Dry Tortugas is beautiful and romantic, it is where the ghosts of slaves cry out for freedom, where the ghosts of pirates commit wild deeds and walk the plank, where the ghosts of murderous conspirators languish in guilt.

The duty of a free press

FEBRUARY 3, 2017

During a May 1962 news conference, President John F. Kennedy was asked to comment on the media's treatment of his administration after 16 months in office.

"Well," he said, "I'm reading more and enjoying it less."

That response, while reflecting quintessential JFK wit, showed that he had difficult times with the press like every president before him. Although JFK's sense of humor made him likable, many journalists regularly called him to account.

What made JFK's relationship with the press unique was that as a voracious reader of the news and as the first president to regularly conduct live televised press conferences, he understood the necessity of a free press, the so-called "fourth estate," in American democracy.

In 1963, NBC's Sander Vanocur asked Kennedy to expound on his "reading more, enjoying it less" remark.

"I think (the press) is invaluable, even though . . . it is never pleasant to be reading things that are not agreeable news," he said. "But I would say that it is an invaluable arm of the presidency, as a check really on what is going on in the administration, and more things come to my attention that cause me concern or give me information.

"So I would think that (Russian Premier) Nikita Khrushchev operating a totalitarian system, which has many advantages as far as being able to move in secret, and all the rest—there is a terrific disadvantage not having the abrasive quality of the press applied to you daily, to an administration, even though we never like it, and even though we wish they didn't write it, and even though we disapprove, there isn't any doubt that we could not do the job at all in a free society without a very, very active press."

Here we are, more than 50 years later, with President Donald Trump, Kennedy's opposite when it comes to a free press.

Trump adviser Stephen Bannon labeled the media the "opposition party." He said we should keep our mouths shut and listen to the new administration. This point of view, which may guide policy, is straight out of the totalitarian tradition and un-American.

As many of my colleagues have written, we should not swallow the White House's bait and get ourselves unhinged by playing the losing game of tit-for-tat. I see Bannon's crude salvo as a challenge for us, especially opinion writers, to become more dispassionate in everything we write.

I vividly recall the information-gathering and gumshoe lessons I learned as a student at the University of Florida College of Journalism and Communications. We were taught to "always get the record," to never totally trust what politicians or other important people said. Show respect for their positions, yes, but be skeptical of their words and motives and pay special attention to their deeds. Go to the courthouse and city hall and other places that held public documents. Find the truth on our own.

In that light, I see Bannon's labeling us the "opposition party" as a challenge to work harder, a challenge for us to fulfill the four essential roles of a free press. Ellen Hume, professor and founder of the Center on Media and Society at the University of Massachusetts Boston, outlines these roles: "holding government leaders accountable to the people; publicizing issues that need attention; educating citizens so they can make informed decisions; and connecting people with each other in a civil society."

We still are the "fourth estate," the watchdog. It is the duty of a free press in a democratic society to be "very, very active," as President Kennedy said.

Kennedy Space Center opens new worlds for grandsons

JUNE 2, 2017

After my 6-year-old twin grandsons graduated from kindergarten last week, I took them and their mother, my daughter, to the Kennedy Space Center Visitor Complex to celebrate. I wanted them to have fun and learn in a welcoming, safe and inspiring environment.

What better place than the space center, where more than 1.5 million visitors come each year from around the world? At the outset, in the parking lot and in the ticket line to enter the 70-acre complex, we could hear the world around us through languages we didn't understand and see it in attire that was unfamiliar.

The boys immediately realized that many other kids were headed to the Children's Play Dome, which has slides, nooks and crannies and a climbing wall. I watched as the boys befriended kids from India, Japan, Poland, Bolivia, Jamaica and elsewhere.

And I watched as my grandsons and their new acquaintances, all sweaty and exhausted, said goodbye. One of my grandsons and an Indian boy held hands and exchanged parting words and smiles. I was moved by their innocence, immersing themselves in the universal act of simple play.

After a cold drink and a few minutes of rest, we visited the Rocket Garden. The boys were awed by the sight of a real *Atlas*, *Jupiter* and *Ti-*

tan II rising above everything else around. Both ran to a replica capsule, climbed inside and pretended they were roaring into space.

Next, we went to one of the IMAX theaters and watched *A Beautiful Planet*, the 3D documentary narrated by Jennifer Lawrence. I thought the boys would be bored, but the 3D experience—with stars, mountains, oceans, forests and other images traveling at high speed toward us—kept them on the edge of their seats.

The Space Shuttle *Atlantis* Zone was extra special. One grandson and I did the Shuttle Launch Experience. It is a motion-master ride, complete with thundering sound effects and the violent shaking approximating what astronauts experienced on the shuttle *Atlantis*.

While the boys enjoyed the Shuttle Slide with other kids, I found a seat and observed. When I saw a science teacher with a group of high school students nearby, I eavesdropped like any good journalist would.

The discussion was about NASA's Technology Transfer Program, how space exploration and inventions impact our daily lives. The teacher discussed, among other NASA contributions, light-emitting diodes (LEDs), artificial limbs advancements, anti-icing systems for airliners, improved radial tires, land mine removal, enriched baby food, freeze-drying technology, water purification and powered lubricants.

Several people sat and stood next to me, and I chatted with some of them. They hailed from Germany, Ireland, China, South Africa, Iceland, Russia, Colombia, Denmark and Australia. All seemed awed by what they were experiencing. My question to each was simple: Why did you come? For each, the space center was a destination, and each saw palpable evidence of America's multifaceted uniqueness, especially our multiculturalism.

The Chinese man, his first time in the United States, said the space center is the "ultimate in human diversity." He said he had never been served by a black person in any capacity. He hadn't known that blacks were astronauts and scientists at NASA. He was surprised that Charles F. Bolden, who's African American, had been a NASA administrator.

My biggest surprise at the space center came when I turned my attention back to my grandsons and saw a Buddhist monk, in a signature saffron robe, zooming down the Shuttle Slide. He stood, adjusted his robe, took a photo of the slide with his phone and walked out of the building.

Later, as we walked to the Moon Rock Cafe for lunch, we saw the monk from the slide sitting on the ground in the shade with six other monks. My grandsons stared at these bald men in saffron robes. I was afraid they were going to ask loud kids' questions about the monks.

But they said nothing and kept walking. Over lunch, I used my phone to learn that Buddhists believe in science, that Buddhism isn't a "religion" at all but rather a way of looking at the world.

I am ashamed for not knowing this simple fact. While I came to the space center with my grandsons to celebrate their kindergarten graduation, I serendipitously learned important lessons about another group of people. I will teach these lessons to my boys.

Although I've been to the space center countless times to cover shuttle launches, I will return often with my grandsons. One said he might become an astronaut.

The MLK paradox

APRIL 2, 2018

Twenty-one Americans have won the Nobel Peace Prize. The first was President Theodore Roosevelt in 1906, and the last was Barack Obama in 2009. All but one of the American laureates received the prize for efforts that had an international focus.

Martin Luther King Jr., who won the prize in 1964, was the anomaly. The reason for his winning the coveted prize was—and remains—a shameful paradox for the United States. The United States props itself up as the global paragon of democracy, human rights, religious freedom and individual dignity. The United States even chastises other nations, taking some to war for not sharing its values.

King won the prize for leading the movement that showed the world that too many white Americans were shameless racists and hypocrites who denied an entire group of citizens, African Americans, the democratic rights that whites took for granted for themselves in their daily lives.

The United States was shown to be as much a land of the marginalized and disenfranchised as it was a land of the free. The ideals enshrined in the nation's honored documents, such as the Declaration of Independence and the Constitution, were shown to be for the benefit and protection of white people.

During his Nobel acceptance speech in Oslo, Norway, King described the essence of the civil rights movement and the reason for his being awarded the prize.

"I accept the Nobel Prize for Peace at a moment when 22 million Negroes of the United States of America are engaged in a creative battle to end the long night of racial injustice. I accept this award on behalf of a civil rights movement which is moving with determination and a majestic scorn for risk and danger to establish a reign of freedom and a rule of justice.

"I am mindful that only yesterday in Birmingham, Alabama, our children, crying out for brotherhood, were answered with fire hoses, snarling dogs and even death. I am mindful that only yesterday in Philadelphia, Mississippi, young people seeking to secure the right to vote were brutalized and murdered. And only yesterday more than 40 houses of worship in the state of Mississippi alone were bombed or burned because they offered a sanctuary to those who would not accept segregation. I am mindful that debilitating and grinding poverty afflicts my people and chains them to the lowest rung of the economic ladder."

A white gunman killed him in Memphis a half century ago Wednesday. On the 50th anniversary of his assassination, King and all he stood for remain as relevant as ever with the ascendancy of Republicans and the election of Donald Trump as president.

"Post-racial" dreams of equality that preceded and briefly followed the election of Barack Obama as the nation's first black president have evaporated. The hopes of blacks have come full circle, back to the acute reality that America is a land of intractable structural injustices.

Voting rights were high on King's agenda. He was present on May 26, 1965, when President Lyndon Johnson signed the Voting Rights Act into law. Today, with the rise of the GOP, attacks on voting rights have returned in full bloom.

Several states in many parts of the country passed measures making it harder for residents—particularly black people, the elderly, students and people with disabilities—to exercise their right to vote.

Although old practices such as poll taxes and literacy tests are gone, their replacements are equally draconian. They include purges of voter rolls, cuts to early voting, voter ID requirements and flawed rules for restoring ex-felons' right to vote. The intent of these measures is clear: to suppress voting.

King also championed economic justice. The Economic Policy Institute, a nonprofit, nonpartisan think tank, found that last year the wage gap between blacks and whites was the worst it had been in nearly 40 years. The main reason for the gap had little to do with access to education, differences in work experience or where someone resided. EPI scholars found "discrimination . . . and growing earnings inequality in general" to be the major factors involved.

"Race is not a skill or characteristic that should have any market value as it relates to your wages, but it does," said Valerie Wilson, the director of the program on Race, Ethnicity and the Economy at the EPI.

During a rally of sanitation workers in Memphis on March 18, 1968, weeks before his death, King said of the wage gap of the time: "Now our struggle is for equality, which means economic equality. For we know now that it isn't enough to integrate lunch counters. What does it profit a man to be able to eat at an integrated lunch counter if he doesn't have enough money to buy a hamburger?"

Blacks always have been victims of unequal access to decent and affordable housing, beginning with their status as "free people" after the Emancipation Proclamation and later, the 13th Amendment.

Before his assassination, King worked with congressional leaders and President Johnson on housing equality. Although he influenced the drafting of the Fair Housing Act, he did not live to see it become law. Fittingly, Johnson used the tragedy of King's death to urge Congress to quickly pass the legislation, which it did.

The legislation was groundbreaking in its intent, prohibiting discrimination related to the sale, rental and financing of housing based on race, religion, national origin or sex.

Today, some major goals of the 50-year-old act are unfulfilled. Access to decent and affordable housing remains unequal, and few African American leaders see any hopes of change with Ben Carson, a right-wing black Republican, heading the Department of Housing and Urban Development.

As to be expected, Carson, in GOP tradition, pejoratively refers to the major portions of the Fair Housing Act as "social engineering."

Although King was not involved in campaigns involving police shootings of unarmed African American males that are common today, leaders of black organizations, such as Black Lives Matter and others, connect with King's vision and methods.

"We are very aware of history, and we build on it," said Charlene Carruthers, national coordinator of the Black Youth Project 100. "We are about reclaiming what MLK means. His work and his image have been sanitized by people who are interested in maintaining the current system of oppression."

Dante Berry, director of the Million Hoodies Movement based in New York, said: "MLK was a radical, very strategic and uncompromising in his strive for justice. We're reclaiming our own history in a way that is truthful. What makes people uncomfortable is that we're challenging people to think about what it looks like—what education, what the justice system, what society—looks like when black lives matter."

Even sports personalities, such as Colin Kaepernick, who initiated the movement to kneel during the national anthem at National Football League games to protest police killings of unarmed black men, are inspired by King's nonviolent disobedience.

Kaepernick's simple kneel is potent, and it will live forever even though the quarterback lost his NFL career.

After all the prayers, the marches, the speeches, the violent confrontations, the nights in jail and his murder at age 39, what is King's legacy? What does his work mean for our time?

Peniel E. Joseph of the *Washington Post* says it well:

"King's lasting gift to the nation—what makes 1968 such an important and resonant year for our time—was his unflinching recognition of America's shortcomings and his persistent belief that the nation could transform itself through collective sacrifice, political struggle and spiritual renewal.

"In an era before mass incarceration weaponized the criminal justice system, King fully understood the depth and breadth of structural racism and that economic inequality required personal sacrifice and steadfast moral courage. Stalking the world stage like a man on fire, King— who had dined with presidents, European and African royalty, and international dignitaries—perished fighting alongside garbage workers and welfare mothers."

The Joy of reading

JANUARY 4, 2019

Parental involvement is key to teaching kids to read and appreciate education.

Finally, a few Pinellas African American leaders, particularly St. Petersburg NAACP president Maria Scruggs, are showing the courage to publicly acknowledge that the lack of engagement by black parents in their children's learning plays a major role in our children's persistent academic failure.

During a recent NAACP meeting, Scruggs was unequivocal: "The (school) district has shown they just can't do it. They have done what they can do, but now it's time for the community to step in." She also said that educating black children cannot happen only during the school day.

Getting the community involved is fine, but it is hardly enough. The key to closing the achievement gap is effective parental involvement. It is essential.

Let me share a few of my life experiences that illustrate the singular benefits of parental involvement.

My father, who died in 1999, dropped out of school in the eighth grade. For the rest of his life, he was a farm laborer. From ages 5 to 11, I traveled with him each growing season, planting and harvesting crops from Florida to Long Island, N.Y.

This uneducated man made all the difference in my life. An avid reader of comic books, *Jet* and *Ebony* magazines, he taught me to read before I entered first grade.

Each night after dinner, he would place me on a knee and read to me. I recall many of the titles—*Green Lantern, Superman, Buster Brown, Captain Marvel, Captain America, Hawk* and *The Flash*. With the patience of Job, he taught me to sound letters, syllables and whole words. I remember when I began to read complete sentences.

I recall reading an *Apache Kid* comic from cover to cover by myself. It was quite an accomplishment for a migrant kid. I was reading—and loving it—before I knew it was a formal activity.

My father's attentiveness had other effects: It stirred my imagination and made life bearable in our isolated, violent labor camps.

Knowingly or not, my father fulfilled a sacred duty of parenthood: He was my first teacher. The love of reading he instilled in me led me to love all learning and to love school.

When I became a parent, I fully understood my role in my daughter's academic life. I was fortunate in that my wife, a child of Mexican immigrants, and I were of one accord. When she was pregnant with our daughter, we read to the child in the womb. We had heard that reading to unborn children may give them a head start. That is what we wanted, a head start for our child.

After our daughter was born, we continued to read to her. We had books and other reading materials in every room. When our daughter was 2 years old, we would bring *Mother Goose Nursery Rhymes* and other colorful, big-lettered books to bed. We would place her between us and take turns reading.

The first advance-level book we read to her was *Alice's Adventures in Wonderland*. She delighted in hearing the descriptions of scenes and characters and the clever dialogue. The next book we read to her was *The Wizard of Oz*. Same thing. She loved it. We moved on to *The Hobbit* and *Grimm's Fairy Tales*.

One night out of the blue, we knew we had crossed over into a magical place when our daughter grabbed a book of her choice, crawled into bed with us and asked us to read to her. She did this regularly.

Reading had become integral to her life.

Today, my daughter is the mother of 8-year-old twin boys. They are avid readers. As far as I can tell, they love school. They perform well on all academic measures, and we have not received any reports of disciplinary problems.

The most important lesson I taught my daughter, which my father taught me, is this: Learning is free. Education—the formal process of attending classes at an institution, completing assignments and taking exams to earn a diploma or degree—costs money.

Learning, on the other hand, can be done by simply finding a comfortable, quiet place to sit and engage. There is nothing inherently difficult or mysterious about it. Just get parents involved.

Empowering women in politics

MAY 3, 2019

I've always thought that women in the United States too often have allowed men to marginalize them and devalue them. After all, women outnumber men in the United States.

I've had many arguments with women, and I have engendered a lot of hostility for asking these questions: You outnumber men, so why do you let men run almost everything, including many aspects of your personal lives, abortion rights being one? Why have you accepted, blithely in some instances, second-class citizenship?

That said, I'm hopeful women will gain real power with the launch of a new women's organization called Supermajority.

The professional histories and political instincts of the three cofounders make the effort instantly legitimate: Cecile Richards, former Planned Parenthood president; Alicia Garza, a cofounder of Black Lives Matter; and Ai-jen Poo, the director of the National Domestic Worker Alliance.

What makes Supermajority different from other such organizations?

In an email, Richards writes: "What's different this time around is just how many women there are: the teachers in Arizona, Oklahoma, California, and West Virginia striking for public education. Women everywhere speaking out against sexual assault and harassment. And of course the millions of women (and our allies) marching all across the country for issues like reproductive rights and equal pay.

"One of my comrades in this effort, Ai-jen Poo, says it best: 'Women have always been forces for change in this country, but we've never run the country.' That's what Supermajority is all about—women coming together across issues and identities to fight for our shared values and demand what we need from those in power."

Richards, the daughter of former Texas Gov. Ann Richards, said the issues women care about most are cast aside. She said despite being the majority of Americans, women are treated as a mere constituency and a special interest group.

Supermajority intends to change that. Going beyond perfunctory meetings and marches, the organization's goal is to professionally train women on basic ways to participate in politics and activism in their communities, both face-to-face and online.

Getting women to run for office and getting women to vote for other women is a winning combination during Donald Trump's presidency, as the 2018 midterm elections clearly demonstrated.

When the 116th Congress convened in January, women composed nearly a quarter of its voting membership. A record 102 women now serve in the House of Representatives, 23.4 percent of the chamber's voting members. This is the highest percentage in history. More good news is that 25 women now serve in the Senate. These increases are the direct result of smart activism.

In a press release, Supermajority stated that a major goal is to create a "women's New Deal for gender equality." It will include issues such as unequal pay, soaring child care costs, family leave and saving the Affordable Care Act.

Notably absent from the release was any mention of reproductive health care or abortion rights. Organizers said these issues remain priorities, but how they are handled for public consumption still needs to be worked out.

Supermajority's cofounders and others will launch a national "listening tour" over the summer, meeting with other women to gather information on issues that are important to them. The hope is to establish the "agenda" that will underpin the group's long-term advocacy.

"In many ways, women have been doing all this work—whether it's running their PTA, or organizing around reproductive health care—but we haven't been doing it together," Richards told the *Washington Post*. "What are we going to do to make this moment not something that is just a fleeting flash point of activism, but actually creating a permanent organizing ability for women?

"The issues we share as women are deep, and they are wide, and they're very similar across the country. But we have to be in rooms with women that we don't know. I know that there are many more of us, even though we don't come from the same backgrounds. I don't know what the model for that is. It's not something that we have done."

A white man hit me, apologized 49 years later

JULY 5, 2019

I was 10 years old, in 1955, when I had my first violent racial encounter.

I had gone with my grandfather to a three-day all-black tent revival in Lake City. On the second day, six boys and I walked to a nearby convenience store. A pickup appeared suddenly, its horn blasting, the white boys in the cab and bed screaming racial epithets.

We ran. I saw a boy in the bed raise a belt with a big shiny buckle. The buckle came down and struck the bridge of my nose. The pain was excruciating. My nose had been broken, exposing bone.

I returned to Lake City 49 years later as part of the Florida Humanities Council public reading titled "Parallel Lives." Novelist Beverly Coyle and I read select passages from our essays that had been published in the council's *Forum* magazine. Ironically, the reading was about race relations during Florida's Jim Crow era, when blacks and whites were legally separated by skin color in nearly every part of daily life.

Beverly, who is white, and I read to an ethnically diverse audience of nearly 200 from our essays we had written.

As we read, I noticed the agitation of a white man in a middle row. After the reading, Beverly and I conducted our routine question-and-answer session. The man raised his hand and acknowledged that he was the boy who had hit me with his buckle. Only someone who had been there could have described the scene in such accurate detail.

After the reading, the man said he had waited all those years to apologize to his victim and to ask for forgiveness.

I am writing about this long-ago experience in light of the Florida Legislature's recent decision not to fund the Humanities Council's request for $500,000, which represents 25 percent of the council's annual funding. Lawmakers rejected the funding even though the governor supported it.

"Parallel Lives," with its focus on racial understanding and reconciliation, was a quintessential Humanities Council program. It would have been difficult to produce without state funding.

Ann Schoenacher, former director of the Florida Center for Teachers and staff member for the Humanities Council, was a facilitator of "Parallel Lives."

Prior to the program, she said, the council typically let local nonprofit community groups attract audiences for events. Predictably, those audiences usually turned out to be over-the-age-of-50 white people.

Council staff sensed that the "Parallel Lives" program would be different because it was about race, one of the nation's most enduring and critical issues. Organizers were certain "Parallel Lives" would inspire deep discussion among attendees.

"We realized, however, that the discussions would be more meaningful if we could create audiences that included a wider demographic than usual," Schoenacher said. "Since the objective of the program was to build bridges between cultures that historically had intersected only through societal inequities, indignities, violence or commerce—whites and African Americans—the task was daunting.

"Our brainstorming sessions resulted in the idea of forming 'curious coalitions' in each town or city that requested the program. The phrase worked in several senses of the word 'curious,' for not only did we want groups that were eager to learn something, were interested and inquiring, but we wanted groups that had never even thought of working together before. At first it might feel strange to them or unsettling. So, we required that each request for the program had to be submitted by a partnership between a 'curious coalition' of two entities: maybe two churches, one black and one white; maybe two volunteer civic groups that usually divided along racial lines."

A pleasant surprise was that audiences were larger than usual, more engaged and more passionate, Schoenacher said. Attendees began to see racial situations and people from perspectives never considered.

Beverly shared stories about her learned contempt for blacks. As a child, she was glad that blacks sat in the balcony of the local movie theater while whites sat downstairs. "Colored only" water fountains and "White only" fountains were the way of the South.

A white store owner in his right mind would never let a Negro woman try on a dress. White men wearing blackface in debasing skits was considered innocent fun.

Beverly's candor, as she read and during our question-and-answer sessions, gave whites the courage and freedom to describe their own racial experiences. For more than two years, no matter the venue, from church to college campus, our audiences had no volatile arguments, shouting matches or caustic recrimination.

Instead of denying the Humanities Council funding, now is the time for the Florida Legislature to fund programs such as "Parallel Lives" that give citizens safe spaces to examine the problems and issues that are ripping Floridians apart.

BILL MAXWELL wrote a twice-weekly syndicated column and editorials for the *St. Petersburg Times* from 1994 to 2009 and a monthly opinion column in the *Tampa Bay Times* from 2010 through 2019. His columns appeared in 200 newspapers worldwide and received many writing awards, including the Florida Press Club's plaque for general excellence in commentary (twice) and the Community Champion Award from the American Trial Lawyers Association. From 1988 to 1994 he wrote for the New York Times Regional Newspaper Group. During and before that period he taught journalism and English for eighteen years, at the University of Illinois (Chicago), Governor's State University (Park Forest, Illinois), Northern Illinois University (DeKalb), Santa Fe Community College (Gainesville, Florida), Broward Community College (Pembroke Pines, Florida), Indian River Community College (Fort Pierce, Florida), Florida Keys Community College (Key West), and in the Florida prison program at Lake City Community College. At various times from 2013 to 2017, he taught writing at St. Petersburg College and Miami-Dade College while writing weekly articles and columns for the National Park Service, Everglades National Park Centennial, and *South Dade News Leader*. He founded Role Models Today Foundation to support journalism students.